Apple BASIC for Business for the Apple II

Alan J. Parker
Professor of Computer Systems
School of Hospitality Management
Florida International University
Miami, Florida

John F. Stewart
Associate Professor of Management Science
School of Business
University of Miami
Coral Gables, Florida

Reston Publishing Company, Inc.
 A Prentice-Hall Company
Reston, Virginia

Apple II is a trademark of Apple Computer.

Library of Congress Cataloging in Publication Data

Parker, Alan J
    Apple BASIC for business for the Apple II

    Includes bibliographical references and index.
    1. Basic (Computer program language)
I. John F. Stewart, joint author. II. Title.
HF5548.5.B2P36   001.6'424   81-1186
ISBN 0-8359-0228-5
ISBN 0-8359-0226-1 (pbk.)

© 1980, 1981 by Alan J. Parker and John F. Stewart

10 9 8 7 6 5

Printed in the United States of America

To our parents, David, Sally, Harold, and Ethel
and to my wife, Ann

Contents

Preface

Courses in computer programming and management information systems are required in most collegiate business schools. Such courses teach the student to think logically and they provide an introduction to computer terminology. But a knowledge of the terminology is not enough to generate an understanding of computers, and logical thinking by itself does not unlock the power of computers. Computers are used to solve problems, and students must learn *how* computers can help them solve problems.

In this text we have presented problems from the business data processing environment as a reason for learning BASIC. Of course, not all facets of a problem can be explained at once, since different parts require different approaches and tools. But step by step, as we look at the many facets of a problem and introduce the necessary BASIC statements, the student will collect the tools needed to solve all these problems.

Because of the emphasis on problem-solving, the focus of this book is the point at which problem elements meet language capabilities. The BASIC language fundamentals, syntax and grammar, are not the dominant elements—they are subordinate to the problem requirements. So language capabilities that do not fit clearly into a problem context were omitted for the purposes of this text.

Unlike most introductory BASIC books, this book uses files extensively. All business applications use files, and most file instructions are different for the various brands of computers. This book was written specifically for the Apple II microcomputer with DOS Version 3.2. All programs presented are compatible with DOS Version 3.3. Since all programs, examples, and problems deal with business, all listings and output were produced using a line printer with 132 character lines.

We would like to express our gratitude to Pat Fiorentino, Parviz Moarefi, Alan Bigio, and Paul Fraynd all with International Computer Systems, Inc., of Coral Gables for their assistance. Our thanks also to Maria Martinez who did an excellent job typing the manuscript.

Our special thanks to Dr. Val Silbey of Ball State University, coauthor of the first book in this series for his valuable contributions.

Alan J. Parker
John F. Stewart

1 / Introduction

At the end of this chapter you should be able to:

Performance
Objectives

- Understand the importance and impact of computer usage
- Sign-on and sign-off the Apple computer
- Understand how the Apple reacts to system commands

Everyone living in the United States today is affected by computers. The federal government uses computers in almost all of its departments. The Social Security Administration and the Internal Revenue Service are highly computerized. State and local governments use computers for tax collections and assessments. Businesses and utilities use computers for customer billing. Banks and other financial organizations use computers to handle customer accounts. Hospitals use computers for hospital administration and patient billing. Unless you live as a hermit in a cave, you are affected everyday in some way by computers.

The computer revolution is approximately thirty years old. Since 1946 when the ENIAC (the first electronic digital computer) began operating, changes that computers have wrought have been prodigious. All areas of society have been, and are being, touched by computers. From the time read the morning newspaper (typeset by computer) until we go to watching television (computer allocated programs), we are constantly using computers either directly or indirectly.

The effect of the Computer Revolution can be compared to the Industrial Revolution, which also radically changed society. Both revolutions changed work and leisure activities. With respect to work, no occupations were left untouched by the Industrial Revolution, except artisan crafts (sculptors, painters, etc.). Now, approximately two hundred years after the beginning of the Industrial Revolution, there are no coopers (barrel makers), wainwrights (horse drivers), millers (flour makers) or weavers (cloth makers) in the old sense of those occupations. The products or services are still supplied, but the methods of production have been radically altered. Work hours at the beginning of the Industrial Revolution were dawn to dusk, six days a week, leaving limited time for leisure activities. Now leisure is available during long weekends and after working hours. The impact of the Industrial Revolution may aid us in imagining the breadth of changes that will result from the computer revolution.

Initially, the few digital computers available were used for numerical calculations ("number crunching") by an elite group of mathematicians, engineers and scientists. Since then, radical changes in the cost, design, and use of computers have occurred. Today, computers are no longer the exclusive tool of mathematicians and scientists. More computers are used in businesses, such as insurance, banking, retailing, utilities, manufacturing and hospitals, than are used in scientific organizations. Almost daily, television and newspapers report new uses of computers. The computer has taken the drudgery out of calculating and printing bills, invoices, paychecks and other record-keeping tasks, freeing people from many of the routine tasks of adding numbers together. With the shift of paperwork from people to computers, some significant implications have become apparent. For society the use of computers is considered by some people to be a mixed blessing. But blaming the computer for human failings is an error. The computer itself is a tool. It is simply a new technology and this technology will be used as society chooses. The first quarter century of the computer revolution has brought us

- Computer controlled air-defense and air traffic control systems
- The landing of men on the moon
- Large scale and inexpensive use of checking accounts
- Credit cards
- Integrated reservation systems for travel
- Computerized hospitals
- A new field of employment (data processing)
- Management Information Systems

But so far we can barely envision what the second quarter century will bring.

Impact of
Computers on
Management

The first computer dedicated to business applications was installed in 1954. Since that time business applications have become more sophisticated. Applications at first consisted of simple clerical functions: preparation of payroll, financial statements, and other bookkeeping tasks. Thousands of clerical jobs were replaced by computers. The computer could do these routine tasks faster, cheaper, and more accurately.

The next major step was the use of computers to make simple decisions, e.g., ordering to restock inventory when a low level has been reached. At the present time, computers are the tools used to implement Management Information Systems (MIS). Management Information Systems transcend routine business applications because attention is focused upon providing management with the proper information for decision making. In many organizations, it is common to see computer terminals in the offices of the president and other senior executives. And MIS will become more common in organizations as computers become less expensive and easier to use. The manager of the future will need some familiarity with computers in order to make use of the great potential of MIS.

WHY USE
BASIC?

BASIC (Beginners All-purpose Symbolic Instruction Code) is a computer language. It was chosen for this text for numerous reasons. The first and most significant reason is that it is the simplest computer language that is widely available. The second reason is that the time required to learn BASIC is the shortest of all the common languages. Additionally, the extensions and enhancements made to BASIC have added power to the language, making BASIC comparable to other, more difficult languages.

A final reason for learning BASIC is that almost all of the manufacturers and vendors of microcomputers and minicomputers provide BASIC for their machines and systems; and these smaller computers are the fastest growing segment of the computer market. Apple alone has sold over 100,000 microcomputers; and every one of these small computers used BASIC for its higher-level language. Computers of this type are used by the hobbyist as well as by the largest organization.

This text is written with an assumption that the student has some basic knowledge of business transactions such as payroll, invoicing, and customer statements. It is also helpful if the student has the ability to think logically. The computer is not affected by emotions. If the student is a disciple of Marshall McLuhan, beware: The computer is not!

Prerequisites

It is *not* important, however, that you possess a mathematical background in order to learn BASIC. (A mathematical background, however, will not penalize a student.) On the basis of the successful completion of this text alone, the reader will probably *not* be able to find employment as a computer programmer or technician; but the student will understand the fundamentals of programming and be able to write programs of reasonable complexity.

In business, one usually wishes to computerize a manual system or function. It is important to understand how the manual system operates in order to successfully perform this function on a computer. Throughout this text, the major example will be the payroll function. It will serve as a vehicle for the introduction of programming (instructing the computer to perform a function, in this case payroll). A payroll system consists of the collection and manipulation of data to pay people for their time spent working. An hourly payroll system will be analyzed and programmed.

HOW TO USE A COMPUTER

The first step in computerizing a payroll is an analysis of the system and a clear definition of the system: The Silpar Company, Inc., has approximately 14 hourly employees used in the fabrication and assembly of computer components. All hourly wages are computed on the basis of hourly rate multiplied by the regular hours worked, plus time-and-a-half for overtime. The normal work week is 40 hours with one paid hour per day for lunch and coffee breaks. An employee may work a maximum of 20 overtime hours per week, if work is available. The payroll system should produce weekly paychecks and the necessary reports for tax and auditing purposes.

It should be obvious that all of the analysis and definition of the computerized payroll system has not been performed in the preceding paragraph. However, enough has been stated to begin the computerization of the payroll system. The first step consists of identifying the data necessary to produce all of the output (paychecks and reports). An examination of the manual system data will provide the answers to our first step.

In the manual system, each employee has a record that contains information such as employee number, social security number, address, marital status, number of dependents, hourly wages, wage payments made during the last year, federal income taxes withheld, FICA (Social Security) and other miscellaneous data. Each week, time cards are used to accumulate the regular and overtime hours worked by each employee. At the end of a pay period (weekly), the time cards are signed by the employee's supervisor and sent to the payroll department for processing. The payroll department computes the employee's pay for the week, the required deductions, issues a check for the employee's net pay (gross pay minus deductions), enters this information into the employee's record, and prepares a payroll register. A payroll register is a listing of the amounts paid to all employees, all deductions subtracted from their pay, and totals for all amounts.

In computerizing the payroll function or any other business application, it is very important to understand that files are used exactly as in the manual system. In the payroll, two files are used. The first is the employee *master file*; it consists of the *records* of all the employees. Each employee record contains data in *fields*. The fields are: employee number, name, hourly rate, etc. It is important to note that all records in one file must contain the same fields in the same order. Also, fields may contain data that is numeric, alphabetic, or both alphabetic and numeric (alphanumeric). The second file is the time *file*; it consists of a record for each employee and contains as fields the regular and overtime hours worked. With these two files and the appropriate program, a payroll register will be produced in Chapter 8.

COMMUNICATING WITH THE APPLE

Sometime in the not too distant future, we may communicate with computers by simply talking. In many science fiction films this is already the case. Unfortunately, technology has not taken us that far yet. As a consequence, we have to communicate with a computer through some sort of mechanical device. The common name for this device is a computer terminal or as it is simply known—a terminal. All terminals have many things in common. One important feature is a keyboard that is similar to a typewriter keyboard.

The keyboard allows us to communicate with the Apple. It takes the information that we transmit by pressing on the keys and transforms it into electronic signals that can be understood by the computer. Conversely, when the Apple communicates with us, the terminal transforms the electronic signals from the computer into characters printed on paper or displayed on a video screen. A short way of referring to the screen is by the initials CRT, which stands for cathode ray tube. The way messages are written on a CRT is similar to the way pictures appear on a TV screen. (A television picture tube is a CRT, but no one calls it that, except technicians.) In the Apple II the computer is housed in the same enclosure as the keyboard.

You should not be timid about using the Apple: The important thing to remember is that *you cannot damage* a computer or do any harm to it by typing *anything* on the keyboard. The only way you can cause any damage is by banging on the keyboard or spilling coffee on it. *You may type anything* on the keyboard and *not harm or "break" the computer system*. Similarly, neither the keyboard nor the computer can harm the user in any physical manner.

Every time you wish to use the Apple, there is a procedure that you must follow. This procedure is called a *sign-on*. Silly as it may sound, your first step, after sitting at the Apple, is to make sure it is on. There are two different sign-on procedures depending upon whether or not your Apple has what is called the *automatic starting option (autostart)*.

Sign-On
Procedure
(SON)

Without Autostart:
Once the Apple is on, an asterisk (*) will appear on the screen. Then place a properly initialized diskette in the drive. (See Appendix E for a description of the initialization procedure.) Close the drive door and type the number 6. Next, hold down the control key (CTRL) and press the P key. Finally, press the "RETURN" key. The Apple will respond, after a short time, with a "prompt" character (]). This tells you that the Apple is ready for you to program. The computer is prompting you to begin.

If the "prompt" character on the screen appears as a ">", type FP and press "RETURN". This will result in the prompt character "]", and you are ready to use the Apple.

The "RETURN" key serves the same function as a carriage return key on a typewriter. When you finish typing a line on a typewriter, you press it. On the Apple, when you press RETURN, you have told the computer that you are at the end of a line. The Apple will then respond with a prompt character (]) or a message.

To recap:

1. Make sure the Apple is turned on.

2. Insert an initialized diskette in the disk drive and close the door.

3. Type 6 followed by "CTRL" P. Press "RETURN".

4. The Apple responds with either "]" or ">".

5. If the response is ">" type FP and press "RETURN".

With Autostart and/or Corvus options:
If you have an Apple with autostart, the sign-on procedure is considerably easier. Simply place an initialized diskette into the disk drive, close the door, and turn on the Apple's power switch. The disk will turn on, and in a few seconds you will see the BASIC prompt character]. If the prompt char-

acter > appears, **type FP** and "RETURN" to get a]. You are now ready to begin typing a BASIC program.

You may also have an Apple hooked up to a Corvus Winchester disk drive. In this case, you can use the same procedure as above. The Apple will respond with the question "PLEASE ENTER YOUR NAME:". Type the name assigned to you and press the "RETURN" key. Next the Apple will say "PLEASE ENTER YOUR PASSWORD:" if a password is required for access to the computer. Enter your assigned password and press "RETURN". Finally the Apple will respond with the BASIC prompt character]. Type "CATALOG,S4" followed by a RETURN. The computer will print out some information on the screen and will again give you the] prompt. You are now ready to begin your terminal session.

Sign-Off Procedure

The only safe way to sign-off, no matter what type of system you have, is to remove your diskette from the drive and turn off the power switch.

Programming in BASIC

In order to write programs (instructions understood by the computer), the sign-on procedure must be used. The program in BASIC is entered through the terminal after the prompt character, line by line.

The greatest problem that people have when first using a computer is that they forget to press the "RETURN" key after entering something on a line. The result is that nothing happens! The "RETURN" *must* be pressed to indicate the end of your message to the computer. Until it is pressed, the computer assumes that you have not finished whatever you are trying to tell it!

2 / Performing Simple Calculations

At the end of this chapter you should be able to:

- Write a program that will do simple calculations
- Enter a program into the computer and use simple BASIC commands (NEW, SAVE, LIST, RUN)
- Use BASIC instructions for data manipulation and calculations (assignment to data fields, addition, subtraction, multiplication, division, output of results, end of program)
- Retrieve and modify an existing program using a BASIC command (LOAD)

The first uses of computers were computational. The power of the computer was used to perform engineering and scientific calculations. In business there are many instances where calculations have to be performed. Computers can perform these calculations very quickly. In this chapter we will show you how to program the computer to perform calculations and how to display the results of these calculations.

The first problem deals with payroll calculations. Starting with elementary calculations, this problem will be expanded to include more and more realistic elements. For the very first problem you are given the hourly rate and the number of hours worked. You are asked to calculate the gross pay for an employee.

One way of showing what a program does is to diagram the general steps of a program. Such a diagram shows the order in which the various steps are performed. Conceptually the execution of a program flows from one instruction to another; hence, the name flowchart. Flowcharts are used throughout this book to illustrate the structure of programs. For simple programs a flowchart may not be necessary; however, for complex programs flowcharts are very helpful. The symbols used in program flowcharting are explained here.

The rectangle is used to describe all processing performed by a computer. The arrow shows the direction of flow in the flowchart. In general the flow is top to bottom and left to right on a page.

 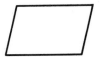

The diamond is used to indicate a decision point where the flow may go in one of two directions depending on the condition in the diamond. The parallelogram is used to indicate input of data to the computer or output of information from the computer. The oval is used for the beginning or end of the program.

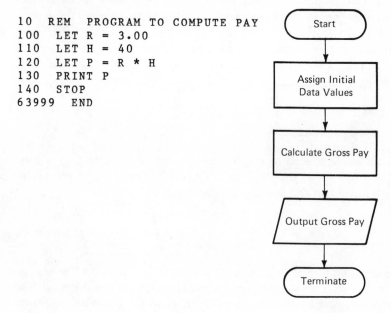

Problem Summary

Input
   Hourly rate: $3.00
   Number of hours worked: 40
Processing
   Multiply hourly rate times hours worked, giving gross pay.
Output
   Gross pay

The paycheck calculation program has to perform the following steps:

1. Assign values to data fields.

2. Calculate the gross pay.

3. Output the gross pay amount.

4. End the program.

The flowchart and a BASIC computer program to perform these four steps is shown below:

```
10     REM   PROGRAM TO COMPUTE PAY
100    LET R = 3.00
110    LET H = 40
120    LET P = R * H
130    PRINT P
140    STOP
63999   END
```

This program consists of seven lines. Each line starts with a number. This number, also called the statement number, is important because it tells the computer the sequence in which this program should be performed. The statement with the lowest number will be performed first, then the statement with the next lowest number, and so on until the end of the program is reached.

In this example the statement numbers go from 10 to 63999. However, any other sequence of numbers that keeps the same order could have been used. As long as the order of the lines is not changed, the lines could have been numbered from 10 to 16. These line numbers would have the same effect as the present numbers in the example program. Each line of the program is now explained:

The first line, 10 REM PROGRAM TO COMPUTE PAY, serves the programmer and not the computer. In fact, all "REM" statements are ignored by the computer. REM is short for remark. It is used to insert comments in a program as an aid to understanding the logic of the program.

The second line, 100 LET R = 3.00, states that the value 3.00 (the hourly rate of $3.00) is assigned to the field called R (for rate). The programmer identifies these fields by giving each a name. In BASIC, field names consist of one letter, or a letter followed by a single-digit number or two letters. Following are examples of field names with explanations of their validity.

Example	*Explanation*
A	Valid field name; one letter
AA	Valid field name; two letters
A1	Valid field name; one letter followed by single-digit number
B2	Valid; one letter and one digit
2B	Invalid; the first character has to be a letter
O0	Valid; letter "O" followed by zero "0" *(but not recommended since it is hard to see the difference)*
I1	Valid; letter "I" followed by number "1" *(also not recommended since it may be difficult to distinguish between I and 1)*

The third line, 110 LET H = 40, sets the value of H (H stands for hours worked) to 40. It is good practice to use field names that will help you to remember what is in that field. Such descriptive names are called mnemonic —memory aids. Of course, with only one letter, two letters, or a letter followed by a number, BASIC is limited in mnemonic capability.

The fourth line, 120 LET P = R * H, performs the calculations for gross pay. First the hourly rate (R) is multiplied by the number of hours worked (H). Then the result of this multiplication is placed in the field P. The asterisk (*) between R and H means multiply. Other arithmetic operations are + (plus) for addition, − (minus) for subtraction, / (slash) for division and ∧ (caret) for raising to a power. Parentheses may be used to separate parts of an arithmetic statement.

The next line, 130 PRINT P, tells the system to display the value of field P. Whatever number has been placed into the field called P, will be written on the screen.

The last two lines are used to terminate the program. The "STOP" tells the computer that the processing is finished. The "END", which must be the last statement of a program, tells the system that the program is finished. The STOP can be found almost anywhere in a program, but the END must be the last statement. That is why the END statement has the line number 63999; 63999 is the highest number available for a line in Apple BASIC.

RUNNING THE
PROGRAM

The next step in the problem-solving process is the entry of the program into the Apple. First, sign-on the system using the procedure from the previous chapter. Once you are on, then type

NEW

Don't forget the "RETURN"! The command NEW tells the system that a new BASIC program will be entered. The computer is now ready to accept the program and responds with]. At this time, type the program, one line at a time, ending each line with "RETURN". The program that you enter will be held in the Apple's memory.

The memory is where anything typed from the keyboard is stored. When the Apple is turned off, all information stored in memory is wiped clean. Think about the memory as a blackboard that is wiped clean when you sign off.

```
10   REM   PROGRAM TO COMPUTE PAY
100   LET R = 3.00
110   LET H = 40
120   LET P = R * H
130   PRINT P
140   STOP
63999   END
```

If a mistake is made in typing a line, the mistake can be corrected by retyping the line. Do not worry, mistakes will occur; to err is human. Merely retype the line correctly.

When the program has been entered into the Apple, type

SAVE PAY

This command places a copy of the program onto the diskette and stores it there under the program name (PAY). You can use up to 30 characters for a program name. The first character must be alphabetic. The program itself is also still in the memory (only a copy of the program exists on the diskette). If you did not SAVE PAY, and turn the Apple off, you would have to retype the program. To see what is in the memory type

LIST

This command will display the program in memory. Each line of the program is written on the screen. The command permits you to check that the program was entered correctly. Errors can be corrected by retyping incorrect lines. When a new line is typed with an old line number, the new line wipes out the old line and takes its place in the program sequence. To tell the computer to do what the program says (i.e., to execute or run the program) type the word

RUN

If you type RUN, and the screen displays the message "SYNTAX ERROR IN 100", it means that you have made an error in typing that line (100). List the program and retype the incorrect line. Syntax errors consist of typing BASIC instructions wrong. For example, if you typed 100 LT R = 3.00, you would get an error message when you try to run the program. Syntax errors are called "dumb errors". The computer will catch these. If you typed 100 LET R = 300, the computer would not catch that type of error.

```
]NEW

]10 REM PROGRAM TO COMPUTE PAY

]100 LET R=3.00

]110 LET H=40

]120 LET P=R*H

]130 PRINT P

]140 STOP

]63999 END

]SAVE PAY
]LIST

10   REM PROGRAM TO COMPUTE PAY
100   LET R = 3.00
120   LET H = 40
```

```
130   LET P = R * H
140   STOP
63999 END

]RUN
120

BREAK IN 140
]
```

Since the terminal session is now complete, sign-off.

When looking at the process that has occurred, some elements become apparent. First the problem has to be precisely specified. In this case the specification included a definition of starting values, hourly rate and hours worked; a statement of the desired output, gross pay; and a statement of how to get the output from the given inputs—multiply hourly rate by hours worked to get gross pay. Second, a program has to be written to perform the actions required to solve the problem. Third, the computer performs the instructions, one at a time in line number sequence. The BASIC instructions that tell the computer what to do were:

The LET statement, which assigns a value to a field
The PRINT statement, which displays the value of a field
The STOP statement, which tells the computer to stop executing
The END statement, which indicates the end of the program

These are all statements in the BASIC language. Furthermore, to work with a program, these BASIC commands were used:

NEW: To tell the system that a new program will be input from the keyboard

SAVE: To tell the system to keep a copy of the program on the diskette

LIST: To display the program currently in the memory

RUN: To tell the system to perform (execute) the program

BASIC commands do not have line numbers; BASIC instructions (statements) must have line numbers. Only after the last command (RUN) is entered does the computer actually perform (execute) the instructions of a program.

Examples

Invoice Example: This example deals with invoice calculations. Initial data are the number of units sold and the price per unit for an item. The output desired is the dollar amount of the invoice.

Problem Summary

Input

    Number of units sold: 50

    Price per unit: $15

Processing

    Multiply number of units sold by price per unit, giving dollar amount of invoice.

Output

    Dollar amount of invoice

```
]NEW

]10 REM THIS PROGRAM COMPUTES INVOICE AM
OUNT

]100 LET U=50

]110 LET P=15

]120 LET D=U*P

]130 PRINT D

]140 STOP

]63999 END

]SAVE INVCE
]LIST

10    REM  THIS PROGRAM COMPUTES IN
          VOICE AMOUNT
100   LET U = 50
110   LET P = 15
120   LET D = U * P
130   PRINT D
140   STOP
63999  END

]RUN
750

BREAK IN 140
]
```

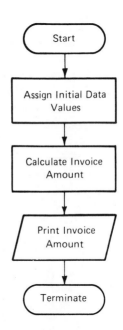

Notice that line 10 in the listing looks different from the line 10 that you typed. When you type in a line, you can type 40 characters across the screen. However, when you LIST the program on the screen, only 33 characters are printed on a line, and the next line contains the rest of the original line. **Note:** All program listings in this book were produced on a line printer for clarity.

Inventory Example: This problem asks for the calculation of ending inventory. The number of units in beginning inventory, the number of units received into inventory and the number of units released from inventory are given.

Problem Summary

Input

Number of units in beginning inventory: 120
Number of units received into inventory: 40
Number of units released from inventory: 45

Processing

Add number of units received to inventory; then subtract number of units released, giving ending inventory.

Output

Number of units in ending inventory

```
 NEW
10 REM THIS PROGRAM COMPUTES ENDING INVENTORY
100 LET B=120
110 LET R1=40
120 LET R2=45
130 LET E=B+R1-R2
140 PRINT E
150 STOP
63999 END
SAVE INVTY

RUN
115

BREAK IN 150
```

Exercises

Note: Save all programs. These exercises will be modified in later problems.

Commission Exercise: Write a program to calculate the commission that a salesman has earned. The initial data are gross sales and the commission rate.

Problem Summary

Input
    Gross sales: $12000
    Commission rate: 0.05

Processing
    Multiply gross sales by commission rate, giving dollar amount of commission.

Output
    Dollar amount of commission

Program:

_____

_____

_____

_____

_____

_____

_____

_____

_____

_____

Run your program, and see if your output matches the following:

```
RUN
600

BREAK IN 150
```

Account Balance Exercise: Retail merchants have to update customer accounts. The update consists of adding new charges to an account balance and subtracting customer payments from an account balance. Write a program that will perform these tasks to arrive at an ending balance for the customer.

Problem Summary

Input

Starting balance: $60

Customer payments: $60

New charges: $45

Processing

Subtract customer payments from starting balance; then add customer charges to balance, giving ending balance.

Output

Ending balance

Program:

_____

_____

_____

_____

_____

_____

_____

_____

_____

_____

_____

Run your program and check your ending balance with the following ending balance:

```
RUN
45

BREAK IN 150
```

MODIFYING THE PROGRAM

To change a program that has already been written requires the use of some new BASIC commands. For the payroll example, a modification is in order, if the problem is changed.

Assume that the output requirement is changed so that the words "GROSS PAY" as well as the amount of gross pay are displayed. This change requires that the print statement in the program be expanded for the output of alphabetic information. Printing aphabetic information is easy: Simply type "PRINT" followed by the alphabetic information enclosed in quotation marks as illustrated in line 125 below. Each PRINT causes one line of output. Therefore to display a line with "GROSS PAY", followed by a line with the amount of gross pay, the new program would look as follows:

```
10 REM PROGRAM TO COMPUTE PAY
100 LET R=3.00
110 LET H=40
120 LET P=R*H
125 PRINT "GROSS PAY"
130 PRINT P
140 STOP
63999 END
```

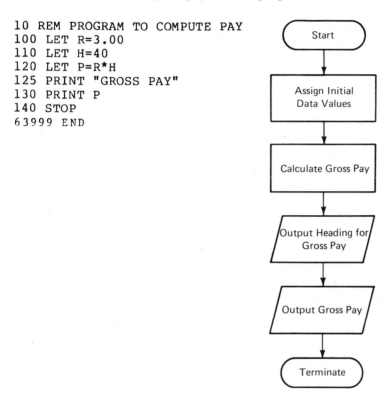

This new program has an extra line. To add this line to the existing program, it will be necessary to get the old program, and make the addition. This modification involves a series of steps.

First, sign-on the system. Next to get a copy of the program from the diskette, type

LOAD PAY

This command will copy your SAVEd program (PAY) from your diskette to memory where you may modify or RUN it.

If you cannot remember the program's name, type

CATALOG

The command CATALOG gives a list of the program names on the diskette.

Once the program is in memory, list it to make sure that it is the correct program. If the old and modified program are both to be retained, it will be necessary to change the program name, since two programs cannot be stored with the same name. To place a copy of the program on the diskette under the name PAY2, type

SAVE PAY2

Now, if the CATALOG command is issued, it will show two programs: PAY and PAY2. The new line can now be inserted into the program. Type the additional line

125 PRINT ''GROSS PAY''

The system will place the line in the proper sequence automatically. In order to provide space for program modifications, the line numbers were initially picked so that there was room for the insertion of additional lines. If the line numbers in the original program had run from 10 to 16, then no open space for program modifications would have been available. To place a copy of the modified program on your diskette the command

SAVE PAY

will have to be used.

After saving the modified program, LIST it; then RUN it. Following is the sequence that performs these tasks.

```
LOAD PAY
SAVE PAY2

125 PRINT "GROSS PAY"
SAVE PAY

LIST
10 REM PROGRAM TO COMPUTE PAY
100 LET R=3.00
110 LET H=40
120 LET P=R*H
125 PRINT "GROSS PAY"
130 PRINT P
140 STOP
63999 END

RUN
GROSS PAY
 120

BREAK IN 140
```

Review of Problem Modification Procedure

The problem modification procedure starts with a change in one of the problem specifications, either a change in initial data, or in the processing requirement, or in the desired output. In this example, the output was changed to include alphabetic information. Then the required changes are identified in the written program.

Next, on the Apple, the old program is retrieved from the diskette and placed in memory. The program is renamed and saved. The new line is added to the program. The changed program is then listed and executed.

Invoice Example: In this problem we want to have a heading for the invoice dollar amount. The remaining problem specifications are unchanged. The procedure for making this modification is given as follows:

Examples

```
LOAD INVCE
SAVE INVCE2

LIST
10 REM THIS PROGRAM COMPUTES INVOICE AMOUNT
100 LET U=50
110 LET P=15
120 LET D=U*P
130 PRINT D
140 STOP
63999 END

125 PRINT "INVOICE AMOUNT"
SAVE INVCE

RUN
INVOICE AMOUNT
 750

BREAK IN 140
```

Sales Tax Example: Many states and municipalities require that a sales tax be added to the purchase price of an item. The initial data for this problem are a dollar amount of taxable sales and the tax rate. The desired output is the total amount of the sale that the customer has to pay.

Problem Summary

Input
    Dollar amount of sale: $10.00
    Tax rate: 4%

Processing
    Multiply tax rate by dollar amount to get taxes. Add taxes to dollar amount, giving total amount of sale.

Output
    Total sale

```
NEW

10 REM THIS PROGRAM COMPUTES THE TOTAL SALE
100 LET S=10.00
110 LET R=.04
120 LET T=S*R
130 LET A=S+T
140 PRINT A
150 STOP
63999 END
SAVE TAX

RUN
 10.4

BREAK IN 150
```

It now becomes desirable to have additional output. Customers would like to see the tax separate from the total. Therefore, the desired output has been changed to include printing of the sales amount and of the tax.

```
LOAD TAX

135 PRINT S
137 PRINT T
SAVE TAX

LIST
10 REM THIS PROGRAM COMPUTES THE TOTAL SALE
100 LET S=10.00
110 LET R=.04
120 LET T=S*R
130 LET A=S+T
135 PRINT S
137 PRINT T
140 PRINT A
150 STOP
63999 END
RUN
 10
 .4
 10.4

BREAK IN 150
```

Exercises   Account Balance Exercise: Change the account balance problem so that the title "ENDING BALANCE" will appear as part of the output. Your output should look similar to the output shown below:

```
RUN
ENDING BALANCE
 45

BREAK IN 150
```

Sales Tax Exercise: Change the sales tax problem to calculate the total sales amount for a tax rate of 5%. The title "TOTAL SALE" should appear in the output. You can check your results with the output shown below.

```
RUN
TOTAL SALE
 10.5

BREAK IN 150
```

PRINTING
MANY VALUES
ON A LINE

The PRINT instruction has already been used to display the value of one field as well as to display alphabetic information. This PRINT statement can also be used to output many field values. To output many fields with one PRINT statement, the fields are separated by commas. This capability is illustrated by taking the initial payroll example and changing the desired output to a display of the hours worked and the hourly rate in addition to the output of gross pay.

Problem Summary

Input
> Hourly rate: $3.00
> Hours worked: 40

Processing
> Multiply hours worked by hourly rate, giving gross pay.

Output
> Hourly rate, hours worked, and gross pay

This change would alter line 130 of the Pay program to

> 130 PRINT R, H, P

To make this change in the program, the required sequence of steps is:

1. Sign-on.

2. Get the old program (LOAD PAY2).

3. Type the new line (130 PRINT R, H, P).

4. Save the program (SAVE PAY2).

5. List the program (LIST).

6. Execute the program (RUN).

7. Sign-off.

This sequence of steps would produce the following output.

```
LOAD PAY2

LIST
10 REM PROGRAM TO COMPUTE PAY
```

```
110 LET H=40
120 LET P=R*H
130 PRINT P
140 STOP
63999 END

130 PRINT R,H,P
SAVE PAY2

LIST
10 REM PROGRAM TO COMPUTE PAY
100 LET R=3.00
110 LET H=40
120 LET P=R*H
130 PRINT R,H,P
140 STOP
63999 END
RUN
 3                      40                      120

BREAK IN 140
```

Notice that with the new PRINT instructions, three numbers are printed on a line. Each of these field values starts at a column position that has been built into the system. The prespecified column positions are 1, 17, and 33. Therefore, three field values can be printed on one line. If the print instruction contains more than three fields, then another line is used to continue output on the screen.

With the prespecified columns, headings and associated data will always line up. As long as the alphabetic information has less than 16 characters, including blanks, any data displayed will fall directly under the headings. This alignment is shown in the revised payroll problem where headings are added to the output.

Problem Summary

Input
    Unchanged
Processing
    Unchanged
Output
    Change output to include headings for hourly rate, hours worked, and gross pay.

This modification requires that a line of headings be added to the program. After sign-on, the steps are:

1. Get the old program.

```
LOAD PAY2
```

2. List the program to see where to make the modification.

```
LIST
10 REM PROGRAM TO COMPUTE PAY
100 LET R=3.00
110 LET H=40
120 LET P=R*H
130 PRINT R,H,P
140 STOP
63999 END
```

3. Make the change. In this example, the data are printed in line 130. Since the headings have to appear before the data, a line has to be added before line 130. The headings consist of the words "Hourly Rate", "Hours Worked", and "Gross Pay". It is good practice to keep headings and data together. Therefore, line number 125 is used to output the headings.

```
125 PRINT "HOURLY RATE","HOURS WORKED","GROSS PAY"
LIST
10 REM PROGRAM TO COMPUTE PAY
100 LET R=3.00
110 LET H=40
120 LET P=R*H
125 PRINT "HOURLY RATE","HOURS WORKED","GROSS PAY"
130 PRINT R,H,P
140 STOP
63999 END
```

4. Execute the program.

```
RUN
HOURLY RATE           HOURS WORKED          GROSS PAY
   3                      40                   120

BREAK IN 140
```

5. Check the output. Although this aspect has not been discussed before, it should be remembered that errors can occur. Therefore, whenever you execute a program for the first time, make sure that the output is correct. If you are satisfied with the output, then the program can be SAVED for future use in the current form.

```
SAVE PAY3
```

6. If you are finished, sign-off.

WHY YOUR SCREEN DIFFERS FROM THE BOOK

Notice that what you see on the screen of your Apple will differ in many cases from what is printed in this book. The differences occur since all program listings and output presented were written on a printer with a 132 character print line while the Apple screen is only 40 characters wide. As you enter a program line, the first 40 characters will print across a line with additional characters being continued on the next line, etc.

Program output can, of course, use many more than 40 spaces. Most programs which generate reports will need more than 40 print positions. While you can write such a program in BASIC with no thought given to whether or not you even have a printer, when you RUN it, the output can look very strange as each printed line takes up two or more lines on the screen.

Program listings are even more mysterious. Listed lines use 33 characters on the first line and 28 on each additional line with lines after the first indented six characters for easier reading. Since a line in Apple BASIC can be up to 239 characters long, a line could be almost six lines long when entered and over eight lines long when listed.

With a little practice, you can learn to read the screen well enough to tell whether or not your program listing is correct or whether a program ran correctly. For final results, though, you would always want to LIST or RUN your program on a printer.

The output on your screen for the last program (Step 4) would look as follows:

```
]RUN
HOURLY RATE      HOURS WORKED
GROSS PAY
3                40                  120

BREAK IN 140
]
```

HANDLING ALPHABETIC TITLES

The headings in the last example were all less than the number of positions available. However, what would happen if the headings were longer? For example, what would the output look like, if the alphabetic titles that you wanted were "Hourly Rate of Pay", "Hours Worked", and "Gross Pay"? To find out what a system would do if requirements change, there is only one valid test—try it. Make the change and execute the program to see what happens. For the payroll problem, the key steps are shown below:

```
LOAD PAY3

125 PRINT "HOURLY RATE OF PAY","HOURS WORKED","GROSS PAY"
RUN
HOURLY RATE OF PAY            HOURS WORKED    GROSS PAY
 3                40           120

BREAK IN 140
```

Oops! The data do not line up. One way of handling this problem is to print the headings on two lines. The heading "HOURLY RATE OF PAY" is separated into two parts "HOURLY" and "RATE OF PAY". The two parts are then printed separately. The procedure for this change involves re-typing line 125 as

125 PRINT "RATE OF PAY", "HOURS WORKED", "GROSS PAY"

and a new line is added as line number 123

123 PRINT "HOURLY"

Now the output from the program would look as follows:

```
125 PRINT "RATE OF PAY","HOURS WORKED","GROSS PAY"
123 PRINT "HOURLY"
RUN
HOURLY
RATE OF PAY            HOURS WORKED            GROSS PAY
 3                     40                      120

BREAK IN 140
SAVE PAY3
```

This is the first example where the screen will not appear as the printout.

Example

Inventory Example: Inventory records typically show more than just the number of units in ending inventory. In this example we want to show the beginning inventory, the number received into inventory, the number issued from inventory, the number in ending inventory and the dollar amount of ending inventory. Furthermore, a general heading for the output is also worked.

Problem Summary

Input

Number of units at beginning: 120
Number received into inventory: 40
Number of units issued from inventory: 45
Cost per unit: $5.20

Processing

Add number received to beginning inventory and subtract number issued from inventory, giving ending inventory. Multiply ending inventory by cost per unit to get dollar amount of inventory.

Output

Heading of "Inventory Status", labels for each field of output "Beginning Inventory", "Receipts", "Issued", "Ending Inventory", and "Dollar Amount" followed by a line of field values.

Note: Five fields are printed on a line in this program. The heading "Inventory Status", should appear centered over the output. Therefore, to align the words "Inventory Status" over the third column, it is necessary to skip to the third built-in tab position. Printing two blank fields will skip to the third column. Similarly, two blank fields are inserted in the print line for "Receipts" and "Issued" since these titles do not have to be split over print lines.

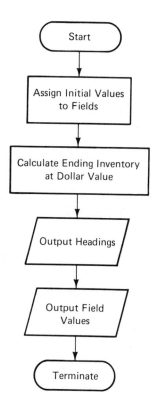

```
LOAD INVTY

LIST

10   REM  THIS PROGRAM COMPUTES ENDING INVENTORY
100    LET B = 120
110    LET R1 = 40
120    LET R2 = 45
130    LET E = B + R1 - R2
140    PRINT E
150    STOP
63999  END

132    LET C = 5.20
134    LET D = E * C
136    PRINT " "," ","INVENTORY STATUS"
138    PRINT "BEGINNING"," "," ","ENDING","DOLLAR"
140    PRINT "INVENTORY","RECEIPTS","ISSUED","INVENTORY","AMOUNT"
142    PRINT B,R1,R2,E,D

LIST
SAVE INV2
10   REM  THIS PROGRAM COMPUTES ENDING INVENTORY
100    LET B = 120
110    LET R1 = 40
120    LET R2 = 45
130    LET E = B + R1 - R2
132    LET C = 5.20
134    LET D = E * C
136    PRINT " "," ","INVENTORY STATUS"
138    PRINT "BEGINNING"," "," ","ENDING","DOLLAR"
140    PRINT "INVENTORY","RECEIPTS","ISSUED","INVENTORY","AMOUNT"
142    PRINT B,R1,R2,E,D
150    STOP
63999  END

RUN
```

		INVENTORY STATUS		
BEGINNING			ENDING	DOLLAR
INVENTORY	RECEIPTS	ISSUED	INVENTORY	AMOUNT
120	40	45	115	598

```
BREAK IN 150
```

Note: In order to have your output appear as shown, it is necessary to use a line printer.

Exercises

Sales Tax Exercise: Change the output of the sales tax problem so that it will print the amount of sale, the tax, and the total with appropriate headings.

```
RUN
SALE                        TOTAL
AMOUNT        TAX           SALE AMOUNT
  10           .5             10.5

BREAK IN 150
```

Account Balance Exercise: Change the account balance problem so that the heading "Beginning Balance", "Payments", "New Charges" and "Ending Balance" will appear over their respective values.

_____

_____

_____

_____

_____

```
RUN
BEGINNING                                   ENDING
BALANCE      CHARGES      PAYMENTS          BALANCE
   60           45           60               45

BREAK IN 150
```

SUMMARY

This chapter has shown you how to use the computer for simple calculations. The instructions of the BASIC language and the BASIC commands are listed below. BASIC commands are used to manipulate a program; they have no line numbers. BASIC instructions are used to manipulate data in a program; they do have line numbers.

Additionally, you have learned, not only how to write a program from scratch, but also ways of changing your program. The method of program modification will be continued throughout this book as the problem requirements and the BASIC capabilities are further developed.

You may be wondering why STOP is used since there is an END statement. By using a STOP, the message "BREAK IN ____" appears at the end of your output. As you proceed through the book, programs become more complex and it is important to know if your program ran to completion. The message "BREAK IN ____" tells us that the program finished as it should.

BASIC Commands Introduced:

NEW	Tells the Apple that the operator is about to type in a new program.
LIST	Gives a printout (listing) of the program.
SAVE PROGRAM NAME	Puts a copy of the program onto the diskette under program name. Must give program name.
RUN	Executes a program, i.e., tells a computer to perform the program instructions.
LOAD PROGRAM NAME	Asks for a copy of a program from the diskette, and places it in memory so that you can modify, run, or list it. Must give program name.

CATALOG   Lists the names of programs on the diskette.

BASIC Instructions Introduced:

Statement	*Explanation*
LET X = Y	Assigns the value of Y to the field X
PRINT X,Y	Displays the values of X and Y
PRINT "XYZ"	Displays the alphabetic information XYZ
STOP	Tells the system to stop
END	Indicates the physical end of a program
REM	Ignored by computer—remarks for programmer

Arithmetic operations

X + Y	Add Y to X
X − Y	Subtract Y from X
X * Y	Multiply X by Y
X / Y	Divide X by Y
X ∧ Y	Raise X to the Y power
( )	Parentheses may be used to group parts of arithmetic statements

Definitions

Field Name:	A field is named by a letter (A − Z), or by a letter followed by a number (A − Z, 0 − 9), or by two letters. Field names used in a program can actually consist of up to 238 characters, as long as the first character is a letter. The Apple simply ignores all but the first two characters.
Program Name:	A program name may be up to 30 characters; the first character must be a letter. Short program names are used in this book to minimize typing.

PROBLEMS   Write programs that will do the following:

1. Write your name.

2. Calculate the amount of a sale where 175 units are sold at $1.19 per unit.

3. Calculate the net amount of a sale where 47 units are sold at $4.56 per unit and a return is made for 3 units at $6.26 per unit.

4. Calculate the average sale for a day in which sales were made for $126.46, $276.19, $197.50 and $252.71. (**Note:** Average = the sum of daily sales divided by the number of sales.)

5. Modify Problem 3 above where the output is labelled Net Sale.

6. Modify Problem 4 above where the output is labelled Average Sale.

7. Modify the inventory program on page 32 so that the amount is printed on a separate line.

8. Calculate the amount of interest that would be earned in one year on $527.26 at 4%, 5%, 6%, 6.5%, and 7% annual interest. Display the results on one line and place headings of the interest rate above the interest amounts. Also center the heading Interest Calculation in your output.

9. In economics, the concept of unit elasticity means that the price times the quantity is a constant. If a product is manufactured by a company whose revenue is $125,000, and output could be 10,000, 8,000, 7,000, or 6,000 units, what would the price be at the four levels of output? Put headings on your output and write the numeric output on one line. (**Note:** pq = r where p = price, q = quantity, r = revenue.)

10. The formula for compound interest is $A = P(1 + i)^n$ where p = principal amount, i = interest rate expressed as a decimal, n = the number of time periods, and A = total amount at the end of n periods. Determine and label the output for p = $1,250, i = .055, and the number of time periods is from 1 to 5.

3 / Data Entry

At the end of this chapter you should be able to:

- Write.a program that will take data from the Apple keyboard
- Write a program that will process many records
- Test data for reasonableness

In many cases the data values are unknown when the program is written. For example, payroll data change from week to week. Consequently, to use the program, the data assignments have to be changed. Quite often in business, the person who runs a program is not the person who wrote the program. Therefore making changes, such as changing the assignment statements, would be cumbersome and awkward. Isn't there a way to give a program to somebody to run so that the person using the program doesn't have to know programming? The answer is yes. There is a way for a program to get data from a terminal. In this chapter, we will show you how to enter data while a program is running, how to process many records at the same time, and how to check field values for reasonableness.

The payroll function must calculate the employee's gross pay and the employee's net pay, the amount of his paycheck. Gross pay is the wages for regular and overtime hours. Net pay is gross pay minus deductions. Deductions include federal income tax and social security contributions (also known as FICA—Federal Insurance Contribution Act). In the following problems you are given the tax rate and the social security withholding rate.

    The program should be written so that the data for the hourly rate, the number of regular hours worked, and the number of overtime hours worked can be entered from a keyboard. The required outputs are gross pay, taxes, social security deductions, and net pay. Gross pay is calculated by adding regular wages to overtime wages. Regular wages are regular hours worked multiplied by the hourly rate. With time-and-a-half for overtime, overtime wages are calculated by multiplying overtime hours by 1.5 and then multiplying by the hourly rate. The deductions are calculated by multiplying gross pay by the appropriate rate. Net pay is calculated by subtracting the deductions from gross pay. The person is identified by name.

Problem Summary

Input
    Social security withholding rate: 6.13% (.0613)
    Federal income tax rate: 15% (.15)
    Hourly rate: $3.00
    Regular hours worked: 40
    Overtime hours worked: 2

Processing
    Multiply regular hours by hourly rate, giving regular wages. Multiply overtime hours times 1.5 and then multiply by hourly rate, giving overtime wages. Add regular wages to overtime wages, giving gross pay.

Multiply gross pay by income tax rate, giving federal income tax deduction. Multiply gross pay by social security rate, giving social security deduction. Subtract federal income tax and social security deductions from gross pay, giving net pay.

Output

Gross pay, payroll deductions, and net pay.

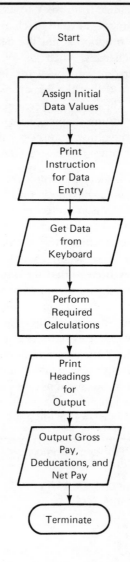

```
10   REM   PROGRAM TO INPUT AND COMPUTE PAY
100    LET F1 = .15
110    LET F2 = .0613
```

```
120    PRINT "TYPE NAME, HOURLY RATE, REGULAR HOURS, OVERTIME HOURS"
130    INPUT N$,R,H1,H2
140    LET G = R * H1 + R * H2 * 1.5
150    LET D1 = G * F1
160    LET D2 = G * F2
170    LET N = G - D1 - D2
180    PRINT "NAME:",N$
190    PRINT "GROSS","F.I.T.","F.I.C.A.","NET"
200    PRINT "PAY","DEDUCTION","DEDUCTION","PAY"
210    PRINT G,D1,D2,N
220    STOP
63999  END
```

This program contains one new BASIC instruction. Line 130 contains the word "INPUT". This instruction tells the computer to ask for data from the keyboard. During program execution, a question mark (?) will be displayed on the terminal. Data values are typed, each field separated by a comma, after the question mark. One value has to be entered for each field of the INPUT statement. In this case, four values separated by commas have to be typed, one value each for name, hourly rate, regular hours and overtime hours. This program also contains a new type of field name (N$), for alphabetic information. In line 130, N$ is used to hold alphabetic information. In line 180 the name is printed. After this program is entered, it can be executed.

Note: When entering dollar amounts, do not use the dollar sign ($) and do not use commas to separate thousands. Commas are used to separate field values; and the "$" has a special meaning in BASIC. It is used to name a field that contains alphabetic or alphanumeric data. The definition of a field name remains the same, but a $ is added.

The arithmetic statement in line 140 computes gross pay. It also could have been written the following way:

$$140 \text{ LET } G = (R*H1) + (R*H2*1.5)$$

The parentheses could have been added; but the computation in the program and the one above with parentheses give us exactly the same result. Arithmetic statements are performed in BASIC in the following sequence: First, exponentiation; next, division or multiplication; and last, subtraction or addition. In the program, G would be calculated in the following way: H2 is multiplied by 1.5, and this result is multiplied by R; H1 is multiplied by R, and this result is then added to the first result, giving us G.

```
RUN
TYPE NAME, HOURLY RATE, REGULAR HOURS, OVERTIME HOURS
?JONES,3.00,40,2
NAME:            JONES
```

```
GROSS            F.I.T.          F.I.C.A.        NET
PAY              DEDUCTION       DEDUCTION       PAY
129              19.35           7.9077          101.7423

BREAK IN 220
]SAVE PAY4
```

Notice that the name, the hourly rate, the regular hours, and .the over-time hours have to be typed *in that order*. The program will take the first typed value and assign it to the first field in the input statement, assign the next value to the next field, and so on, until it has assigned a value to each field. With the capability of entering data during program execution, it is not necessary for you, the programmer, to know what the specific data values will be. You can write the logic of processing and use it for different data values. By this approach you achieve a generally more useful program, since changes in data values do not require changes in the program. However, the person who uses the program must know what the data values are and the order in which they must be entered.

Examples   Invoice Example: This example deals with invoice calculations. The data to be input during execution are the number of units sold and the price per unit for an item. The output desired is the dollar amount of the invoice.

Problem Summary

Input
Number of units sold: 50
Price per unit: $15

Processing
Multiply number of units sold by price per unit, giving dollar amount of invoice.

Output
Dollar amount of invoice

```
10  REM   DETERMINE DOLLAR AMOUNT OF INVOICE
100    PRINT "TYPE NUMBER OF UNITS, PRICE PER UNIT"
110    INPUT U,P
120    LET D = U * P
130    PRINT "AMOUNT"
140    PRINT D
150    STOP
63999 END

]SAVE INVCE3
```

```
RUN
TYPE NUMBER OF UNITS, PRICE PER UNIT
?50,15.00
AMOUNT
750

BREAK IN 150
```

The flowchart to derive this program follows.

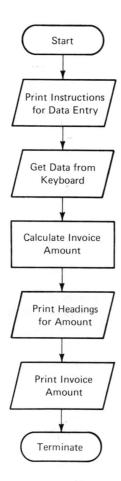

Inventory Example: This problem requires the calculation of ending inventory. The number of units in beginning inventory, the number of units received into inventory and the number of units released from inventory are given.

Problem Summary

Input

Number of units in beginning inventory: 120
Number of units received into inventory: 40
Number of units released from inventory: 45

Processing

Add number of units received to inventory; subtract number of units released, giving ending inventory.

Output

Number of units in ending inventory

```
10   REM   CALCULATE ENDING INVENTORY
100   PRINT "TYPE BEGINNING UNITS, UNITS RECEIVED, UNITS RELEASED"
110   INPUT B,R1,R2
120   LET E = B + R1 - R2
130   PRINT "ENDING INVENTORY"
140   PRINT E
150   STOP
63999 END

]RUN
TYPE BEGINNING UNITS, UNITS RECEIVED, UNITS RELEASED
?120,40,45
ENDING INVENTORY
115

BREAK IN 150
```

Exercises   Commission Exercise: Write a program to calculate the commission that a salesman has earned. The data are gross sales and the commission rate; both should be input during execution with instructions on the order of input. Label the output "Commission."

Problem Summary

Input

Gross sales: $12000
Commission rate: 0.05

Processing

Multiply gross sales by commission rate, giving dollar amount of commission.

Output

Dollar amount of commission

Program:

_____

_____

_____

_____

_____

_____

_____

_____

_____

_____

_____

Run your program, and see if your output matches the following output.

```
TYPE GROSS SALES, COMMISSION RATE
? 12000,.05
COMMISSION
 600

BREAK IN 150
```

Account Balance Exercise: Retail merchants have to update customer accounts. The update consists of adding new charges to the account balance and subtracting customer payments from the account balance. Write a program that will perform these tasks to arrive at an ending balance for the customer. The data should be input during execution. Label the output "Account Balance."

Problem Summary

Input

    Starting balance: $60
    Customer payments: $60
    New charges: $45

Processing

    Subtract customer payments from starting balance and add customer charges to balance, giving ending balance.

Output

    Ending balance

Program:

_____

_____

_____

_____

_____

_____

_____

_____

_____

_____

_____

_____

Run your program and check your ending balance with the ending balance given below.

```
TYPE STARTING BALANCE, CUSTOMER PAYMENT, NEW CHARGES
? 60,60,45
ACCOUNT BALANCE
 45

BREAK IN 150
```

PROCESSING MANY RECORDS

Let's assume that you have collected the weekly payroll data. You have a stack of time cards, with each card containing the weekly data on a person. Depending on the size of the organization, the stack of time cards may contain anywhere from 20 to 2,000 records. Therefore, to do the calculations for the weekly payroll, you would have to run your payroll program 20 to 2,000 times. In this section we will show you how to write a program to process many records in one run.

The assignment for this problem is similar to the previous problem. But instead of data for only one person, the weekly time records of many people have to be processed. The data are listed in Table 3–1. A program for processing all the data in one run follows.

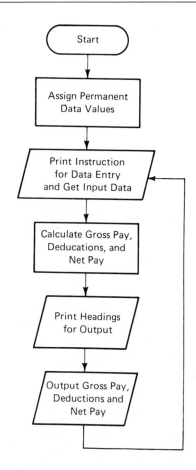

Weekly Payroll Data

Table 3-1

Name	Hourly Rate	Regular Hours Worked	Overtime Hours Worked
1. Adams	5.00	40	0
2. Baker	5.60	40	4
3. Cohen	6.25	38	0
4. Johnson	3.75	40	0
5. Tanner	4.25	36	0

```
10   REM  PROGRAM TO INPUT AND COMPUTE PAY
100    LET F1 = .15
110    LET F2 = .0613
120    PRINT "TYPE NAME, HOURLY RATE, REGULAR HOURS, OVERTIME HOURS"
130    INPUT N$,R,H1,H2
```

```
140   LET G = R * Hl + R * H2 * 1.5
150   LET Dl = G * Fl
160   LET D2 = G * F2
170   LET N = G - Dl - D2
180   PRINT "NAME:",N$
190   PRINT "GROSS","F.I.T.","F.I.C.A.","NET
200   PRINT "PAY","DEDUCTION","DEDUCTION","PAY"
210   PRINT G,Dl,D2,N
215   GOTO 120
220   STOP
63999 END
```

This program contains one new BASIC instruction," GOTO 120," found in line 215. The instruction means exactly what it says: When the computer reaches line 215, it is instructed there to go back to line 120. When the program is run, the computer executes lines 100 to 210 in sequence; when it reaches line 215, it goes back to line 120 and executes from 120 onwards.

This repetition is shown in the flowchart by the arrow that takes the flow back to steps that have already been executed. Thus the computer effectively processes one payroll record, and, since more than one employee is involved, it goes back to get the next employee record. To stop the program, after the last employee record has been processed, type C while holding down the control key (CTRL) when asked for data by the input statement. Nothing will appear on the screen. Then press the "RETURN" key. The logical end of the program is therefore entered during execution—after the last piece of data has been processed and more data is requested.

Since this program is only a one line change from the previous program, the modification is accomplished speedily. The change and execution actions are shown as follows:

```
LOAD PAY4

215 GO TO 120
SAVE PAY5

RUN
TYPE NAME, HOURLY RATE, REGULAR HOURS, OVERTIME HOURS
?ADAMS,5.00,40,0
NAME:           ADAMS
GROSS           F.I.T.          F.I.C.A.          NET
PAY             DEDUCTION       DEDUCTION         PAY
200             30              12.26             157.74
TYPE NAME, HOURLY RATE, REGULAR HOURS, OVERTIME HOURS
?BAKER,5.60,40,4
```

```
NAME:              BAKER
GROSS              F.I.T.              F.I.C.A.            NET
PAY                DEDUCTION           DEDUCTION           PAY
257.6              38.64               15.79088            203.16912
TYPE NAME, HOURLY RATE, REGULAR HOURS, OVERTIME HOURS
?COHEN,6.25,38,0
NAME:              COHEN
GROSS              F.I.T.              F.I.C.A.            NET
PAY                DEDUCTION           DEDUCTION           PAY
237.5              35.625              14.55875            187.31625
TYPE NAME, HOURLY RATE, REGULAR HOURS, OVERTIME HOURS
?JOHNSON,3.75,40,0
NAME:              JOHNSON
GROSS              F.I.T.              F.I.C.A.            NET
PAY                DEDUCTION           DEDUCTION           PAY
150                22.5                9.195               118.305
TYPE NAME, HOURLY RATE, REGULAR HOURS, OVERTIME HOURS
?TANNER,4.25,36,0
NAME:              TANNER
GROSS              F.I.T.              F.I.C.A.            NET
PAY                DEDUCTION           DEDUCTION           PAY
153                22.95               9.3789              120.6711
TYPE NAME, HOURLY RATE, REGULAR HOURS, OVERTIME HOURS
?

BREAK IN 130
```

Invoice Example: In this problem we want a heading for the invoice dollar
amount and to process four records. The remaining problem specifications
are unchanged. The procedure for making this modification is given below.

Examples

Problem Summary

Input

Units sold	Price per unit
50	$15.00
20	$14.00
120	$ 1.20
30	$ 6.00

Processing

Perform calculations for four records.

Output

Unchanged

```
LOAD INVCE3

]LIST

10   REM   DETERMINE DOLLAR AMOUNT OF INVOICE
100   PRINT "TYPE NUMBER OF UNITS, PRICE PER UNIT"
110   INPUT U,P
120   LET D = U * P
130   PRINT "AMOUNT"
140   PRINT D
150   STOP
63999 END

]145 GO TO 100

]SAVE INVCE4


  RUN
TYPE NUMBER OF UNITS, PRICE PER UNIT
?50,15.00
AMOUNT
750
TYPE NUMBER OF UNITS, PRICE PER UNIT
?20,14.00
AMOUNT
280
TYPE NUMBER OF UNITS, PRICE PER UNIT
?120,1.2
AMOUNT
144
TYPE NUMBER OF UNITS, PRICE PER UNIT
?30,6
AMOUNT
180
TYPE NUMBER OF UNITS, PRICE PER UNIT
?

BREAK IN 110
```

Sales Tax Example: Many states and municipalities require that a sales tax be added to the purchase price of an item. The initial data for this problem are a dollar amount of taxable sales and the tax rate. The desired output is the total amount of the sale that the customer has to pay. Six records should be processed.

Problem Summary

Input

Dollar amount of sale: $10.00, $42.00, $57.00, $2.50, $726.32, $9.27
Tax rate: 4%

Processing

Multiply tax rate by the dollar amount to get the taxes; add the taxes to dollar amount, giving the total amount of sale.

Output

Total sale

```
100    PRINT "TYPE AMOUNT OF SALE"
110    INPUT S
120    LET R = .04
130    LET T = R * S
140    LET A = S + T
150    PRINT "TOTAL SALE"
160    PRINT A
170    GOTO 100
180    STOP
63999 END

]RUN
TYPE AMOUNT OF SALE
?10.00
TOTAL SALE
10.4
TYPE AMOUNT OF SALE
?42.00
TOTAL SALE
43.68
TYPE AMOUNT OF SALE
?57
TOTAL SALE
59.28
TYPE AMOUNT OF SALE
?2.50
TOTAL SALE
2.6
TYPE AMOUNT OF SALE
?726.32
TOTAL SALE
755.3728
TYPE AMOUNT OF SALE
?9.27
TOTAL SALE
9.6408
TYPE AMOUNT OF SALE
?

BREAK IN 110
```

Account Balance Exercise: Change the Account Balance Problem so that five records are input.   Exercise

---

Problem Summary

Input

Starting balance	60	130	59.95	22.50	37.62
Customer payment	60	120	59.95	22.50	0.00
New charges	45	60	39.75	0.00	42.97

Processing

Perform calculations for five records.

Output

Unchanged

Program:

_____

_____

_____

_____

_____

_____

_____

_____

_____

_____

_____

_____

```
TYPE STARTING BALANCE, CUSTOMER PAYMENT, NEW CHARGES
?60,60,45
ACCOUNT BALANCE
45
TYPE STARTING BALANCE, CUSTOMER PAYMENT, NEW CHARGES
?130,120,60
ACCOUNT BALANCE
70
TYPE STARTING BALANCE, CUSTOMER PAYMENT, NEW CHARGES
?59.95,59.95,39.75
ACCOUNT BALANCE
39.75
TYPE STARTING BALANCE, CUSTOMER PAYMENT, NEW CHARGES
?22.50,22.50,0.00
ACCOUNT BALANCE
0
```

```
TYPE STARTING BALANCE, CUSTOMER PAYMENT, NEW CHARGES
?37.62,0,42.97
ACCOUNT BALANCE
80.59
TYPE STARTING BALANCE, CUSTOMER PAYMENT, NEW CHARGES
?

BREAK IN 20
```

When a program is written, it is necessary to make sure it performs its intended function. In the examples given so far, the numbers have been sufficiently simple so that the calculations can be checked by hand. It is good practice to check all calculations of a program whenever possible.

PROGRAM VERIFICATION

Errors do occur in complex programs. Errors crop up in the specification of a problem: For example, if salesman commissions are defined as a percentage of gross margin (sales minus cost of goods sold), then a specification of commission on the basis of gross sales would be in error. Errors can happen when the program is first written: For example, if receipts were subtracted from rather than added to beginning inventory, then a design error would exist. Errors can happen when the program is entered into the computer: Hitting the wrong key on the keyboard can cause many problems. These errors, called syntax errors, are caught when the program is first run. Other errors will be caught when the program tries to do something and can't. Logical errors like these will show up during execution.

But many errors, such as the erroneous calculation of inventories will not give any error messages. In those cases it is necessary to do the calculations by hand to make sure that the output is correct. However, even hand calculation will not catch problem specification errors. The salesman commission error—the calculation of commission on the basis of gross sales instead of gross margin—would require a comparison of the specifications with the actual operations of the company.

Errors in programs, called "bugs", bedevil even experienced programmers. But the largest number of errors in data processing is caused by bad data. This source of errors has been immortalized by the phrase "garbage in, garbage out." In this section we show you how to catch some of the "garbage in." The concept is known as "range checking."

HOW TO CATCH SOME ERRORS IN DATA

Range checking assumes that you know the permissible range of data values. Range checks make sure that data are not too high or too low. But range checking can not catch errors when the erroneous data is within the range. A transposition error (for example, $3.69 is entered incorrectly as $3.96) will not be caught by range checks if the erroneous data is within range. In the case of the payroll example, we know that regular hours worked cannot exceed 40 hours. Therefore, we can check to make sure that values for regular hours worked are not larger than 40. The permissible ranges for the data fields are:

Field	Low Value	High Value
Hourly rate	3.05	10.00
Regular hours	0	40
Overtime hours	0	20

Checking range values of input fields is only part of the task. Once an error has been found, it must be identified so that the keyboard operator can correct the mistake. By accident, such as misinterpreting handwritten numbers, or through carelessness, erroneous data may have been typed. Range checks help to catch input that is obviously wrong. But the operator also needs to be told that the input is wrong. Hence, appropriate error messages must be printed. Following are flowcharts (Figs. 3–1 and 3–2) and a program that perform these additional requirements:

```
10    REM   PROGRAM TO INPUT AND COMPUTE PAY
100   LET F1 = .15
110   LET F2 = .0613
120   PRINT "TYPE NAME, HOURLY RATE, REGULAR HOURS, OVERTIME HOURS"
130   INPUT N$,R,H1,H2
131   IF R < 3.05 THEN 138
132   IF R > 10 THEN 138
133   IF H1 < 0 THEN 138
134   IF H1 > 40 THEN 138
135   IF H2 < 0 THEN 138
136   IF H2 > 20 THEN 138
137   GOTO 140
138   PRINT "ERROR IN INPUT DATA"
139   GOTO 120
140   LET G = R * H1 + R * H2 * 1.5
150   LET D1 = G * F1
160   LET D2 = G * F2
170   LET N = G - D1 - D2
180   PRINT "NAME:",N$
190   PRINT "GROSS","F.I.T.","F.I.C.A.","NET
200   PRINT "PAY","DEDUCTION","DEDUCTION","PAY"
210   PRINT G,D1,D2,N
215   GOTO 120
220   STOP
63999   END
```

The difference between this program and the previous program on page 47 is in lines 131 to 139. Here we test the data with a series of IF statements. An IF statement compares two values.

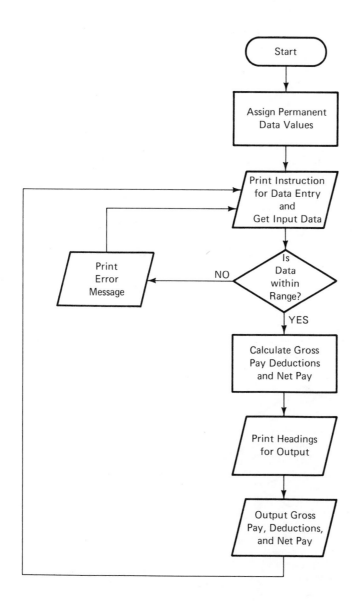

Flowchart of Range Test Program

Figure 3-1

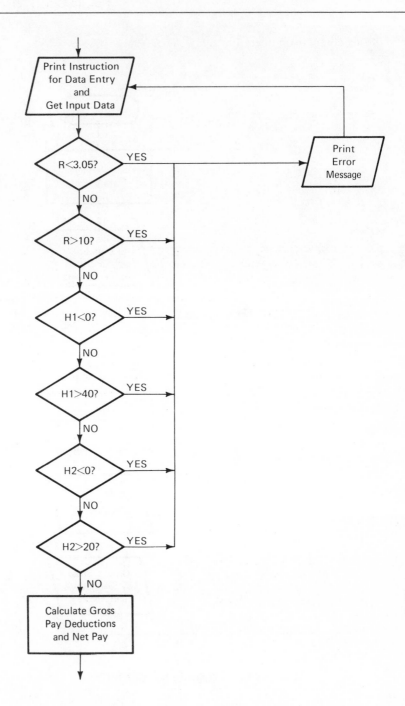

Figure 3–2

Range Tests:
Expansion of Decision—"Is Data Within Range?"

The six comparison operators are:

$=$	Equal
$<$	Less than
$<=$	Less than or equal
$>$	Greater than
$>=$	Greater than or equal
$<>$	Not equal

The comparison is followed by THEN and a line number. The "THEN line number" means GOTO the line number indicated if the comparison is true. If the comparison is not true, the next line is executed (see Fig. 3–2). Fields are compared with values or with other fields. Thus we can read line 131 as, "IF the hourly rate (R) is less than 3.05 THEN go to line 138." Similarly, line 132 means: "IF the hourly rate (R) is greater than 10 THEN go to line number 138." In line 138 an error message is printed. The error message is followed by a return to the instruction (line 120) for data entry.

Notice the GOTO 140 in line 137. This GOTO directs control to line 140 for the processing of valid data. When the computer reaches line 137, the data must be valid because it passed all the tests in lines 131 to 136. If line 137 did not exist, then valid records would also print the error message.

These changes to the old program are shown below:

```
LOAD PAY5

SAVE PAY6


131   IF R < 3.05 THEN 138
132   IF R > 10 THEN 138
133   IF H1 < 0 THEN 138
134   IF H1 > 40 THEN 138
135   IF H2 < 0 THEN 138
136   IF H2 > 20 THEN 138
137   GOTO 140
138   PRINT "ERROR IN INPUT DATA"
139   GOTO 120


]SAVE PAY6

 LIST
```

```
10    REM   PROGRAM TO INPUT AND COMPUTE PAY
100   LET F1 = .15
110   LET F2 = .0613
120   PRINT "TYPE NAME, HOURLY RATE, REGULAR HOURS, OVERTIME HOURS"
130   INPUT N$,R,H1,H2
131   IF R < 3.05 THEN 138
132   IF R > 10 THEN 138
133   IF H1 < 0 THEN 138
134   IF H1 > 40 THEN 138
135   IF H2 < 0 THEN 138
136   IF H2 > 20 THEN 138
137   GOTO 140
138   PRINT "ERROR IN INPUT DATA"
139   GOTO 120
140   LET G = R * H1 + R * H2 * 1.5
150   LET D1 = G * F1
160   LET D2 = G * F2
170   LET N = G - D1 - D2
180   PRINT "NAME:",N$
190   PRINT "GROSS","F.I.T.","F.I.C.A.","NET
200   PRINT "PAY","DEDUCTION","DEDUCTION","PAY"
210   PRINT G,D1,D2,N
215   GOTO 120
220   STOP
63999 END
```

Example
Inventory Example: We want to modify the inventory example in Chapter 2 to process three records and check the appropriateness of their values. The high values were determined by examining the capacity of the company to store and handle inventory. The low values cannot be negative, and the lowest cost of an item of inventory is $1.00.

Problem Summary

Input

Number of units at beginning:	120	20	60
Number received into inventory:	40	70	20
Number of units issued from inventory:	45	100	80
Cost per unit:	$5.00	$7.00	$3.25

Processing

Test the data for reasonableness.

Data Ranges

Field	Low Value	High Value
Units at Beginning	0	10,000
Units Received	0	3,000
Units Issued	0	*
Cost	$1.00	$10.00

*Number of Units in Inventory = Units at Beginning + Units Received.

Output

Unchanged

```
10    REM   THIS PROGRAM CALCULATES ENDING INVENTORY VALUE
100   PRINT "TYPE BEGINNING UNITS, UNITS RECEIVED, UNITS RELEASED"
105   PRINT "AND COST SEPARATED BY COMMAS"
110   INPUT B,R1,R2,C
111   IF B < 0 THEN 120
112   IF B > 10000 THEN 120
113   IF R1 < 0 THEN 120
114   IF R1 > 3000 THEN 120
115   IF R2 < 0 THEN 120
116   IF R2 > (B + R1) THEN 120
117   IF C < 1.00 THEN 120
118   IF C > 10.00 THEN 120
119   GOTO 130
120   PRINT "ERROR IN INPUT DATA"
121   GOTO 100
130   LET E = B + R1 - R2
134   LET D = C * E
136   PRINT " "," ","INVENTORY STATUS"
138   PRINT "BEGINNING"," "," ","ENDING","DOLLAR"
140   PRINT "INVENTORY","RECEIPTS","ISSUED","INVENTORY","VALUE"
142   PRINT B,R1,R2,E,D
143   GOTO 100
150   STOP
63999 END


RUN
TYPE BEGINNING UNITS, UNITS RECEIVED, UNITS RELEASED
AND COST SEPARATED BY COMMAS
?120,40,45,5.00
                              INVENTORY STATUS
BEGINNING                                   ENDING        DOLLAR
INVENTORY        RECEIPTS        ISSUED      INVENTORY     VALUE
120              40              45          115           575
TYPE BEGINNING UNITS, UNITS RECEIVED, UNITS RELEASED
AND COST SEPARATED BY COMMAS
?20,70,100,7.00
ERROR IN INPUT DATA
```

```
TYPE BEGINNING UNITS, UNITS RECEIVED, UNITS RELEASED
AND COST SEPARATED BY COMMAS
?60,20,80,3.25
                            INVENTORY STATUS
BEGINNING                                    ENDING          DOLLAR
INVENTORY          RECEIPTS        ISSUED    INVENTORY       VALUE
60                 20              80        0               0
TYPE BEGINNING UNITS, UNITS RECEIVED, UNITS RELEASED
AND COST SEPARATED BY COMMAS
?

BREAK IN 110
```

Review of
Validity Check
Operations
and Deleting
Obsolete
Programs

This sequence of actions starts with the sign-on procedure. The old program is copied from the diskette and placed into the memory with the command

LOAD PAY5

When the system indicates that it is ready with a prompt, the program name is changed and a copy of the program with its new name is placed on the diskette. This SAVE action is taken as a security precaution. If anything should go wrong while you are working with the program PAY6 then you can recover by calling PAY5, and then repeat the modification steps.

After PAY6 has been saved, the new lines between 130 and 140 are typed. The SAVE and LIST commands save a copy of the modified PAY6 and provide a display of the program so that you can visually verify your modifications. If an error has occurred, you can call the old PAY5 program and make the modifications again. This same sequence is used for the inventory example.

Note that only the program in memory is changed. The diskette is not affected unless you SAVE a program. SAVE copies a program from the memory to the diskette. You can find out what programs are stored for you on the diskette by typing the BASIC command CATALOG.

You can also delete programs from the diskette with the DELETE command. Old programs that have been superseded by newer programs should be removed. Look at the catalog. See if you have programs that you no longer need. If there are obsolete programs in your catalog that you want to remove, then type DELETE followed by the program name. When the system responds with the prompt character, the program has been deleted from the diskette.

SUMMARY

This chapter covered four new techniques:

● How to get data from a keyboard
● How to process many records

- How to check records for reasonableness
- How to delete obsolete programs

All these techniques make your programs more realistic because they add generality and flexibility. No longer do you need to know specific data values when you write a program. The specific data can be entered when the program is used. No longer does a program have to be re-run for each record. A loop controlled by a GOTO can process many records in one run. And with range checks, some of the errors in input data will be caught. Therefore, programs written this way use the computer more flexibly and provide important assistance to the users.

BASIC Commands Introduced:

DELETE **PROGRAM NAME**	Eliminates a program from the diskette. Must use program name.

BASIC Instructions Introduced:

Statement	Explanation
INPUT X,Y	Takes numeric values for fields X and Y from the keyboard.
INPUT X$,Y$	Gets alphabetic values for fields X$ and Y$ from the keyboard.
GOTO nnn	Tells the system to go to line number nnn for the next instruction.
IF x THEN nnn	If x is true then go to line nnn for the next instruction, otherwise (if x is false) go to the next line in sequence.

Comparison operators	Result of comparison
X = Y	Result is true if X equals Y
X < Y	Result is true if X is strictly less than Y
X < = Y	Result is true if X is less than or equal to Y
X > Y	Result is true if X is strictly greater than Y
X > = Y	Result is true if X is greater than or equal to Y
X < > Y	Result is true if X is not equal to Y

Rather than stating the comparison result as true or false, yes or no may be used.

PROBLEMS   Write a program to do the following:

1. Modify the invoice problem in this chapter to check the value of the price per unit. The price should not be less than zero or more than $20. Data to be input at execution time

Units	20	12	34	27	100
Price	1.50	21.22	14.50	1.95	2.56

2. Modify the commission problem in this chapter to check the values of gross sales and commission rate. Gross sales may range from 0 to $100,000. The commission rate varies from 2% to 6%. Data to be input at execution time

Gross sales	2,476	29,650	400,000	97,727
Commission rate	4%	4.2%	2.1%	6.7%

Error messages should indicate whether the error detected is in gross sales or the commission rate.

3. Modify the payroll example on page 54 to output specific error messages such as "HOURLY RATE TOO HIGH", "HOURLY RATE TOO LOW", "HOURS TOO HIGH", "HOURS TOO LOW", "OVERTIME TOO HIGH", "OVERTIME TOO LOW". Use the following data:

Name	Hourly Rate	Regular Hours	Overtime
Able	$1.95	40	0
Baker	2.96	42	26
Charlie	11.65	−4	0
Fern	5.50	40	25
Graak	7.20	40	10

4. In Problem 3 above, a single error will result in not processing a person's data. Modify your program so that multiple errors in a person's data will be detected and result in appropriate error messages. Use the same data. **Note:** Process invalid records.

5. Modify the inventory example on page 59 to output specific error messages such as "BEGINNING INVENTORY TOO HIGH", "BEGINNING INVENTORY TOO LOW", "UNITS RECEIVED TOO HIGH", "UNITS RECEIVED TOO LOW", "UNITS ISSUED TOO HIGH", "UNITS ISSUED TOO LOW", "COST TOO HIGH", "COST TOO LOW". Use the following data:

Beginning Inventory	Units Received	Units Issued	Cost
100	20	60	$ 4.00
20	3,500	4,000	$ .75
500	200	600	$12.00
20	−40	60	$ 1.50
−100	200	700	$14.00

6. Modify your program in Problem 5 so that multiple errors in a data re-cord (a line of input) will be indicated. Use the same data. **Note:** Process invalid records.

4 / Sequential Files

At the end of this chapter you should be able to:

- Use files to store data
- Write a program that will put data in a file
- Write a program that will read data from a file
- Find a record in a file

To use a computer, it is necessary to get data into the computer. In many cases when the amount of data is large, a computer file has to be set up to store the data. With files, the same data can be used again and again.

With files, entry of data is separated from the processing of data. Therefore, the data can be entered into a computer file at one time to be processed later.

But the files that a computer uses are different from the files used by people. Data is stored in a computer file in electromagnetic form. And people can't read electromagnetic data directly.

It is necessary to write a program to enter data into files and to write programs that read data from files. In this chapter, we will show you how to set up a file for computer processing. The type of file used is a sequential file. The file is called a sequential file because it is organized in a particular sequence, one record next to another. In a later chapter another type of file, a direct access file, will be discussed.

The payroll problem will illustrate the capabilities of BASIC to handle files. In this case, we want to write a program that lets a terminal (data entry) operator enter data into a file. Later, we will use the data in the file for calculations and reports. When files are used, only one record at a time is read or written.

The payroll data for this problem consists of records with the following fields. Field names are in parentheses.

- Employee number (N)
- Employment department number (D)
- Employee name (N$)
- Hourly rate of pay (H)
- Regular hours worked (R)
- Overtime hours worked (V)

The processing consists of entering data through a terminal and placing it in a file. For output, messages telling the operator what to do are necessary.

Problem Summary

Input	Valid Range
Employee number	100 to 999
Employee department number	1 to 20

Employee name	anything
Hourly rate	3.05 to 15.00
Regular hours worked	0 to 40
Overtime hours worked	0 to 20

Processing
Take data from a keyboard and place valid data in a file. Check the data for validity.

Output
Instructions for operator and data on a computer file.

Therefore the program has to be able to:

1. Set up a new file.

2. Get data from the terminal when an operator types it.

3. Write the data into a file that the computer can use.

4. Stop when all the data has been entered.

See the flowchart (Fig. 4–1) and program to do all of these actions below:

```
10    REM   THIS PROGRAM TAKES DATA FROM THE KEYBOARD AND
20    REM             PLACES IT IN THE EMPLOY FILE
100   PRINT  CHR$ (4);"OPEN EMPLOY"
110   PRINT "TYPE EMPLOYEE NUMBER, DEPARTMENT NUMBER, EMPLOYEE NAME"
120   PRINT "HOURLY RATE,REGULAR HOURS"
130   PRINT "OVERTIME HOURS SEPARATED BY COMMAS"
140   PRINT "WHEN FINISHED TYPE 99,99,AA,99,99,99"
150   INPUT N,D,N$,H,R,V
160   IF N = 99 THEN 400
170   IF N < 100 THEN 290
180   IF N > 999 THEN 290
190   IF D < 1 THEN 290
200   IF D > 20 THEN 290
210   IF H < 3.05 THEN 290
220   IF H > 15.00 THEN 290
230   IF R < 0 THEN 290
240   IF R > 40 THEN 290
250   IF V < 0 THEN 290
260   IF V > 20 THEN 290
265   PRINT  CHR$ (4);"WRITE EMPLOY"
270   PRINT N;",";D;",";N$;",";H;",";R;",";V
275   PRINT  CHR$ (4)
280   GOTO 110
290   PRINT "ERROR IN INPUT DATA, PLEASE RETYPE"
300   GOTO 110
400   PRINT  CHR$ (4);"CLOSE EMPLOY"
63999  END
```

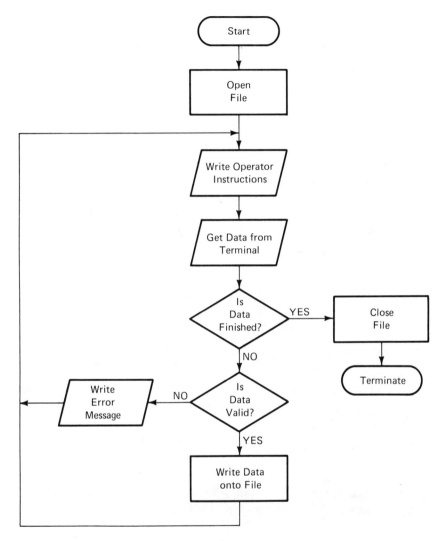

Flowchart for Setting Up a File   Figure 4–1

This program contains three new statements:

- Line 100 opens a file.
- Lines 265–275 write data into a file.
- Line 400 closes a file.

Let's look closely at these three statements.

Open a file: Line 100 is PRINT CHR$(4); "OPEN EMPLOY". This statement is used to open a file for either reading or writing. If we do not have a file, then the computer creates one. The statement says to open a file and that this file will be called "EMPLOY".

This instruction is always written the same way. The only change necessary from program to program is the file name after OPEN. The instruction looks strange because it appears to be a PRINT instruction, but as you will see PRINT CHR$(4) is not an ordinary PRINT instruction. It is the method by which we tell the computer that we want to use a file.

The file name is limited to 30 alphanumeric characters. The first character must be alphabetic. Examples of valid and invalid file names are shown in the following list. (**Note:** The rules for filenames are the same as the rules for program names!)

Example	*Explanation*
A	Valid file name. You can use up to 30 characters, but you don't have to use all 30.
A1	Valid file name. Numbers are also alphanumeric characters. The file names A and A1 are not recommended since they may be confused with field names.
LIST	Valid file name; but not recommended since it is a BASIC command and therefore a possibility of confusion exists.
ACCREC	Valid file name. Good choice of a name since ACCREC for Accounts Receivable has mnemonic (helps you remember) characteristics.
2PAYROLL	Invalid file name. File names must begin with a letter.

At the end of this program you will find that your catalog contains not only programs but also the data file "EMPLOY".

Write into a file: Line 265 PRINT CHR$(4); "WRITE EMPLOY" tells the computer that it should write on the file "EMPLOY". Line 270 PRINT N; ","; D; ","; N$; ";"; H; ","; R; ","; V looks similar to most PRINT instructions. However, since it follows line 265, it will PRINT the values of the fields N, D, N$, H, R and V on the "EMPLOY" file. The strange-looking punctuation between field names (;",";) tells the computer how to store the field values in the file. This punctuation must always be used to separate fields when writing a sequential file. Line 275 PRINT CHR$(4) tells the computer to stop writing on the file so that when line 110 is executed the message will be written on the screen.

Close a file: Line 400 closes a file. That tells the computer that it can now store the file. Storing a file in this case means that the file is placed onto your diskette. That way the file will be available to you for processing. It will remain there until you decide that you no longer need the file. Until then, you can always gain access to it with an OPEN statement.

The file instructions for the program are:

```
100   PRINT CHR$(4); "OPEN EMPLOY"
265   PRINT CHR$(4); "WRITE EMPLOY"
270   PRINT N; ","; D; ","; N$; ","; H; ","; R; ","; V
275   PRINT CHR$(4)
400   PRINT CHR$(4); "CLOSE EMPLOY"
```

Each instruction starts with PRINT, but only one line, 270, actually writes information on to the file. The other lines are necessary to prepare or finish handling the file "EMPLOY". In order to write information to any file, the above sequence should be used. All you have to change is the file name and the field names.

One last explanation before you try this program. In line 140 the operator is instructed to type "99,99,AA,99,99,99" when no more data has to be entered. This entry generates a last record. In effect, we have a dummy record. It is used to indicate that the data input to the file is finished.

But the computer doesn't know that you have chosen a record with 99's and an AA in each field to end the data. This record is called a dummy record since it does not contain usable payroll data. To the machine, it looks like any other record. We know that this record indicates the end of data because that's what we told the operator to do in line 140 in order to end data input. We could have told the operator to enter any other values in line 140 to indicate the end of data. But whatever we told the operator, we have to pick carefully. The dummy record should be invalid so that it stands out. It should be the same every time so that when the data changes, we don't have to rewrite the program.

The instruction to type 99's and AA serves to end the data for the payroll problem. When such a record is reached, we know that it is time to close the file since data entry is finished. The end of data is tested in line 160. If N, the field for employee number, has a 99 then we assume that no more data will be forthcoming, and we go to line 400 to close the file.

Sign-on the system and type the program. Once you have finished typing the program and given the RUN command, enter the payroll data shown below in Table 4–1.

Table 4-1   Payroll Data

Employee Number	Department Number	Employee Name	Hourly Rate	Regular Hours	Overtime Hours
101	1	Adams	$5.00	40	0
103	12	Baker	5.60	40	4
104	17	Bravo	4.00	40	2
108	16	Cohen	6.25	38	0
172	2	Johnson	3.75	40	0
198	1	Tanner	4.25	36	0
202	16	Wilson	4.00	40	0
206	7	Lester	5.25	40	0
255	12	Schmidt	5.60	40	4
281	12	Miller	6.00	40	0
313	7	Smith	4.25	40	4
347	12	Gray	6.00	38	0
368	1	Weaver	3.50	40	2
422	1	Williams	4.00	40	0

Better yet, write the program and talk somebody else into entering the data from a keyboard. By having somebody else enter the data, you have a closer approximation to how things are actually done in organizations. If an error occurs during data entry, then you must stop the program and run it again from the beginning. So be careful. In the last section of this chapter you will learn how to correct records in a data file.

Example

Inventory Example: Create a file called "INV" with five fields per record.

Problem Summary

Input

Part Number	Beginning Units	Units Received	Units Issued	Cost
101	120	40	45	$5.00
210	20	70	100	7.00
219	60	60	80	3.25
226	5	110	90	2.95
235	100	0	50	6.20
347	0	50	20	4.60

Data ranges remain the same as in Chapter 3.

Processing

Take data from keyboard and place valid records in a file named "INV".

Output
Instructions for data entry and a file named "INV".

```
100    REM   THIS PROGRAM PUTS DATA INTO THE INV FILE
110    PRINT  CHR$ (4);"OPEN INV"
120    PRINT "TYPE PART NUMBER,BEGINNING UNITS,UNITS RECEIVED,UNITS ISSUED";
130    PRINT " AND COST, WITH COMMAS IN BETWEEN"
140    PRINT "WHEN FINISHED TYPE 1,1,1,1,99"
150    INPUT P,B,R,I,C
160    IF C = 99 THEN 350
170    IF B < 0 THEN 270
180    IF B > 1000 THEN 270
190    IF R < 0 THEN 290
200    IF R > 3000 THEN 290
210    IF I < 0 THEN 310
220    IF I > B + R THEN 310
230    IF C < 1 THEN 330
240    IF C > 10 THEN 330
245    PRINT  CHR$ (4);"WRITE INV"
250    PRINT P;",";B;",";R;",";I;",";C
255    PRINT  CHR$ (4)
260    GOTO 120
270    PRINT "ERROR IN BEGINNING UNITS-RETYPE"
280    GOTO 120
290    PRINT "ERROR IN UNITS RECEIVED-RETYPE"
300    GOTO 120
310    PRINT "ERROR IN UNITS ISSUED-RETYPE"
320    GOTO 120
330    PRINT "ERROR IN COST-RETYPE"
340    GOTO 120
350    PRINT  CHR$ (4);"CLOSE INV"
360    STOP
63999  END
```

```
]RUN
TYPE PART NUMBER, BEGINNING UNITS, UNITS RECEIVED, UNITS ISSUED
 AND COST, WITH COMMAS IN BETWEEN
WHEN FINISHED TYPE 1,1,1,1,99
?101,120,40,45,5.00
TYPE PART NUMBER, BEGINNING UNITS, UNITS RECEIVED, UNITS ISSUED
 AND COST, WITH COMMAS IN BETWEEN
WHEN FINISHED TYPE 1,1,1,1,99
?210,20,70,100,7.00
ERROR IN UNITS ISSUED-RETYPE
TYPE PART NUMBER, BEGINNING UNITS, UNITS RECEIVED, UNITS ISSUED
 AND COST, WITH COMMAS IN BETWEEN
WHEN FINISHED TYPE 1,1,1,1,99
?219,60,60,80,3.25
```

```
TYPE PART NUMBER, BEGINNING UNITS, UNITS RECEIVED, UNITS ISSUED
  AND COST, WITH COMMAS IN BETWEEN
WHEN FINISHED TYPE 1,1,1,1,99
?226,5,110,90,2.95
TYPE PART NUMBER, BEGINNING UNITS, UNITS RECEIVED, UNITS ISSUED
  AND COST, WITH COMMAS IN BETWEEN
WHEN FINISHED TYPE 1,1,1,1,99
?235,100,0,50,6.20
TYPE PART NUMBER, BEGINNING UNITS, UNITS RECEIVED, UNITS ISSUED
  AND COST, WITH COMMAS IN BETWEEN
WHEN FINISHED TYPE 1,1,1,1,99
?347,0,50,20,4.60
TYPE PART NUMBER, BEGINNING UNITS, UNITS RECEIVED, UNITS ISSUED
  AND COST, WITH COMMAS IN BETWEEN
WHEN FINISHED TYPE 1,1,1,1,99
?1,1,1,1,99

BREAK IN 360
```

Exercises   Account Balance Exercise: Set up a customer statement file ("CUST") with six records that contains the data specified below.

Problem Summary

Input

Customer Number	Customer Name	Balance	Payments	Charges
2741	Fernwood	120	120	40
2937	Blakey	0	0	90
3246	Grey	250	130	170
3359	Phillips	90	40	100
3426	Bird	180	180	200
3527	Lombard	100	100	250

Processing

Take data from keyboard and place it in a file named "CUST".

Output

Instructions for data entry and a file named "CUST".

Sales Commission Exercise: Set up a sales file called "SALES" that contains seven records with the data specified below.

Problem Summary

Input

Sales Territory	Salesman	Gross Sales	Commission Rate
1	Bill	$12,050	.05
1	Joe	5,270	.045
2	Tom	6,940	.04
2	Phil	11,200	.055
3	Clyde	7,340	.04
3	Harry	9,460	.045
3	Bob	14,690	.05

Processing

Take data from keyboard and place it in a file named "SALES".

Output

Instructions for data entry and a file named "SALES".

_____

_____

_____

_____

_____

_____

_____

_____

_____

_____

_____

_____

_____

_____

_____

_____

_____

_____

_____

_____

READING A FILE

In the previous section, you learned how to set up a computer file. To know what is in a computer file, it is necessary to write a program. The program will read a file and print its contents.

The processing for this program consists of reading a file, record by record, and then printing the records. The program continues reading and printing records until there are no more records in the file.

A program to do that is shown below:

```
10    REM   THIS PROGRAM READS AND PRINTS THE EMPLOY FILE
100    PRINT   CHR$ (4);"OPEN EMPLOY"
105    PRINT   CHR$ (4);"READ EMPLOY"
110    INPUT N,D,N$,H,R,V
115    PRINT   CHR$ (4)
120    PRINT N,D,N$,H,R,V
130    GOTO 105
250    PRINT   CHR$ (4);"CLOSE EMPLOY"
500    STOP
63999  END
```

This program contains one new instruction:

    105   PRINT CHR$(4); "READ EMPLOY"

This instruction has the same form as the file write instruction. This instruction is used with an INPUT statement (line 110) to read from a file. The sequence of file commands is the same as when we wrote on the file.

To write a file

    100   PRINT CHR$(4); "OPEN EMPLOY"
    265   PRINT CHR$(4); "WRITE EMPLOY"
    270   PRINT N; ","; D; ","; N$; ","; H; ","; R; ","; V
    275   PRINT CHR$(4)
    400   PRINT CHR$(4); "CLOSE EMPLOY"

Sequence of File Commands

To read a file

    100   PRINT CHR$(4); "OPEN EMPLOY"
    105   PRINT CHR$(4); "READ EMPLOY"
    110   INPUT N,D,N$,H,R,V
    115   PRINT CHR$(4)
    250   PRINT CHR$(4); "CLOSE EMPLOY"

When we run this program, the content of the file is printed:

101	1	ADAMS	5	40	0
103	12	BAKER	5.6	40	4
104	17	BRAVO	4	40	2
108	16	COHEN	6.25	38	0
172	2	JOHNSON	3.75	40	0
198	1	TANNER	4.25	36	0
202	16	WILSON	4	40	0
206	7	LESTER	5.25	40	0
255	12	SCHMIDT	5.6	40	4
281	12	MILLER	6	40	0
313	7	SMITH	4.25	40	4
347	12	GRAY	6	38	0
368	1	WEAVER	3.5	40	2
422	1	WILLIAMS	4	40	0

```
END OF DATA

BREAK IN 110
```

You'll note that, at the end of the file, a message is printed stating that the end of data has been reached at line 110.

To eliminate the error message, some more new statements are needed. We need to specify what to do in case of error. And we need to identify what error has occurred. Adding the following five statements to the program will remove the "end of data" message.

```
20 ONERR GO TO 200
200 REM ***ERROR CHECKING ROUTINE
210 Y=PEEK(222)
215 IF Y=5 THEN 250
220 PRINT "UNUSUAL ERROR CONDITION",Y
```

This segment contains two new statements. Line 20 tells the computer where to go if an error crops up. And line 210 checks which error has occurred. PEEK(222) is a BASIC instruction that tells us the error number of the error condition that has occurred. If the error number is 5 (IF Y=5) then the error condition is caused by an attempt to read beyond the end of the file. (A listing of all error numbers and their messages is Appendix C.) If the error is error number 5, then processing resumes with line 250, otherwise "UNUSUAL ERROR CONDITION" is printed.

Below you have a listing of the program and its output.

```
10    REM  THIS PROGRAM READS AND PRINTS THE EMPLOY FILE
20    ONERR  GOTO 200
100   PRINT  CHR$ (4);"OPEN EMPLOY"
105   PRINT  CHR$ (4);"READ EMPLOY"
110   INPUT N,D,N$,H,R,V
115   PRINT  CHR$ (4)
120   PRINT N,D,N$,H,R,V
130   GOTO 105
200   REM  ***ERROR CHECKING ROUTINE
210 Y =  PEEK (222)
215 · IF Y = 5 THEN 250
218   PRINT  CHR$ (4)
220   PRINT "UNUSUAL ERROR CONDITION",Y
250   PRINT  CHR$ (4);"CLOSE EMPLOY"
500   STOP
63999  END
```

```
] RUN
101        1          ADAMS        5           40          0
103        12         BAKER        5.6         40          4
104        17         BRAVO        4           40          2
108        16         COHEN        6.25        38          0
172        2          JOHNSON      3.75        40          0
198        1          TANNER       4.25        36          0
202        16         WILSON       4           40          0
206        7          LESTER       5.25        40          0
255        12         SCHMIDT      5.6         40          4
281        12         MILLER       6           40          0
313        7          SMITH        4.25        40          4
347        12         GRAY         6           38          0
368        1          WEAVER       3.5         40          2
422        1          WILLIAMS     4           40          0

BREAK IN 500
```

Inventory Example: Read the file "INV" and print each record in that file.   Example

```
10    REM   THIS PROGRAM READS THE INV FILE AND PRINTS IT
20    ONERR   GOTO 200
100   PRINT   CHR$ (4);"OPEN INV"
105   PRINT   CHR$ (4);"READ INV"
110   INPUT P,B,R,I,C
115   PRINT   CHR$ (4)
120   PRINT P,B,R,I,C
130   GOTO 105
200   REM   ***ERROR CHECKING ROUTINE
210   Y =   PEEK (222)
215   IF Y = 5 THEN 250
218   PRINT   CHR$ (4)
220   PRINT "UNUSUAL ERROR CONDITION",Y
250   PRINT   CHR$ (4);"CLOSE INV"
500   STOP
63999  END
```

```
]RUN
101           120          40          45          5
219           60           60          80          3.25
226           5            110         90          2.95
235           100          0           50          6.2
347           0            50          20          4.6

BREAK IN 500
```

Account Balance Exercise: Read the customer statement file "CUST" and   Exercises
print each record.

_____

_____

_____

_____

_____

_____

_____

_____

_____

_____

_____

_____

_____

_____

Sales Commission Exercise: Read the sales file "SALES" and print each record.

_____

_____

_____

_____

_____

_____

_____

_____

_____

_____

_____

_____

_____

FINDING A RECORD IN A FILE

A file of data is created for some purpose. Files are not created to be placed on a shelf in the corner to collect dust. Files are used to hold data until there is a need for it. When there is a need for data, we must be able to go to a file and pull data, with the desired characteristics, out of the file.

Suppose that Smith, employee number 313, wanted to know how many hours of overtime he had worked. Smith is one of the people in the file "EM-PLOY". To answer his question, we need to write a program that will locate his record and print it out. But to locate his record in a sequential file, all preceding records will have to be read.

Problem Summary

Input

The file "EMPLOY" with each record having six fields:

- Employee identification number
- Department number
- Employee name
- Hourly rate
- Regular hours worked
- Overtime hours worked

Processing

Search the file until the record with employee number 313 is found. Print that record and stop.

Output

If the search is successful, the desired record is printed. If the search is not successful (the record is not in the file) then a "RECORD NOT FOUND" message is printed.

The logic of the program for finding a record in a sequential file is:

1. Link to the file.

2. Read a record.

3. If it is the record we want, then print it; otherwise, read the next record.

4. Stop when the search is finished.

A flowchart (Fig. 4–2) and program to do these tasks are shown below:

```
10   REM   PROGRAM TO FIND AN EMPLOYEE RECORD
15 D$ =   CHR$ (4)
110   PRINT D$;"OPEN EMPLOY"
120   ONERR   GOTO 230
125   PRINT D$;"READ EMPLOY"
130   INPUT N,D,N$,H,R,V
135   PRINT D$
140   IF N = 313 THEN 170
150   GOTO 125
160   REM   PRINT THE RECORD FOUND
170   PRINT "EMPLOYEE","EMPLOYEE","HOURLY","REGULAR","OVERTIME"
180   PRINT "NUMBER","NAME","RATE","HOURS","HOURS"
190   PRINT N,N$,H,R,V
200   PRINT D$;"CLOSE EMPLOY"
210   STOP
220   REM   ERROR CHECKING ROUTINE
230 Y =   PEEK (222)
235   IF Y = 5 THEN 280
240   PRINT "UNUSUAL ERROR CONDITION",Y
250   PRINT D$;"CLOSE EMPLOY"
260   STOP
270   REM   RECORD NOT IN FILE
```

```
280   PRINT "END OF DATA - RECORD NOT FOUND"
290   PRINT D$;"CLOSE EMPLOY"
300   STOP
63999 END
```

RUN EMPLOYEE NUMBER	EMPLOYEE NAME	HOURLY RATE	REGULAR HOURS	OVERTI HOURS
313	SMITH	4.25	40	4

```
BREAK IN 210
```

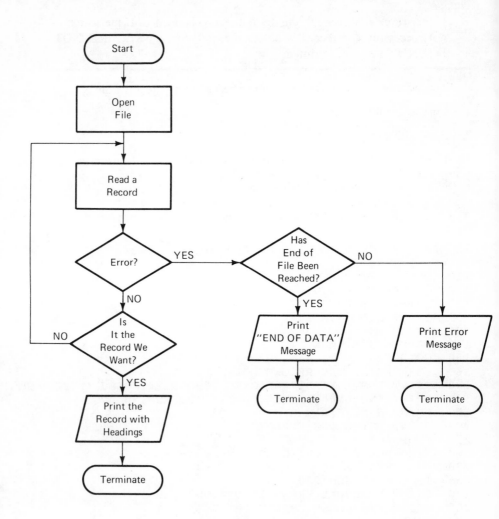

Figure 4–2   Flowchart of Finding a Record

In this program all of the file commands start with PRINT D$ rather than PRINT CHR$(4). In line 15 D$=CHR$(4), we have defined an alphabetic field D$ to consist of CHR$(4). When the PRINT D$ is encountered after line 15 in the program, the D$ is interpreted as CHR$(4). This is simply a method of reducing the amount of typing you have to do for file instructions. If you eliminate line 15 from the program and replace D$ with CHR$(4), the program will run exactly the same.

The key to the search program lies in statement 140. Here the employee number of the record that was read from the file is compared to 313, Smith's employee number. If there is a match (i.e., the value of N, the employee number, is 313), then we know that the desired record has been found and can be printed in lines 170–190. Or, if the employee number is not 313, the next record in the file is read and the check for a match is repeated.

But notice that we also need to consider the possibility that Smith is not in the file. Maybe he was on vacation or sick leave and did not work that week. Or maybe his time card was lost and not entered into the file. Hence, we must include instructions telling the computer what to do if the end of file is reached. The ONERR condition in line 120 and the statements following line 220 take care of that possibility.

No matter the result, whether the desired record is found, or the desired record is not in the file, or the program "bombs" (fails), the file must be closed and the program must be terminated.

We have repeated this same logic in the next example. Look it over, and try the exercises that follow.

Inventory Example: Read the file "INV", find and print out the record for part number 235 with suitable headings.

Example

```
100   REM   TO FIND INVENTORY RECORD
105 D$ =   CHR$ (4)
110   PRINT D$;"OPEN INV"
120   ONERR   GOTO 230
130   PRINT D$;"READ INV"
135   INPUT P,B,R,I,C
140   IF P = 235 THEN 170
150   GOTO 135
160   REM   PRINT THE RECORD FOUND
170   PRINT D$
172   PRINT "PART NUMBER","BEG. UNITS","UNITS REC."
175   PRINT P,B,R
177   PRINT
178   PRINT
180   PRINT "UNITS ISSUED","COST"
185   PRINT I,C
190   PRINT
200   PRINT D$;"CLOSE INV"
205   PRINT
206   PRINT
```

```
210   STOP
220   REM  ERROR CHECKING ROUTINE
230   Y =  PEEK (222)
235   IF Y = 5 THEN 280
240   PRINT "UNUSUAL ERROR",Y
250   PRINT D$;"CLOSE INV"
260   STOP
270   REM  RECORD NOT IN FILE
280   PRINT "END OF DATA - RECORD NOT FOUND"
290   PRINT D$;"CLOSE INV"
300   STOP
63999 END

]RUN
PART NUMBER        BEG. UNITS         UNITS REC.
235                100                0


UNITS ISSUED       COST
50                 6.2
```

```
BREAK IN 210
```

Exercises

Account Balance Exercise: Read the customer statement file "CUST", find and print out the record for customer number 2741 with suitable headings.

_____

_____

_____

_____

_____

_____

_____

_____

_____

_____

_____

_____

Sales Commission Exercise: Read the sales file, "SALES", find and print out the record for salesman Clyde with suitable headings.

CORRECTING
RECORDS IN
A FILE

Once a file has been created it is good practice to check it by writing a program that reads and prints the file. Then you can look at what is in the file to see that all records have been entered correctly. Although the range checks will catch some errors in data entry, they do not catch errors if the incorrect value entered is within the range specified. These errors can be caught by comparing the records in a file with what the data should have been. To correct them, a program has to be written.

Assume that the "EMPLOY" file had an error: for some reason the regular hours for Gray, employee number 347, was entered as 38 when it should have been 40. A program to correct that error is shown below:

```
10   REM   PROGRAM TO CORRECT THE HOURS WORKED FOR GRAY
12   REM
15 D$ =   CHR$ (4)
120  REM   LINK TO FILES
130  REM
140  PRINT D$;"OPEN EMPLOY"
150  PRINT D$;"OPEN EMPLCR"
160  REM
170  REM   READ THE RECORDS FROM EMPLOY
180  REM
190  ONERR  GOTO 380
200  PRINT D$;"READ EMPLOY"
205  INPUT N,D,N$,H,R,V
210  REM
220  REM   DETERMINE WHETHER ITS THE RECORD FOR GRAY
230  REM
```

```
240  IF N <  > 347 THEN 330
250  REM
260  REM   IT IS THE RECORD FOR GRAY, EMPLOYEE NUMBER 347,
270  REM   THEREFORE ASSIGN THE CORRECT HOURS WORKED
280  REM
290 R = 40
300  REM
310  REM   PUT RECORD INTO EMPLCR -- THE CORRECT FILE
320  REM
330  PRINT D$;"WRITE EMPLCR"
335  PRINT N;",";D;",";N$;",";H;",";R;",";V
340  GOTO 200
350  REM
360  REM   *** ERROR CHECKING ROUTINE ***
370  REM
380 Y =  PEEK (222)
382  IF Y = 5 THEN 410
385  PRINT D$
390  PRINT "UNUSUAL ERROR",Y
400  STOP
410  PRINT D$;"CLOSE EMPLOY"
420  PRINT D$;"CLOSE EMPLCR"
430  STOP
63999 END

]RUN

BREAK IN 430
```

If you now change the program that prints the "EMPLOY" file in lines 100, 105 and 250 to

```
100   PRINT D$; "OPEN EMPLCR"
105   PRINT D$; "READ EMPLCR"
250   PRINT D$; "CLOSE EMPLCR"
```

and run it, you can list the "EMPLCR" file as follows:

101	1	ADAMS	5	40	0
103	12	BAKER	5.6	40	4
104	17	BRAVO	4	40	2
108	16	COHEN	6.25	38	0
172	2	JOHNSON	3.75	40	0
198	1	TANNER	4.25	36	0
202	16	WILSON	4	40	0
206	7	LESTER	5.25	40	0
255	12	SCHMIDT	5.6	40	4
281	12	MILLER	6	40	0
313	7	SMITH	4.25	40	4
347	12	GRAY	6	40	0
368	1	WEAVER	3.5	40	2
422	1	WILLIAMS	4	40	0

```
END OF DATA

BREAK IN 110
```

The logic for this program is illustrated in Fig. 4–3 (below). This program is designed to find a specific record, employee number 347, and to change the value of the regular hours in that record. When you look at the program two differences from earlier programs emerge:

1. Two files are opened.

2. A LET seems to be missing in line 290.

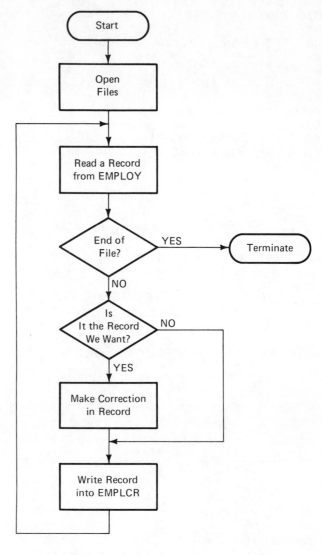

Figure 4–3   Flowchart for Correcting Records in a File

The program runs despite the apparent error in line 290. It runs because the LET is optional. Many computer systems permit you to assign values to a field without the keyword LET. A few systems do not. In Apple BASIC, the LET is optional. Since the LET is optional, you do not have to use it, and by this omission you can save time, and energy, not to mention the added possibility of making typographical errors. In all subsequent programs we have omitted the LET.

Two files are necessary because sequential files can only be used for input to the program or for output from the program, but not both. Therefore to correct an error, we need to read the old file and place the correct data in a new file.

In this program, lines 140 and 150 open the two files. You can open up to 16 files in a program, but each file must be unique (a filename should appear only once). At the end, both files are closed.

The logic of this program takes a record from "EMPLOY". Line 240 checks whether it is the record with an error. If it is, the error is corrected; the statement in line 290 assigns the correct value to R thereby erasing the old, incorrect value of R. And correct records are written into "EMPLCR". The process continues until all records have been read from "EMPLOY" and written into "EMPLCR".

You may notice that a statement seems to be missing. After line 335 we do not have a line with PRINT D$. It is not needed in this program because nothing is expected to be printed on the screen. However, line 385 PRINT D$ appears in the program so that if "UNUSUAL ERROR" has to be written on the screen, it will do so. If line 385 was omitted and the error was not number 5, the error message would be written on the file rather than the screen and you would not know the unusual error occurred.

After this program has been run, both files will appear in your catalog—"EMPLOY" with its error, and "EMPLCR" with only correct records. In effect we have copied the "EMPLOY" file.

A more general error correction program is the next example.

Inventory Example: It has been discovered that when the file "INV" was initially created, two errors were made. The units received for part number 219 should have been 160 instead of 60; and the beginning units for part number 235 should have been 90 instead of 100. These records must be corrected. Part numbers to be corrected should be entered in ascending order.

Example

Problem Summary

Input

The file "INV" where each record has five fields:
- Part number
- Beginning units
- Units received

- Units issued
- Unit cost

Correct field values for erroneous records.

Processing

Get the identification number for incorrect records from the terminal. Search the file until the desired record has been found. Get correct data for incorrect records from the terminal. Place correct records into file "INVCR".

Output

Instructions for data entry and the file "INVCR" with correct inventory records.

```
100   REM   THIS PROGRAM CORRECTS ERRORS IN THE INV FILE
110   REM
115   D$ = CHR$ (4)
120   REM   LINK TO FILES
130   REM
140   PRINT D$;"OPEN INV"
150   PRINT D$;"OPEN INVCR"
160   REM
170   REM   GET PART NUMBER OF RECORD TO BE CORRECTED
180   REM
190   PRINT "TYPE PART NUMBER OF RECORD TO BE CORRECTED"
200   PRINT "WHEN FINISHED -- TYPE 99"
210   INPUT N
220   REM
230   REM   CHECK IF ERROR CORRECTIONS ARE FINISHED
240   REM
250   IF N = 99 THEN 550
260   REM
270   REM   GET A RECORD FROM INV
280   REM
290   PRINT D$;"READ INV"
295   INPUT P,B,R1,R2,C
300   ONERR  GOTO 610
310   REM
320   REM   CHECK IF THE RECORD NEEDS TO BE CORRECTED
330   REM
340   IF P = N THEN 420
350   REM
360   REM   WRITE A RECORD INTO THE INVCR FILE
370   REM
380   PRINT D$;"WRITE INVCR"
385   PRINT P;",";B;",";R1;",";R2;",";C
390   GOTO 290
400   REM
```

```
410    REM
420    PRINT D$
425    PRINT "FOR PART NUMBER ";P
430    PRINT "ENTER BEGINNING UNITS, UNITS RECEIVED"
440    PRINT "UNITS ISSUED AND COST"
450    INPUT B,R1,R2,C
460    PRINT D$;"WRITE INVCR"
465    PRINT P;",";B;",";R1;",";R2;",";C
468    PRINT D$
470    REM
480    REM    GET PART NUMBER FOR NEXT RECORD TO BE CORRECTED
490    REM
500    GOTO 190
510    REM
520    REM    CORRECTIONS FINISHED, COPY REMAINING RECORDS
530    REM    FROM INV TO INVCR
540    REM
550    PRINT D$;"READ INV"
555    INPUT P,B,R1,R2,C
560    PRINT D$;"WRITE INVCR"
565    PRINT P;",";B;",";R1;",";R2;",";C
570    GOTO 550
580    REM
590    REM    ERROR CHECKING ROUTINE
600    REM
610    PRINT D$
615 Y =    PEEK (222)
618    IF Y = 5 THEN 670
620    PRINT "UNUSUAL ERROR",Y
630    STOP
640    REM
650    REM    TERMINATE
660    REM
670    PRINT D$;"CLOSE INV"
680    PRINT D$;"CLOSE INVCR"
690    STOP
63999 END
```

```
TYPE PART NUMBER OF RECORD TO BE CORRECTED
WHEN FINISHED -- TYPE 99
?219
FOR PART NUMBER 219
ENTER BEGINNING UNITS, UNITS RECEIVED
UNITS ISSUED AND COST
?60,160,80,3.25
TYPE PART NUMBER OF RECORD TO BE CORRECTED
WHEN FINISHED -- TYPE 99
?235
FOR PART NUMBER 235
ENTER BEGINNING UNITS, UNITS RECEIVED
```

```
UNITS ISSUED AND COST
?90,0,50,6.20
TYPE PART NUMBER OF RECORD TO BE CORRECTED
WHEN FINISHED -- TYPE 99
?99

BREAK IN 690
```

If the old program to list the "INV" file is changed as follows:

100 PRINT D$; "OPEN INVCR"
105 PRINT D$; "READ INVCR"
250 PRINT D$; "CLOSE INVCR"

and run, the "INVCR" file is printed as follows:

101	120	40	45	5
219	60	160	80	3.25
226	5	110	90	2.95
235	90	0	50	6.2
347	0	50	20	4.6

```
BREAK IN 500
```

This program can correct any number of erroneous records. No matter which records are wrong or which fields have false values, the program can correct them. However, the operator must know in which records the errors have occurred and what the correct field values are. Both items have to be entered by the operator from the terminal.

The program finds a record specified by the operator by searching through the file. As it searches, records that have a lower identification number are placed in the new file. When the record to be corrected has been found, the operator is instructed to enter the data for that record. The data received from the terminal is then placed into the new file. This cycle is repeated until there are no more records to be corrected. At that time any records still remaining in the old file are copied into the new file.

COPYING
A FILE

At times it is necessary to make a copy of a file for back up. Then if the first file is accidentally destroyed the copy can be retrieved and used. In the previous section, where errors in records were corrected, a revised version of a file was created.

The general approach to error corrections is also appropriate to copying a file:

• Link to the desired files
• Read data from one file
• Write the data into the other file
• When no more data remains in the first file, then close both files and terminate.

These steps are included in both examples and in both exercises of the previous section. They are particularly obvious in lines 550–570 of the last program (page 91) where the records remaining in file "INV" are copied to file "INVCR".

This chapter introduces you to sequential files. Sequential files are very economical when large volumes of data have to be processed. You have seen how to set up files and how to enter data into a file. Next the data file was read and printed. Finding a record in a file is an elementary operation that has uses in many applications. In this chapter finding a record was used to correct erroneous data. The chapter concluded by pointing out that error correction has to copy a file. Copying a file is necessary in error correction because sequential files should only be read or written, not both.

SUMMARY

BASIC Instructions Introduced:

Statement	Explanation
PRINT CHR$(4); "OPEN filename"	Opens the file identified by the filename. The filename can be from 1 to 30 characters.
PRINT CHR$(4); "READ filename" INPUT fieldname1, fieldname2, etc. PRINT CHR$(4)	Reads a record from the file. Records are specified by their fieldnames.
PRINT CHR$(4); "WRITE filename" PRINT fieldname1;","; fieldname2;","; etc. PRINT CHR$(4)	Writes a record on the file. The fields of the record will be separated by ;",";.
PRINT CHR$(4); "CLOSE filename"	Closes the file and stores it on the diskette.
ONERR GO TO line number	Tells the computer to go to *line number* when an error is encountered.
Y=PEEK(222) IF Y=N THEN line number	Tells the computer that if the error encountered is N, then processing should resume at the line number given. PEEK (222) gives the error number.

PROBLEMS

1. Set up a file called "XK1" and enter the following data:

I.D. Number	Time 1	Time 2
101	40	0
103	40	4
104	40	2
108	38	0
172	40	0
198	36	0
202	40	0
281	40	0
347	38	0
422	40	0

2. Print out the contents of file XK1.

3. Write a simple program that will set up a file "TOP" with the input data (below) and print out the file.

I.D.	Name
247	Farnsworth
262	Lowell
264	Fergerson
275	Fong

4. Read the sales file, "SALES". Find and print out the record for salesman Joe with suitable headings.

5. Read the inventory file. Find and print out the records for part numbers 219 and 347 with suitable headings. The END OF DATA–RECORD NOT FOUND message will be printed.

6. Read the "XK1" file from Problem 1, above. Find and print out the record for I.D. number 172 with suitable headings.

For problems 7–10 below, write an additional program to read and print the file:

7. Write a program that will read the customer statement file "CUST" and place that data in a new file "CUST1" so that you have two files with exactly the same data. Verify by printing "CUST1".

8. Write a program that will read the customer statement file "CUST" and place only customer data that have customer numbers from 3000 to 4000 into a new file "CUST2". Verify by printing "CUST2".

9. Write a program that will read the sales commission file "SALES" and place the name and gross sales data into a new file "SALE1". However, the company has instituted a new sales policy so that the commission rate for all salesmen will be 6%. Verify by printing "SALES1".

10. Write a program that will read the payroll file "EMPLOY" and place the following data fields into a new file "EMPL1": Employee number, department number, name, hourly rate.

5 / Writing Reports from Sequential Files

At the end of this chapter you should be able to:

- Calculate totals and subtotals for a file
- Produce reports that are clear and legible

Data is the lifeblood of a business. Without data, a business could not operate. For example, customer orders tell a firm what items to ship to a customer. They also tell a business who to bill and how much the customer owes the business. Data, such as customer orders, direct the operations of a business.

There are many other items of data that have the same characteristic, i.e. they support business operations. Production orders, inventory transactions, vendor invoices, time cards, and the like all serve to direct the activities of the firm.

But data is also used to support management decision making. From a management perspective, it is not enough to know that one customer has ordered one item. For decision making it is necessary to keep track of all customers. It is necessary to look at inventories as a whole. It is necessary to judge and evaluate all products. It is necessary to plan and control the operations of the firm as a whole.

Data to support management decisions has to be collected and processed. The processed data has to be presented to management as information in a report that will help management keep track of the activities of a firm. For example, a customer report allows management to determine their best customers. A product-line sales summary would tell management which products are selling well and which products are selling poorly.

This chapter shows you how sequential files are processed to produce reports. It will show you how to accumulate totals for the whole file and how to calculate subtotals for parts of the file. And it will show you how to use additional PRINT capabilities to make your reports neat and orderly.

In order to understand the programming involved in accumulating totals, the following example illustrates what is required.

Problem Summary

Input
  "EMPLOY" file
Processing
  Accumulate the total number of regular hours worked for all employees.
Output
  Total regular hours worked with an appropriate heading.

See the flowchart (Fig. 5–1) and program to do this on the next page.

```
10   REM   PROGRAM TO TOTAL REGULAR HOURS WORKED FOR
11   REM   ALL EMPLOYEES; R1 WILL BE THE ACCUMULATION
12   REM   OF ALL REGULAR HOURS
15  D$ =   CHR$ (4)
100   PRINT D$;"OPEN EMPLOY"
110  R1 = 0
120   PRINT D$;"READ EMPLOY"
125   INPUT N,D,N$,H,R,V
130   ONERR   GOTO 160
140  R1 = R1 + R
150   GOTO 125
160  Y =   PEEK (222)
162   PRINT D$
165   IF Y = 5 THEN 190
175   PRINT "UNUSUAL ERROR CONDITION",Y
180   STOP
190   PRINT "TOTAL REGULAR HOURS ";R1
200   PRINT D$;"CLOSE EMPLOY"
210   STOP
63999 END
```

This program is very similar to the last payroll program with the exception of lines 110 and 140.

$$110 \ R1 = 0$$

Line 110 sets the value of R1 to zero. This is called initializing an accumulation. Most computer systems will do this automatically, however some systems will not. Therefore it is worth the slight additional effort to put in an initialization statement. The choice of the name, R1 in this case, is up to the programmer. Any name could be used provided it is not used to define any other field. R1 seems a reasonable choice since R is the name assigned to the regular hours field.

$$140 \ R1 = R1 + R$$

This statement looks strange until you remember that the equal sign (=) is not an equal sign in algebraic terms. This statement looks the same as the algebra statement $a = a + b$; however, it is different. The equal sign in BASIC is an assignment. Line 140, if translated into English means take the value that you found in field R, add its value to the current value of R1, and assign the sum to R1. If we look at the first four records in EMPLOY the values of R are: 40 for Adams, 40 for Baker, 40 for Bravo, and 38 for Cohen.

When the computer executes line 110 it sets the value of R1 to 0, at line 120 the value of R for Adams is 40. At line 140 the values to the right of the equal sign are 0 and 40 which sum to 40. The value 40 is now assigned to R1; after line 140 has been executed, R1 has the new value of 40. The program then directs that the next record be input (Baker). Again at 120 the value of R for Baker is 40. In line 140 R1 is 40 and R is 40. When they are

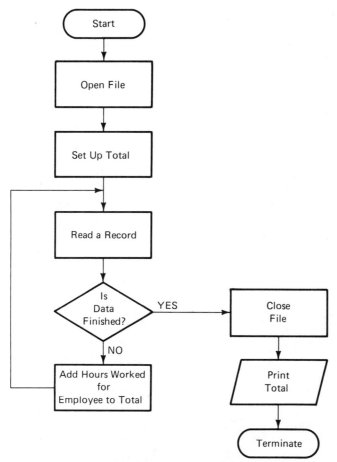

Flowchart for Accumulating Totals   Figure 5–1

summed, the new value of R1 is 40 + 40 which is 80. The program directs that the next record be input (Bravo). At line 120 the value of R for Bravo is 40. At line 140, R1 is now 80 and R is 40. These values are summed and the new value of R1 is assigned as 120. The next record is input (Cohen). The value of R is 38, R1 is 120. The new value of R1 is assigned as 158.

This process repeats until the end of the file is reached and Y=5 is detected. Then the file is closed and the following output is produced:

TOTAL REGULAR HOURS 552

BREAK IN 210

As a second example, let us increase the number of totals. For this case, we want to calculate the total hours worked (both regular and overtime) and the total wages earned by everyone. The "EMPLOY" file will again be used.

Now, we need to add the regular and overtime hours worked by each employee to get their totals, also we need to add the wages earned by each employee to get the total wages earned.

Problem Summary

Input
   "EMPLOY" file

Processing
   Accumulate regular hours worked, overtime hours worked, and wages earned by each employee to get totals.

Output
   Totals for regular hours worked, overtime hours worked, and wages earned with appropriate headings.

The program therefore has to:

1. Link to the "EMPLOY" file.

2. Set up fields for the totals.

3. Read the records in the file.

4. Accumulate totals.

5. Print the totals with appropriate headings.

The program to perform these steps is shown below:

```
10   REM   THIS PROGRAM ACCUMULATES TOTALS FOR REGULAR HOURS
11   REM   OVERTIME HOURS AND TOTAL WAGES EARNED IN THE EMPLOY FILE
15 D$ =   CHR$ (4)
100   PRINT D$;"OPEN EMPLOY"
120 R1 = 0
130 V1 = 0
140 W1 = 0
150   PRINT D$;"READ EMPLOY"
155   INPUT N,D,N$,H,R,V
160   ONERR  GOTO 220
170 R1 = R1 + R
180 V1 = V1 + V
190 W1 = W1 + H * R + 1.5 * H * V
200   GOTO 155
210   REM  ERROR CHECKING ROUTINE
220   PRINT D$
225 Y =   PEEK (222)
230   IF Y = 5 THEN 250
235   PRINT "UNUSUAL ERROR CONDITION",Y
240   STOP
```

```
250   PRINT "TOTAL REGULAR HOURS WORKED ";R1
260   PRINT "TOTAL OVERTIME HOURS WORKED ";V1
270   PRINT "TOTAL WAGES EARNED BY ALL EMPLOYEES ";W1
280   PRINT D$;"CLOSE EMPLOY"
290   STOP
63999 END

]RUN
TOTAL REGULAR HOURS WORKED 552
TOTAL OVERTIME HOURS WORKED 16
TOTAL WAGES EARNED BY ALL EMPLOYEES 2771.7

BREAK IN 290
```

The first group of statements, lines 120, 130, and 140, sets the fields called R1, V1, and W1 to zero. R1 will be used to accumulate regular hours. V1 will be used to accumulate overtime hours. And W1 is used, later in the program, to accumulate the wages earned. Again, as in the preceding example, before you read a record, you have to initialize these fields to zero anywhere before the loop.

The second group of statements performs the accumulation of totals. As each record is read, the data from the record is added to the fields that are used to hold the accumulation. Remember the $=$ symbol is an assignment symbol and not an equal sign! What line 170 tells the computer to do is: Take the value that is currently in R1, add to this the value that is currently in R, and place the sum back into R1.

A similar operation occurs in lines 180 and 190. In line 180, the current contents of V1 is added to the current contents of V; and the result is placed into V1. In line 190, a somewhat more complicated procedure is involved:

First, the regular wages are computed when the hourly rate is multiplied by the hours worked (H*R).

Next, the computer calculates overtime wages when it multiplies the overtime hours (V) by one-and-a-half times the hourly rate (1.5*H).

Then, the regular wages and the overtime wages are added to the current wage total (W1).

Finally, that sum is stored again in W1.

In this way, the wages of all employees are accumulated, but only one at a time.

The third group of statements, in lines 250–270, prints what has been accumulated in R1, V1, and W1, with appropriate headings, of course.

To further illuminate this process, here is another example. To highlight how the accumulation procedure works, let's take a simple data file and generate the totals of that file.

Assume you have a file called "SALORD", that contains sales orders. Further assume that each sales order has just two fields—order number and dollar amount of order. The file of data could look like this:

Sales Order Number	Dollar Amount of Sale
20473	1800.00
20474	450.00
20475	600.00
20476	150.00
20477	500.00

Of course, a *real* sales order would have many more fields. For example, a sales order would have to identify the customer, the customer address, the salesman who made the sale (for commission calculation if needed), where to ship the items, who to bill for the sale, and so on. And obviously, a *real* sales order file would contain many more records than the five that are shown. For our simple example, this file will be adequate.

Now, what we need to do is write a program that will accumulate the total dollar amount of sales, and then print out this total. But let's also print the value of sales and the value for the total as we are accumulating.

A program to perform this task is given below:

```
100   REM   PROGRAM TO TOTAL SALES ORDERS
105 D$ =   CHR$ (4)
110   PRINT D$;"OPEN SALORD"
120 T = 0
130   PRINT D$;"READ SALORD"
135   INPUT N,S
138   PRINT D$
140   ONERR   GOTO 180
150 T = T + S
160   PRINT "S=";S,"T=";T
170   GOTO 130
180 Y =   PEEK (222)
185   IF Y = 5 THEN 210
190   PRINT "UNUSUAL ERROR CONDITION",Y
200   STOP
210   PRINT "THE TOTAL DOLLAR SALES ARE ";T
220   PRINT D$;"CLOSE SALORD"
230   STOP
63999 END
```

If you now type RUN, the program will give the following output.

```
S=1800            T=1800
S=450             T=2250
S=600             T=2850
S=150             T=3000
S=500             T=3500
THE TOTAL DOLLAR SALES ARE 3500

BREAK IN 230
```

Look again at the program. We'll go over the steps that it performs one by one, and we'll trace what happens to the fields labelled N, S, and T.

After opening the file, line 120 sets the field T to zero. So, picture a box called T and put a zero into it.

$$T\ \boxed{\ 0\ }$$

Line 130 reads two values from the file and puts these values into N and S. Thus:

$$N\ \boxed{\ 20473\ }\qquad S\ \boxed{\ 1800\ }$$

Line 150 (we skipped 140 because it's not yet pertinent) then takes the value of field T. Look at the box called T above. It contains a zero—right? So, it takes the zero and adds to it the content of the box called S. S contains 1800. So, 1800 is added to zero and now T would look like:

$$T\ \boxed{\ 1800\ }$$

In line 160, we print the contents of S and T. And line 170 gets us back to line 130. At line 130, the next set of values is placed into the fields N and S:

$$N\ \boxed{\ 20474\ }\qquad S\ \boxed{\ 450\ }$$

Line 140 then adds what is in T (the 1800) to the contents of S (the 450). And the result (2250) is placed into the field T.

$$T\ =\ 2250$$

Line 160 outputs S and T before line 170 takes us back for another cycle.

You can now repeat these steps on your own. Use the boxes below for the third, fourth and fifth records.

ending

3rd	starting T	2250	N ⬜	S ⬜	T ⬜
4th			N ⬜	S ⬜	T ⬜
5th			N ⬜	S ⬜	T ⬜

Note the pattern that is followed in accumulating a total. Start by setting a field to zero. Then, add one item at a time to that field until you are out of data. When you next PRINT that field, the grand total is output.

Example

Problem Summary

Input
   "SALES" file

Processing
   Accumulate the total sales commissions that must be paid to the salesmen.

Output
   Total of all the commissions suitably labelled.

```
10   REM   THIS PROGRAM ACCUMULATES IN C1
11   REM   THE TOTAL COMMISSION PAID TO ALL SALESMEN
12   REM   IN THE FILE SALES
15 D$ =   CHR$ (4)
100   PRINT D$;"OPEN SALES"
110 C1 = 0
120   PRINT D$;"READ SALES"
125   INPUT D,S$,S,C
130   ONERR  GOTO 200
140 C1 = C1 + S * C
150   GOTO 125
180   REM   ERROR CHECKING ROUTINE
200 Y =   PEEK (222)
202   PRINT D$
205   IF Y = 5 THEN 250
210   PRINT "UNUSUAL ERROR CONDITION",Y
230   STOP
250   PRINT "TOTAL COMMISSION PAID ";C1
260   PRINT D$;"CLOSE SALES"
270   STOP
63999 END

RUN
TOTAL COMMISSION PAID          3187.05
BREAK IN 270
```

Exercises

Inventory Value Exercise:

Problem Summary

Input
   "INV" file

Processing

Accumulate the beginning units, units received, and units issued; calculate the total inventory value at the beginning of the period.

Output

Totals for beginning units, units received, units issued, and beginning inventory value, with appropriate headings.

```
TOTAL BEGINNING UNITS              305
TOTAL UNITS RECEIVED               330
TOTAL UNITS ISSUED                 385
TOTAL VALUE OF THE BEGINNING INVENTORY        1569.75
```

Account Balance Exercise:

Problem Summary

Input data
   "CUST" file

Processsing
   Accumulate balances, payments, charges, and new balances for the file.

Output
   Totals for balances, payments, charges and new balances, with appropriate headings.

```
TOTAL BEGINNING BALANCES     740
TOTAL PAYMENTS               570
TOTAL CHARGES     850
TOTAL NEW BALANCES          1020

BREAK IN 300
```

In many cases, summaries of the file as a whole are too gross to make any decisions. A more refined breakdown of the data is needed. But the detail is not at the individual record level. Instead of totals for the file as a whole or detail at the individual record level, we need an intermediary categorization of the data. Subtotals provide such intermediary categorizations.

Again, we look to the payroll problem for an illustrative example. Look at the payroll data file. It contains values for employee number, department number, employee name, etc. For our example, we need a summary of employee wages by department.

Departmental subtotals furnish an intermediary breakdown of the data.

HOW TO
CALCULATE
SUBTOTALS

They are not as aggregate as file totals, neither are they as detailed as the earnings by individual employee. Instead, they fit someplace between the employee level detail and the all encompassing aggregation of file totals.

But before subtotals can be calculated with sequential files, the data has to be reorganized. Table 5–1 shows how the EMPLOY file would look once it's been placed into department number sequence.

Table 5–1   Employee File Sorted by Department Number

Employee Number	Dept. Number	Employee Name	Hourly Rate	Regular Hours	Overtime Hours
422	1	Williams	$4.00	40	0
368	1	Weaver	3.50	40	2
198	1	Tanner	4.25	36	0
101	1	Adams	5.00	40	0
172	2	Johnson	3.75	40	0
313	7	Smith	4.25	40	4
206	7	Lester	5.25	40	0
347	12	Gray	6.00	38	0
281	12	Miller	6.00	40	0
255	12	Schmidt	5.60	40	4
103	12	Baker	5.60	40	4
202	16	Wilson	4.00	40	0
108	16	Cohen	6.25	38	0
104	17	Bravo	4.00	40	2

The process used to order the data in a particular sequence is called sorting. (Sorting is a complex subject, so we will not cover the logic of sorting a data file. Instead, Appendix B contains a sort program with instructions on how to use it. We will indicate where a sort is needed, but sorting itself is left to your discretion.)

Problem Summary

Input

"EMPLOY" file in department number sequence, which will be called "EMPLDP".

Processing

Accumulate regular hours worked, overtime hours worked, and wages earned by department and for the file as a whole.

Output

Subtotals and totals accumulated.

The program will have to:

1. Link to the "EMPLDP" file.

2. Set up fields for subtotals and totals.

3. Read the records in the file.

4. Accumulate subtotals by department.

5. Print the subtotals.

6. Accumulate totals for the file.

7. Print the totals.

8. Terminate.

The flowchart for the program is shown in Figure 5–2. A program to do these steps is shown below.

```
10   REM   PROGRAM TO ACCUMULATE SUBTOTALS FOR THE
11   REM   PAYROLL PROBLEM AND TO ACCUMULATE TOTALS
12   REM   OF THE SUBTOTALS
15 D$ =   CHR$ (4)
130  PRINT D$;"OPEN EMPLDP"
140 R1 = 0
150 V1 = 0
160 W1 = 0
170 R2 = 0
180 V2 = 0
190 W2 = 0
200 D1 = 0
210  PRINT "DEPARTMENT","REGULAR","OVERTIME","WAGES"
220  PRINT "NUMBER","HOURS","HOURS","EARNED"
230  PRINT "------","-----","-----","------"
240  REM  READ THE DATA IN THE FILE
250  PRINT D$;"READ EMPLDP"
255  INPUT N,D,N$,H,R,V
260  ONERR  GOTO 480
265  REM  SET UP FOR FIRST DEPARTMENT
270  IF D1 > 0 THEN 280
275 D1 = D
280  IF D1 < D THEN 350
290  REM  THEN DEPARTMENT THE SAME AS FOR THE PREVIOUS RECORD
300  REM  THEREFORE ACCUMULATE SUBTOTALS FOR THE DEPARTMENT
310 R1 = R1 + R
320 V1 = V1 + V
330 W1 = W1 + H * R + 1.5 * H * V
331  REM  READ THE NEXT RECORD
340  GOTO 250
341  REM  PRINT DEPARTMENT SUBTOTALS
350  PRINT D$
360  PRINT D1,R1,V1,W1
361  REM  ADD SUBTOTALS TO TOTALS
370 R2 = R2 + R1
```

```
380 V2 = V2 + V1
390 W2 = W2 + W1
400  REM  SET SUBTOTALS TO ZERO FOR NEXT DEPARTMENT
410 R1 = 0
420 V1 = 0
430 W1 = 0
440  REM  SET DEPARTMENT TO CURRENT DEPARTMENT
450 D1 = D
460  GOTO 310
470  REM  ERROR CHECKING ROUTINE
480  PRINT D$
485 Y =  PEEK (222)
490  IF Y = 5 THEN 520
495  PRINT "UNUSUAL ERROR CONDITION",Y
500  STOP
510  REM  PRINT SUBTOTALS FOR LAST DEPARTMENT
520  PRINT D1,R1,V1,W1
530  REM  ADD SUBTOTALS FOR LAST DEPARTMENT TO TOTALS
540 R2 = R2 + R1
550 V2 = V2 + V1
560 W2 = W2 + W1
570  REM  PRINT THE TOTALS
580  PRINT "TOTAL",R2,V2,W2
590  REM  TERMINATE THE PROGRAM
600  PRINT D$;"CLOSE EMPLDP"
610  STOP
63999 END
```

```
]RUN
```

DEPARTMENT NUMBER	REGULAR HOURS	OVERTIME HOURS	WAGES EARNED
1	156	2	663.5
2	40	0	150
7	80	4	405.5
12	158	8	983.2
16	78	0	397.5
17	40	2	172
TOTAL	552	16	2771.7

```
BREAK IN 610
```

We can trace the logic of this program to see what it does. You'll note the same elements that existed in the process of getting totals.

First, the fields that are used to hold the subtotals (as well as those for the totals) are set to zero in lines 140–190. Next, they are used to accumulate the running totals in lines 310–330. Then they are printed in line 360; used in the accumulation of totals in lines 370–390; and set to zero for the accumulation of subtotals for the next department in lines 410–430.

As you can see, calculating subtotals is identical to the process used to

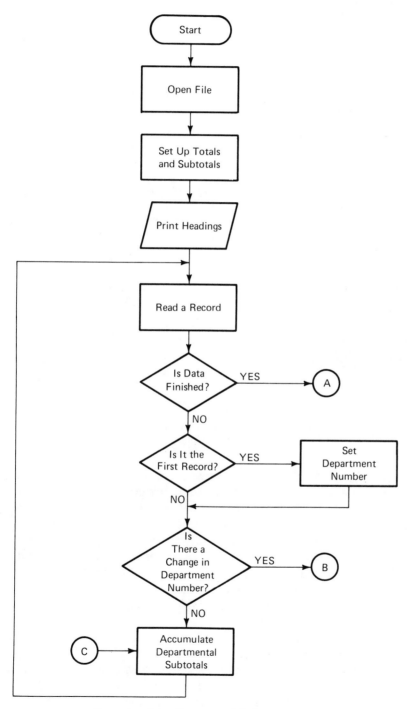

Flowchart for Program DEPSUB   Figure 5-2

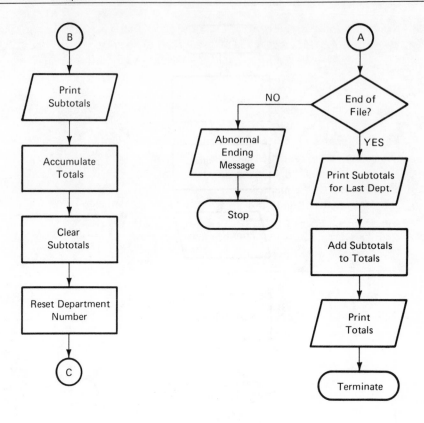

Figure 5-2   Flowchart for Program DEPSUB (Cont'd.)

calculate totals. The key difficulty lies in determining when to start and when to stop accumulating for one department.

How do we know we have finished with a department? Look at Table 5-1, the employee file sorted by department number. Cover up the table (with a sheet of paper or your hand) except for the titles. Now look at the first record. Move your sheet of paper down the table one record at a time (because that is the way the computer does it—the computer sees the whole file, but only one record at a time). And herein lies the clue for determining the end of a department. We are finished with one department when we arrive at the next department.

Try it again. Look at Table 5-1, one record at a time. Look only at the department number. We start with department number 1. Remember that number. Look at the next record. It is still department 1. And the next one. Still 1. Look at the fourth record. Department number is 1. Read the next record. The department number is no longer one. Therefore, we know that we are finished with department one.

Now let's look at the program. The process that you have just gone through is in lines 255, 270, 275, 280, and 450. The statement in line 255 reads a record. Line 280 compares the department number of the record just read with a prior department number. The prior department number is defined in lines 270 and 275 for the first record read, and it is set in line 450 after each department break. (A "break" in this context refers to the point where a number changes from one value to another.)

So, D1 "remembers" the previous department number. And when in line 280 a different department number (D) is encountered (D1 not equal to D) then the accumulated values in R1, V1, and W1 represent the subtotals for the previous department. Hence, the logic flows to line 350 where the subtotals are printed. Note the use of the PRINT D$ in line 350 to direct printing to the screen or printer.

One more item needs to be mentioned: printing the last department. We know we have finished accumulating the subtotals for the last department when we run out of data. But at that point, while the accumulation is complete, the answer resides in the computer. To get it out, it has to be printed. But a print different from line 360 has to be used. (If we did go to line 360, then the end of data would be ignored.) Hence, the "GO TO 480" to check on the error before printing the last set of subtotals.

Look over the inventory example and then try the exercises.

Inventory Example: In the "INV" file, assume that part numbers 100–199 belong to department one (1), numbers 200–299 belong to department two (2), and numbers 300–399 belong to department three (3). Calculate the dollar value of the beginning and ending inventory for each department and print these values as well as their grand totals. We want to write a program that will calculate the departmental subtotals for the value of the beginning and ending inventory values, as well as the grand totals.

Example

Problem Summary

Input
    "INV" file

Processing
    Accumulate beginning and ending inventory dollar values by department for the file.

Output
    Departmental subtotals and grand totals suitably labelled.

The steps in this program are the same as in the previous payroll program in that the program will have to:

1. Link to the INV file.

2. Set up fields for subtotals and totals.

3. Read the records in the file.

4. Accumulate subtotals by department.

5. Print the subtotals.

6. Accumulate totals for the file.

7. Print the totals.

8. Terminate.

```
10   REM   THIS PROGRAM ACCUMULATES SUBTOTALS FOR BEGINNING
11   REM   AND ENDING INVENTORY VALUES BY DEPARTMENT
12   REM   AND ACCUMULATES TOTALS FOR THE FILE
15 D$ =   CHR$ (4)
100   PRINT D$;"OPEN INV"
110 B1 = 0
120 E1 = 0
130 B2 = 0
140 E2 = 0
145 D1 = 0
150   PRINT "DEPARTMENT","BEGINNING","ENDING"
160   PRINT "NUMBER","INVENTORY","INVENTORY"
170   PRINT "-------","----------","----------"
180   REM  READ IN DATA IN THE FILE
210   PRINT D$;"READ INV"
215   INPUT N,B,R1,R2,C
218   PRINT D$
220   ONERR  GOTO 430
225 N =   INT (N / 100)
230   IF D1 > 0 THEN 260
250 D1 = N
260   IF D1 < N THEN 330
270   REM   DEPARTMENT NUMBER IS THE SAME AS THE PREVIOUS RECORD
280   REM   THEREFORE ACCUMULATE THE TOTALS
290 B1 = B1 + B * C
300 E1 = E1 + B * C + R1 * C - R2 * C
305   REM  READ THE NEXT RECORD
310   GOTO 210
320   REM  PRINT DEPARTMENT SUBTOTALS
330   PRINT D1,B1,E1
340   REM  ADD THE SUBS TO THE TOTALS
350 E2 = E2 + E1
360 B2 = B2 + B1
370   REM  SET SUBS TO ZERO FOR THE NEXT DEPARTMENT
380 B1 = 0
390 E1 = 0
400   REM  SET D1 EQUAL TO THE NEXT DEPARTMENT NUMBER
410 D1 = N
420   GOTO 290
430   REM  ERROR CHECKING ROUTINE
```

```
440 Y =  PEEK (222)
445  IF Y = 5 THEN 470
450  PRINT D$
455  PRINT "UNUSUAL ERROR",Y
460  STOP
470  REM   END OF FILE REACHED -- PRINT SUBTOTALS FOR LAST DEPARTMENT
480  PRINT D1,B1,E1
490  REM   ADD SUBTOTALS FROM LAST DEPARTMENT TO TOTALS
500  E2 = E2 + E1
510  B2 = B2 + B1
520  REM   PRINT TOTALS FOR FILE
530  PRINT "TOTAL BEGINNING AND ENDING INVENTORIES ";B2,E2
540  PRINT D$;"CLOSE INV"
63999 END
```

```
RUN
DEPARTMENT             BEGINNING      ENDING
NUMBER                 INVENTORY      INVENTORY
-------                ---------      ---------
  1                      600            575
  2                      829.75         513.75
  3                      0              138
TOTAL BEGINNING AND ENDING INVENTORIES        1429.75        1226.75
```

The only difference in logic between this program and the previous payroll program is the test for a new department. Before, department numbers were given in a field; in this example, the department number is determined from the part number. The instruction in line 225 does this. The statement

$$N = INT(N/100)$$

illustrates the use of a new type of BASIC statement. INT is called a function. It makes an integer (whole number) out of what appears in parenthesis after it, by dropping anything after the decimal point. For example, if we had the number 2.73 appearing in the parenthesis after INT, that is, if we had INT(2.73), the resulting value would be 2. In the particular case of the expression in this program, when the first record is input, N is equal to 101. INT(N/100) divides the value 101 by 100, giving 1.01, and the integer function makes an integer (1) out of this value.

So D1 has the value 1. In this way all parts with values 100–199 will be accumulated. When the second record with part number 219 is input, at line 250 D1 is equal to 1 so that we go to line 330 where departmental subtotals (for one) are printed. Then in line 410 D1 has the value of 2 and the program continues to accumulate the subtotals for department two. Similarly, when the last record with part number 347 is input, N in line 250 will have the value of 3. The department subtotals (for two) will be printed and D1 in line 410 will have the value 3. The subtotals for department 3 will be calculated and the next record (EOF) read. Since there are no more records, the end of file (Y = 5) occurs and the subtotals for department 3 as well as the grand totals are printed.

Exercises   Sales Commission Exercise:

Problem Summary

Input
   "SALES" file
Processing
   Accumulate sales and commissions by sales territory and for the file as a whole.
Output
   Territory subtotals and grand totals suitably labelled.

_____
_____
_____
_____
_____
_____
_____
_____
_____

(Attach additional paper to complete your program.)

TERRITORY NUMBER	TERRITORY SALES	COMMISSIONS PAID
1	17320	839.65
2	18140	893.6

Account Balance Exercise: The department is indicated by the first digit of the customer number.

Problem Summary

Input
    "CUST" file

Processing
    Accumulate initial balances and final balances by department and for the file as a whole.

Output
    Department subtotals and grand totals suitably labelled.

_____
_____
_____
_____
_____

(Attach additional paper to complete your program.)

```
DEPARTMENT           BEGINNING            ENDING
NUMBER               BALANCE              BALANCE
------               -------              -------
  2                    120                  130
  3                    620                  890
TOTAL BEGINNING AND ENDING BALANCES          740             1020

BREAK IN 510
```

So far the output of all the programs has been labelled in a manner that identifies it. The output of the programs up to now has been brief and satisfactory for programmer purposes. The output would be unsatisfactory for management purposes because it is too brief and is not self-explanatory to a manager. Managers do not read programs. It is important that the output be self-explanatory with appropriate headings and follow general business formats.

The output to the second payroll example consists of the following:

```
TOTAL REGULAR HOURS WORKED      552
TOTAL OVERTIME HOURS WORKED      16
TOTAL WAGES EARNED BY ALL EMPLOYEES        2771.7

BREAK IN 290
```

The program can be modified so that the function of the program can be made clear in the output. The supporting data that resulted in that output can also be printed. The report that we want to produce is usually called a payroll report.

Problem Summary

Input
  "EMPLOY" file

Processing
  Accumulate regular hours, overtime hours, and wages for the company.

Output
  An easily readable and understandable payroll report.

```
100  REM   THIS PROGRAM ACCUMULATES TOTALS FOR REGULAR HOURS
110  REM   OVERTIME HOURS AND TOTAL WAGES IN THE EMPLOY FILE
115 D$ =   CHR$ (4)
120  PRINT
130  PRINT
140  PRINT   TAB( 30);"PAYROLL REPORT"
150  PRINT
160  PRINT
170  PRINT "EMPLOYEE  DEPT","NAME","HOURLY","REGULAR   OVERTIME   GROSS"
180  PRINT "NUMBER    NUMBER"," ","RATE","HOURS     HOURS     PAY"
190  PRINT "-------------------------------------------------------------------------"
200  PRINT D$;"OPEN EMPLOY"
210 R1 = 0
220 V1 = 0
230 W1 = 0
240  PRINT D$;"READ EMPLOY"
245  INPUT N,D,N$,H,R,V
248  PRINT D$
250  ONERR   GOTO 330
260 R1 = R1 + R
270 V1 = V1 + V
280 W = H * R + 1.5 * H * V
```

```
290  W1 = W1 + W
295  W =  INT (100 * W + 0.5) / 100
300  PRINT N; SPC( 6);D,N$,H,R; SPC( 8);V; SPC( 7);W
310  GOTO 240
320  REM  ERROR CHECKING ROUTINE
330  Y =  PEEK (222)
335  IF Y = 5 THEN 360
340  PRINT "UNUSUAL ERROR",Y
360  PRINT D$;"CLOSE EMPLOY"
370  PRINT "*******************************************************************************"
380  PRINT "TOTALS"," "," ",R1; SPC( 7);V1; SPC( 7);W1
63999  END
```

PAYROLL REPORT

EMPLOYEE NUMBER	DEPT NUMBER	NAME	HOURLY RATE	REGULAR HOURS	OVERTIME HOURS	GROSS PAY
101	1	ADAMS	5	40	0	200
103	12	BAKER	5.6	40	4	257.6
104	17	BRAVO	4	40	2	172
108	16	COHEN	6.25	38	0	237.5
172	2	JOHNSON	3.75	40	0	150
198	1	TANNER	4.25	36	0	153
202	16	WILSON	4	40	0	160
206	7	LESTER	5.25	40	0	210
255	12	SCHMIDT	5.6	40	4	257.6
281	12	MILLER	6	40	0	240
313	7	SMITH	4.25	40	4	195.5
347	12	GRAY	6	38	0	228
368	1	WEAVER	3.5	40	2	150.5
422	1	WILLIAMS	4	40	0	160

```
**********************************************************************
```
| TOTALS | | | | 552 | 16 | 2771.7 |

There are two new BASIC functions in this program—TAB and SPC. Both of these functions only appear in print statements and are used to make the output more readable. In line 140 PRINT TAB(30); "PAYROLL REPORT", the TAB is used to position the heading of the report. The first "P" of "PAYROLL REPORT" will start printing in column 30. TAB works the same way as setting manual tabs on a typewriter. The number in parentheses indicates the column in which you want the printing to start.

The SPC function is used to place spaces between fields on a line of output. In line 300 the SPC function specifies six spaces between the N and D fields; eight spaces between the R and V fields; and seven spaces between the V and W fields. Spaces should only be inserted between numeric fields where you know the number of characters in that field will be constant, otherwise, the characters will not line up neatly in columns.

Line 295 W=INT (100*W+0.5)/100 is used to round gross pay to dollars and cents. Assume that the value of W is \$198.6666 at line 280. It would be printed with four sixes to the right of the decimal. INT(100*W+0.5) multiplies 198.6666 by 100 giving 19866.66, then adds .5 giving 19867.16.

INT(19867.16) is 19867 and division by 100 results in 198.67. So we have rounded off gross pay to dollars and cents.

The program does not have a STOP instruction before the END. This STOP instruction was removed after the program was tested so that the message BREAK IN 390 would not appear on the report. You may remove the final STOP instruction after you run the program and it is correct. Then run the program a final time and the message will not appear at the bottom of the report.

The preceding program is one example of how a report may be printed so that it is more readable. There are still some shortcomings in the output: the department numbers that are single digits should be one column over, and all decimal numbers should have decimal points and two decimal characters. In Chapter 11, you will be shown how to make the output look even better.

SUMMARY

In this chapter you have been shown how to accumulate subtotals and totals for a file. A use of the BASIC instruction INT has been explained for cases where department numbers are part of some identification number. Finally you have seen how to produce reports for management that are easily readable and understandable.

BASIC Instructions Introduced:

Statement	Explanation
INT(X)	The value X is made into an integer (whole number).
SPC(X)	Allows X spaces between two fields.
TAB(X)	Starts printing in the Xth column. X must be 40 or less.

PROBLEMS

1. Use the "XK1" file from the first problem in Chapter 4 (page 94) to accumulate the totals from Time 1 and Time 2. Output these totals suitably labelled.

2. Use the "XK1" file to accumulate departmental subtotals from Time 1 and Time 2 assuming that departments are defined as follows:

Department	I.D. Number
1	100–199
2	200–299
3	300–399
4	400–499

Output these totals suitably labelled.

3. Use the "INV" file to accumulate department subtotals and grand totals for units received. Assume department one has part numbers 100–199, department two has part numbers 200–299, department three has part numbers 300–399. Output the totals suitably labelled.

4. Modify your program that produces sales and commission department subtotals and grand totals from the "SALES" file so that it may be read by management. Title it: Sales and Commission Report.

5. Modify your program that produces initial balances and final balances by department and grand totals from the "CUST" file so that it may be read by management. Title it: Customer Sales Report.

6. Modify the program that produces beginning and ending inventory value by department and grand totals from the "INV" file so that it may be read by management. Title it: Inventory Value Report.

7. Modify your program in Problem 3 above so that you produce a management report. Title it: Units Issued by Departments.

6 / Adding and Deleting Records

At the end of this chapter you should be able to:

- Add records to sequential files
- Delete records from sequential files

Files are not static. The contents of files change as the business changes. In the payroll example, employees are hired and new employee records are added to the files. People also leave or retire, and the old employee records have to be dropped from the file. Customers are acquired and new customer records have to be inserted into a file. Or a product becomes obsolete and it must be deleted from the file.

In this chapter we will show you how to add and delete records using sequential files.

An accidental omission has occured. When the data for the employee payroll (Table 4–1, Chapter 4) was given, two records were lost. Now they have been found. Fortunately, the payroll has not been prepared. But these two records have to be added to the file before the payroll program can be run.

This hypothetical situation (it would never occur in real life, would it?) serves as the basis for showing you how to add records to a file. Let's assume that the two missing records are the following:

Employee Number	Department Number	Employee Name	Hourly Rate	Regular Hours	Overtime Hours
425	17	Jones	4.80	40	2
426	17	Cooper	4.25	38	0

As you can see, Jones and Cooper belong at the end of the "EMPLOY" file. So we need to find the end of the file and add the records at that point.

But here we run into a limitation of sequential files. We can either read from a file or print into a file, but we cannot both read and print the *same* sequential file unless we are only adding records to the end of a file. If records are to be added between existing records or old records are to be changed, we need to read from one file and print into another file. Since this is the most typical situation we will use the two file approach in this chapter.

The problem has two sets of input data. First, the payroll file with its records of six fields:

- Employee number
- Department number
- Employee name
- Hourly rate of pay
- Regular hours worked
- Overtime hours worked

Secondly, the two omitted records with the same fields (which must be added from the keyboard). For output the problem requires a complete file as well as messages to the keyboard operator.

The processing consists of reading the records in the old file and writing them into a new file. When the end of data has been reached in the old file, then records are entered from the keyboard and added to the new file.

Problem Summary

Input Data
1. "EMPLOY" file with six fields per record:
   - Employee number
   - Employee department number
   - Employee name
   - Hourly rate
   - Regular hours
   - Overtime hours

   No validity checks necessary since all fields have already been checked.
2. New records to be added to the file, each record consisting of six fields.

Field name	Valid Range
Employee number	100 to 999
Employee department number	1 to 20
Employee name	—
Hourly rate	3.05 to 15.00
Regular hours worked	0 to 40
Overtime hours worked	0 to 20

Processing

Take data from the old file and write into new file until end of data is reached. Then take data from keyboard and place valid records into new file.

Output

Instructions for operator and complete payroll data file.

The program, therefore, has to be able to:

1. Link to the file "EMPLOY".
2. Set up a new file.
3. Read from the old file and write into new file until end of data is reached.
4. Get data from terminal and check it for valid range.
5. Write valid records into new file.
6. Stop when new records have been added.

The flowchart for the program is given in Figure 6–1.

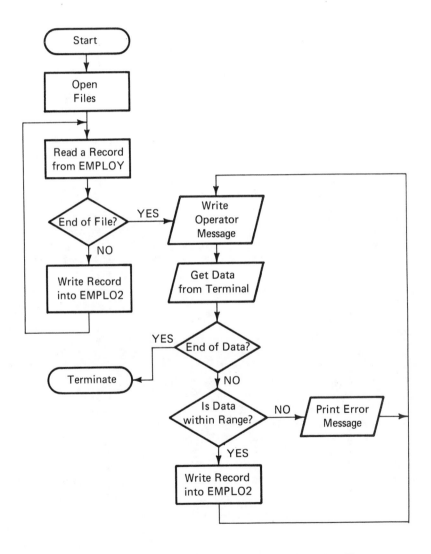

Flowchart for Adding Records to the End of a File   Figure 6–1

```
100   REM   THIS PROGRAM APPENDS RECORDS TO A FILE
110   REM
115 D$ =   CHR$ (4)
120   REM   OPEN FILES FOR INPUT AND OUTPUT
130   PRINT D$;"OPEN EMPLOY"
140   PRINT D$;"OPEN EMPLO2"
150   REM
160   REM   READ THE FILE EMPLOY
170   REM   CHECK FOR END OF FILE
180   REM   AND PRINT INTO THE FILE EMPLO2
190   REM
200   PRINT D$;"READ EMPLOY"
205   INPUT N,D,N$,H,R,V
210   ONERR  GOTO 250
220   PRINT D$;"WRITE EMPLO2"
225   PRINT N;",";D;",";N$;",";H;",";R;",";V
230   GOTO 200
250   PRINT D$
255 Y =  PEEK (222)
260   IF Y = 5 THEN 300
265   PRINT "UNUSUAL ERROR CONDITION",Y
270   GOTO 590
280   REM   READ DATA FROM THE KEYBOARD AND
290   REM   ADD IT TO FILE EMPLO2
295   PRINT D$;"READ EMPLOY"
300   PRINT "TYPE EMPLOYEE NUMBER, DEPARTMENT NUMBER"
310   PRINT "EMPLOYEE NAME, HOURLY RATE, REGULAR HOURS"
320   PRINT "AND OVERTIME HOURS SEPARATED BY COMMAS"
330   PRINT "WHEN FINISHED TYPE 99,99,AA,99,99,99"
340   INPUT N,D,N$,H,R,V
350   REM
360   REM   CHECK FOR END OF DATA
380   IF N = 99 THEN 590
390   REM
400   REM   CHECK THE DATA FOR VALIDITY
410   REM
420   IF N < 100 THEN 540
430   IF N > 999 THEN 540
440   IF D < 1 THEN 540
450   IF D > 20 THEN 540
460   IF H < 3.05 THEN 540
470   IF H > 15.00 THEN 540
480   IF R < 0 THEN 540
490   IF R > 40 THEN 540
500   IF V < 0 THEN 540
510   IF V > 20 THEN 540
520   PRINT D$;"WRITE EMPLO2"
525   PRINT N;",";D;",";N$;",";H;",";R;",";V
530   PRINT D$
535   GOTO 300
```

```
540    PRINT "***ERROR IN INPUT DATA -- PLEASE RETYPE"
550    GOTO 300
560    REM
570    REM   TERMINATE PROGRAM
580    REM
590    PRINT D$;"CLOSE EMPLOY"
595    PRINT D$;"CLOSE EMPLO2"
600    STOP
63999 END

]RUN
TYPE EMPLOYEE NUMBER, DEPARTMENT NUMBER
EMPLOYEE NAME, HOURLY RATE, REGULAR HOURS
AND OVERTIME HOURS SEPARATED BY COMMAS
WHEN FINISHED TYPE 99,99,AA,99,99,99
?425,17,JONES,4.80,40,2
TYPE EMPLOYEE NUMBER, DEPARTMENT NUMBER
EMPLOYEE NAME, HOURLY RATE, REGULAR HOURS
AND OVERTIME HOURS SEPARATED BY COMMAS
WHEN FINISHED TYPE 99,99,AA,99,99,99
?426,17,COOPER,4.25,38,0
TYPE EMPLOYEE NUMBER, DEPARTMENT NUMBER
EMPLOYEE NAME, HOURLY RATE, REGULAR HOURS
AND OVERTIME HOURS SEPARATED BY COMMAS
WHEN FINISHED TYPE 99,99,AA,99,99,99
?99,99,AA,99,99,99

BREAK IN 600
```

In order to determine whether the program worked, print the "EMPLO2"
file with the following program.

```
15  D$ =  CHR$ (4)
20   ONERR  GOTO 200
100    PRINT D$;"OPEN EMPLO2"
110    PRINT D$;"READ EMPLO2"
120    INPUT N,D,N$,H,R,V
125    PRINT D$
130    PRINT N; SPC( 2);D,N$,H,R,V
135    GOTO 110
200    REM   ***ERROR CHECKING ROUTINE
205    PRINT D$
210 Y =  PEEK (222)
215    IF Y = 5 THEN 250
220    PRINT "UNUSUAL ERROR CONDITION",Y
250    PRINT D$;"CLOSE EMPLO2"
500    STOP
63999 END
```

```
]RUN
101   1          ADAMS        5          40        0
103   12         BAKER        5.6        40        4
104   17         BRAVO        4          40        2
108   16         COHEN        6.25       38        0
172   2          JOHNSON      3.75       40        0
198   1          TANNER       4.25       36        0
202   16         WILSON       4          40        0
206   7          LESTER       5.25       40        0
255   12         SCHMIDT      5.6        40        4
281   12         MILLER       6          40        0
313   7          SMITH        4.25       40        4
347   12         GRAY         6          38        0
368   1          WEAVER       3.5        40        2
422   1          WILLIAMS     4          40        0
425   17         JONES        4.8        40        2
426   17         COOPER       4.25       38        0


BREAK IN 500
```

This program contains no new statements. The Apple allows a much shorter version of this program only if we want to add records to the end of the file. Instead of opening the "EMPLOY" file, the instruction PRINT D$; "APPEND EMPLOY" could be used. This causes each print to the file to add the record to the end of "EMPLOY" without the use of a second file. This is a much easier program but in order for you to better understand the logic of the next program, this program was written the long way.

Look again at the program. As you can see, it transfers all of the records from the old file to the new file before it gets any data from the terminal. But what if the employees Jones and Cooper had employee numbers 154 and 232 respectively? Then the program would still place their records at the end of the file, but at the end of the file, their records would be out of sequence by employee number.

We must change the program so that new records fit into the middle of the new file. The location of these records is determined by the sequence of identification numbers, in this case employee number. Records to be added fit into the file after records with lower numbers, and before records with higher numbers.

However, the computer cannot see the whole file. It operates on the file *one record at a time.* It will know where to insert a record only after it has read a record from the old file with a *higher* identifying number.

Let's look at an example to illustrate this point. Below you have the employee numbers of a section of the payroll file. And the employee numbers of the records to be added.

Employee Number in File	*New Employee Numbers of Records to be Added*
104	154
108	232
172	
198	
202	
206	
255	
282	

Now look at the first number in each column. Remember, the employee number stands for the complete record. With the first number in each column you have the whole record. You can see that record 154 belongs after record 104. Hence 104 is transferred to the new file.

Now read the next record in the file—108. Again, since it is less than the record to be added—154, it gets transferred to the new file. When you now read the next record, we have the following position.

Record to be Added	*Record from Old File*	*Records in New File*
154	172	104
		108

Here the record from the old file is greater than the record to be added. Therefore the record to be added is placed into the new file. The new file now consists of three records in sequential (ascending) order—104, 108 and 154.

Since we do not know where the next record will fit, until we have read it, a new record to be added is obtained and the comparison is repeated. In our example, the record to be added is 232. But it could just as easily have been record 155 or 163 or 171. In that case, the record also should be placed prior to record 172.

Think your way through the process of placing record 232 into the new file. Read the old file, one record at a time. Move all records with lower employee numbers to the new file. Once you read a record with a higher ID number, then place the record to be added into the new file.

You have been playing "computer" when you think through a problem in this excruciatingly detailed way. And very simple thinking also; but that is the way the simple-minded computer works: one elementary operation at a time on small amounts of data.

The general pattern of record insertion hinges on two things:

1. The old records are in ascending order.

2. The program must find a record that is larger than the one that has to be inserted into the sequence.

The program therefore has to transfer all records with lower employee numbers to the new file. Then the record to be added can be written into the new file. *Then* the record with a higher employee number is written into the new file. Finally, another record to be added is input and the process continued.

A program to add records to a file is shown below. The range checks of the records to be added have been removed for brevity and to highlight the program logic.

Problem Summary

Input

"EMPLOY" file in employee number sequence. Records to be added, also in employee number sequence.

Processing

Place records to be added into their proper location in the file.

Output

Data entry operator instructions and complete file of payroll records.

Here is the program and flowchart (Fig. 6–2) for placing records in the middle of a file:

```
10   REM   THIS PROGRAM ADDS RECORDS TO THE MIDDLE OF THE FILE
15 D$ =   CHR$ (4)
100  REM   OPEN THE FILES
110  REM
130  PRINT D$;"OPEN EMPLOY"
140  PRINT D$;"OPEN EMPLO3"
150  REM   GET A RECORD FROM THE TERMINAL
160  REM
170  REM
180  PRINT "TYPE EMPLOYEE NUMBER, DEPARTMENT NUMBER, EMPLOYEE NAME"
190  PRINT "HOURLY RATE, REGULAR HOURS, OVERTIME HOURS"
200  PRINT "SEPARATED BY COMMAS"
210  PRINT "WHEN FINISHED TYPE 99,99,AA,99,99,99"
220  INPUT N1,D1,N1$,H1,R1,V1
230  REM
240  REM   CHECK FOR END OF DATA FROM TERMINAL
250  REM
260  IF N1 = 99 THEN 670
270  REM
280  REM   SEARCH THE FILE FOR NUMBER SEQUENCE
290  REM
300  PRINT D$;"READ EMPLOY"
305  INPUT N,D,N$,H,R,V
```

```
310   ONERR  GOTO 650
320   IF N1 < N THEN 420
330   REM
340   REM   RECORD FROM FILE LESS THAN RECORD FROM TERMINAL
350   REM
360   PRINT D$;"WRITE EMPLO3"
365   PRINT N;",";D;",";N$;",";H;",";R;",";V
370   GOTO 300
380   REM
390   REM   RECORD FROM TERMINAL IS LOWER THAN THE ONE IN THE FILE
400   REM   PRINT THE RECORD IN THE NEW FILE
410   REM
420   PRINT D$;"WRITE EMPLO3"
425   PRINT N1;",";D1;",";N1$;",";H1;",";R1;",";V1
428   PRINT D$
430   REM
440   REM   GET ANOTHER RECORD FROM THE TERMINAL
450   REM
470   PRINT "TYPE EMPLOYEE NUMBER, DEPARTMENT NUMBER, EMPLOYEE"
480   PRINT "NAME, HOURLY RATE, REGULAR HOURS, OVERTIME HOURS"
490   PRINT "WHEN FINISHED TYPE 99,99,AA,99,99,99"
510   INPUT N1,D1,N1$,H1,R1,V1
520   IF N1 = 99 THEN 580
530   GOTO 320
540   REM
550   REM   NO MORE RECORDS TO BE ADDED
560   REM   TRANSFER REMAINING RECORDS TO THE NEW FILE
570   REM
580   PRINT D$;"WRITE EMPLO3"
585   PRINT N;",";D;",";N$;",";H;",";R;",";V
590   PRINT D$;"READ EMPLOY"
595   INPUT N,D,N$,H,R,V
610   GOTO 580
620   REM
640   REM
650   PRINT D$
655 Y =  PEEK (222)
660   IF Y = 5 THEN 670
665   PRINT "UNUSUAL ERROR",Y
670   PRINT D$;"CLOSE EMPLOY"
675   PRINT D$;"CLOSE EMPLO3"
700   STOP
63999 END


]RUN
TYPE EMPLOYEE NUMBER, DEPARTMENT NUMBER, EMPLOYEE NAME
HOURLY RATE, REGULAR HOURS, OVERTIME HOURS
SEPARATED BY COMMAS
WHEN FINISHED TYPE 99,99,AA,99,99,99
?154,17,JONES,4.80,40,2
TYPE EMPLOYEE NUMBER, DEPARTMENT NUMBER, EMPLOYEE
NAME, HOURLY RATE, REGULAR HOURS, OVERTIME HOURS
```

```
WHEN FINISHED TYPE 99,99,AA,99,99,99
?232,17,COOPER,4.25,38,0
TYPE EMPLOYEE NUMBER, DEPARTMENT NUMBER, EMPLOYEE
NAME, HOURLY RATE, REGULAR HOURS, OVERTIME HOURS
WHEN FINISHED TYPE 99,99,AA,99,99,99
?99,99,AA,99,99,99

BREAK IN 700
```

To determine whether the program worked, print the "EMPLO3" file. This may be done by modifying your program that prints the "EMPLO2" file. The change necessary is

100   PRINT D$; "OPEN EMPLO3"
110   PRINT D$; "READ EMPLO3"
250   PRINT D$; "CLOSE EMPLO3"

Then run the changed program.

101	1	ADAMS	5	40	0
103	12	BAKER	5.6	40	4
104	17	BRAVO	4	40	2
108	16	COHEN	6.25	38	0
154	17	JONES	4.8	40	2
172	2	JOHNSON	3.75	40	0
198	1	TANNER	4.25	36	0
202	16	WILSON	4	40	0
206	7	LESTER	5.25	40	0
232	17	COOPER	4.25	38	0
255	12	SCHMIDT	5.6	40	4
281	12	MILLER	6	40	0
313	7	SMITH	4.25	40	4
347	12	GRAY	6	38	0
368	1	WEAVER	3.5	40	2
422	1	WILLIAMS	4	40	0

```
BREAK IN 500
```

Let's take another look at this program. Notice how the end of data in the file (EOF) for the old file and the end of data from the terminal (EOD) decisions appear a number of times. The program is made complicated by having to consider all possibilities:

1.   There are no records to be added.

2.   The file is empty when more records have to be added. (In our example, the program merely terminated when that happened; see line 310 and line 660. The extension of handling such records is left as an exercise for you.)

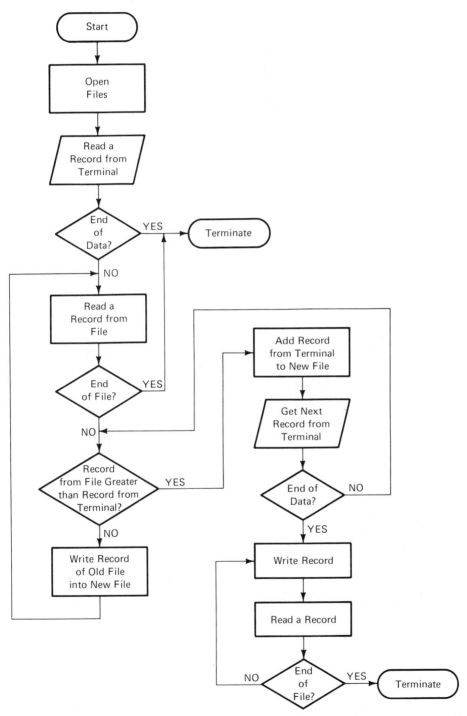

Flowchart for Adding a Record into the Middle of a File

Figure 6-2

3. No more records have to be added while there are still records in the file.

4. The file is empty and no records need to be added.

For all four cases the program has to provide a means of reaching a satisfactory conclusion. In our example, the program merely terminates without telling the operator what has happened. Maybe you can think of some way to modify the program so that a message appears that would identify why the program stopped.

Example   Inventory Example: To the inventory file ("INV"), add the following two records.

Problem Summary

Input

	Part Number	Beginning Units	Units Received	Units Issued	Cost
Record 1	112	0	50	10	8.25
Record 2	300	0	150	70	6.85

"INV" file

Processing

Place records to be added into their proper sequence in the file.

Output

Data entry operator instructions
New file "INV1"
Print the file "INV1"

```
100   REM   PROGRAM TO ADD RECORDS TO THE MIDDLE OF THE INVENTORY FILE
110   REM
115 D$ =   CHR$ (4)
120   REM   LINK TO FILES
130   REM
140   PRINT D$;"OPEN INV"
150   PRINT D$;"OPEN INV1"
160   REM
170   REM   GET RECORD TO BE ADDED FROM TERMINAL
180   REM
190   PRINT "ENTER PART NUMBER, BEGINNING UNITS, UNITS RECEIVED"
200   PRINT "UNITS ISSUED AND UNIT COST -- SEPARATED BY COMMAS"
210   PRINT "WHEN FINISHED -- TYPE 99 FOR EACH FIELD"
220   INPUT P9,B9,R9,I9,C9
230   REM
240   REM   CHECK FOR END OF DATA FROM TERMINAL
250   REM
260   IF P9 = 99 THEN 1130
270   REM
280   REM   SEARCH FILE FOR PLACE TO ADD NEW RECORD
```

```
290   REM
300   ONERR   GOTO 990
310 T = 1
320   PRINT D$;"READ INV"
325   INPUT P,B,R1,R2,C
330   IF P9 < P THEN 440
340   REM
350   REM    RECORD FROM TERMINAL GREATER THAN RECORD FROM FILE
360   REM    THEREFORE PLACE RECORD FROM FILE INTO INV1
370   REM
380   PRINT D$;"WRITE INV1"
385   PRINT P;",";B;",";R1;",";R2;",";C
390   GOTO 320
400   REM
410   REM    RECORD FROM TERMINAL LESS THAN RECORD FROM FILE
420   REM    THEREFORE PLACE RECORD FROM TERMINAL INTO INV1
430   REM
440   PRINT D$;"WRITE INV1"
445   PRINT P9;",";B9;",";R9;",";I9;",";C9
448   PRINT D$
450   REM
460   REM    GET ANOTHER RECORD FROM TERMINAL
470   REM
480   PRINT "ENTER PART NUMBER, BEGINNING UNITS, UNITS RECEIVED"
490   PRINT "UNITS ISSUED AND UNIT COST -- SEPARATED BY COMMAS"
500   PRINT "WHEN FINISHED -- TYPE 99 FOR EACH FIELD"
510   INPUT P9,B9,R9,I9,C9
520   REM
530   REM    CHECK FOR END OF DATA ENTRY
540   REM
550   IF P9 = 99 THEN 620
560   GOTO 330
570   REM
580   REM    NO MORE RECORDS TO BE ADDED, BUT RECORDS STILL IN INV
590   REM    TRANSFER REMAINING RECORDS FROM INV
600   REM    INTO INV1
610   REM
620 T = 2
630   PRINT D$;"WRITE INV1"
635   PRINT P;",";B;",";R1;",";R2;",";C
640   PRINT D$;"READ INV"
645   INPUT P,B,R1,R2,C
650   GOTO 630
660   REM
780   REM
790   REM    NEW FILE HAS BEEN GENERATED SO PRINT IT OUT
800   REM
810   PRINT D$;"CLOSE INV"
815   PRINT D$;"CLOSE INV1"
820   PRINT D$;"OPEN INV1"
830   REM
840   REM    PRINT HEADINGS
```

```
850   REM
860   PRINT
870   PRINT
880   PRINT
890   PRINT "PART","BEGINNING","UNITS","UNITS","UNIT"
900   PRINT "NUMBER","UNITS","RECEIVED","ISSUED","COST"
910   PRINT "------","-----","--------","------","----"
920 T = 3
930   PRINT D$;"READ INV1"
935   INPUT P,B,R1,R2,C
938   PRINT D$
940   PRINT P,B,R1,R2,C
950   GOTO 930
960   REM   *****************************
970   REM   *** ERROR CHECKING ROUTINES ***
980   REM   *****************************
990   PRINT D$
995 Y =  PEEK (222)
1000   IF Y = 5 THEN 1080
1005   PRINT "UNUSUAL ERROR",Y
1010   STOP
1020   REM
1030   REM   CHECK WHERE END OF FILE WAS ENCOUNTERED
1040   REM   IF T=1 THEN INV IS EMPTY BUT ADD MORE DATA
1050   REM   IF T=2 THEN INV IS EMPTY AND DATA ENTRY FINISHED
1060   REM   IF T=3 THEN NEW FILE INV1 HAS BEEN WRITTEN
1070   REM
1080   IF T = 1 THEN 480
1090   IF T = 2 THEN 810
1100   REM
1110   REM   T MUST BE 3 -- TERMINATE PROGRAM
1120   REM
1130   PRINT D$;"CLOSE INV1"
1140   STOP
63999 END


]RUN
ENTER PART NUMBER, BEGINNING UNITS, UNITS RECEIVED
UNITS ISSUED AND UNIT COST -- SEPARATED BY COMMAS
WHEN FINISHED -- TYPE 99 FOR EACH FIELD
?112,0,50,10,8.25
ENTER PART NUMBER, BEGINNING UNITS, UNITS RECEIVED
UNITS ISSUED AND UNIT COST -- SEPARATED BY COMMAS
WHEN FINISHED -- TYPE 99 FOR EACH FIELD
?300,0,150,70,6.85
ENTER PART NUMBER, BEGINNING UNITS, UNITS RECEIVED
UNITS ISSUED AND UNIT COST -- SEPARATED BY COMMAS
WHEN FINISHED -- TYPE 99 FOR EACH FIELD
?99,99,99,99,99
```

PART NUMBER	BEGINNING UNITS	UNITS RECEIVED	UNITS ISSUED	UNIT COST
------	-----	--------	------	----
101	120	40	45	5
112	0	50	10	8.25
219	60	60	80	3.25
226	5	110	90	2.95
235	100	0	50	6.2
300	0	150	70	6.85
347	0	50	20	4.6

BREAK IN 1140

This example contains two new features:

● A file is opened, closed, and reopened.

● A test value is used to determine where an error (end of file) occurs.

In line 150 the file "INV1" was opened and the program wrote into the file. However, the problem summary specifies that the file should also be printed. Therefore "INV1" must be opened again, as shown in line 820. But before a file can be changed from writing to reading, it must be closed as in line 815.

It is perfectly legal for a program to open a file first for writing, close it, and then open it again for reading. When it is opened again, the records are read starting at the beginning of the file.

The second feature, the use of a test value, is necessary because the program hinges on where the error was encountered. The ONERR in line 300 tells the computer to go to line 990 if an error occurs. If we focus only on the end-of-file error ($Y = 5$), then three locations in the program are possible.

1. The EOF was encountered in line 325.

2. The EOF was encountered in line 645.

3. The EOF was encountered in line 935.

If the culprit is line 325, then we have run out of data in "INV", but there are more records to be added. If line 645 was the cause of the error, then we have run out of data in the file "INV" and no more records have to be added. If line 935 caused the error, then the program was printing out the new file "INV1".

In the first case, error caused by line 325, the program should get more records from the terminal and add them to "INV1". In the second case, error caused by line 645, data entry is finished and the program should close the files and start to print out "INV1". In the third case, error caused by line 935, the program is finished and it should terminate.

To distinguish between these three possible EOF conditions a test value is used. T is set to 1 in line 310 to indicate the first condition. T is set to 2 in 620 to indicate the second condition. It is set a last time to 3 in line 920.

When any error occurs, the computer goes to line 990. If it is an EOF error ($Y = 5$) then it checks the T value in lines 1080 and 1090 to determine which action has to be taken. Depending on the value of T, the program directs the computer to

- Line 480 to get more data from the terminal
- Line 810 to close the files and print "INVl"
- Next line in succession (line 1130) if T is neither 1 nor 2, to terminate the program

With this logic the program can add records to the middle of a file.

Exercises

Account Balance Exercise: The firm has acquired two new customers. Write a program to add their records to the customer file.

Problem Summary

Input

	Customer Number	Name	Balance	Payments	Charges
Record 1	2995	Jones	0	0	50
Record 2	3370	Moats	0	0	75

Old "CUST" file

Processing

Get new customer data from the terminal and place it at the end of the "CUST1" file.

Output

Instructions for data entry
New customer file "CUST1"
Print the "CUST1" file

_____

_____

_____

_____

_____

_____

_____

_____

_____

_____

_____

_____

_____

_____

_____

_____

_____

_____

_____

_____

_____

(Attach additional paper to complete your program.)

```
TYPE CUSTOMER NUMBER, CUSTOMER NAME, BALANCE
PAYMENTS, CHARGES --- SEPARATED BY COMMAS
WHEN FINISHED TYPE 999,AAA,999,999,999
?2995,JONES,0,0,50
TYPE CUSTOMER NUMBER, CUSTOMER NAME, BALANCE
PAYMENTS, CHARGES --- SEPARATED BY COMMAS
WHEN FINISHED TYPE 999,AAA,999,999,999
?3370,MOATS,0,0,75
TYPE CUSTOMER NUMBER, CUSTOMER NAME, BALANCE
PAYMENTS, CHARGES --- SEPARATED BY COMMAS
WHEN FINISHED TYPE 999,AAA,999,999,999
?999,AAA,999,999,999
```

CUSTOMER NUMBER	CUSTOMER NAME	BALANCE	PAYMENTS	CHARGES
2741	FERNWOOD	120	120	40
2937	BLAKEY	0	0	90
2995	JONES	0	0	50
3246	GREY	250	130	170
3359	PHILLIPS	90	40	100
3370	MOATS	0	0	75
3426	BIRD	180	180	200
3527	LOMBARD	100	100	250

BREAK IN 1050

Sales Commission Exercise: The firm has added two salesmen. Add their records to the file.

Problem Summary

Input

	Sales Territory	Salesman	Gross Sales	Commission Rate
Record 1	1	Kevin	2500	.045
Record 2	2	Jack	500	.05

"SALES" file

Processing

Get the data from the terminal and place it in the file ("SALES1") by sales territory.

Output

Instructions for data entry
New "SALES1" file
Print the "SALES1" file

(Attach additional paper to complete your program.)

```
TYPE SALES TERRITORY, SALESMAN, GROSS
SALES AND COMMISSION RATE --- SEPARATED BY COMMAS
WHEN FINISHED TYPE 0,AA,0,0
?1,KEVIN,2500,.045
TYPE SALES TERRITORY, SALESMAN, GROSS
SALES AND COMMISSION RATE --- SEPARATED BY COMMAS
WHEN FINISHED TYPE 0,AA,0,0
?2,JACK,500,.05
TYPE SALES TERRITORY, SALESMAN, GROSS
SALES AND COMMISSION RATE --- SEPARATED BY COMMAS
WHEN FINISHED TYPE 0,AA,0,0
?0,AA,0,0
```

SALES TERRITORY	SALESMAN	GROSS SALES	COMMISSION RATE
1	BILL	12050	.05
1	JOE	5270	.045
1	KEVIN	2500	.045
2	TOM	6940	.04
2	PHIL	11200	.055
2	JACK	500	.05
3	CLYDE	7340	.04
3	HARRY	9460	.045
3	BOB	14690	.05

```
BREAK IN 1140
```

DELETING RECORDS FROM A FILE

Sometimes it is necessary to delete records from sequential files. Employees quit or retire. Occasionally an employee may be fired. Items in inventory become obsolete. Suppliers may be dropped. Old customers may shift their buying elsewhere. There are many instances when files need to be purged of records that are no longer needed.

In such cases it is necessary to find the records and delete them. Here again the nature of computer files places a burden on the programmer. Reading a record does not remove it from a file.

Therefore to delete a record, we have to read all of the records in a sequential file, and write all of the records into a new file—*except* those records that should be deleted.

Another aspect to consider is that sequential files are in sequence—and you can't go back. Once a record has been processed, it can only be found again if we start from the beginning of the file.

Therefore if there is more than one record that has to be deleted, they also must be in sequence. Otherwise, the whole file has to be read for each record to be removed.

So let's assume that we have to delete some records from our payroll file, for example, records with employee numbers 104 and 202. A flowchart (Fig. 6–3) and program to do this follow:

```
100   REM   PROGRAM TO DELETE RECORDS FROM A FILE
110   REM
115   D$ =  CHR$ (4)
120   REM   OPEN FILES
130   REM
140   PRINT D$;"OPEN EMPLOY"
150   PRINT D$;"OPEN EMPLO4"
160   REM
170   REM   GET THE ID NUMBER OF THE RECORD TO BE DELETED
180   REM
190   PRINT
200   PRINT
210   PRINT "TYPE THE ID NUMBER OF THE RECORD TO BE DELETED"
220   PRINT "IF FINISHED -- TYPE 99"
230   INPUT N1
240   IF N1 = 99 THEN 570
250   REM
260   REM   READ A RECORD FROM THE EXISTING FILE
270   REM
280   PRINT D$;"READ EMPLOY"
285   INPUT N,D,N$,H,R,V
290   REM
300   REM   TEST FOR END OF FILE
310   REM
320   ONERR  GOTO 500
330   REM
340   REM   CHECK IF RECORD SHOULD BE DELETED
350   REM
360   IF N1 = N THEN 450
370   REM
380   REM   SINCE ID NUMBERS ARE NOT EQUAL THE RECORD REMAINS
390   REM
400   PRINT D$;"WRITE EMPLO4"
405   PRINT N;",";D;",";N$;",";H;",";R;",";V
410   GOTO 280
420   REM
430   REM   ID NUMBERS EQUAL; RECORD IS REMOVED
440   REM
450   PRINT D$
455   PRINT "RECORD REMOVED ";N; SPC( 2);D,N$,H,R; SPC( 2);V
460   GOTO 190
470   REM
480   REM   END OF FILE REACHED WITH THE RECORD NOT FOUND
490   REM
500   PRINT D$
505   PRINT "END OF FILE REACHED"
510   PRINT "RECORD ";N1;" NOT FOUND"
520   GOTO 640
530   REM
540   REM   NO MORE RECORDS TO BE DELETED, TRANSFER REMAINING
550   REM   RECORDS FROM THE OLD FILE TO THE NEW FILE
560   REM
570   ONERR  GOTO 640
```

```
580    PRINT D$;"READ EMPLOY"
585    INPUT N,D,N$,H,R,V
590    PRINT D$;"WRITE EMPLO4"
595    PRINT N;",";D;",";N$;",";H;",";R;",";V
600    GOTO 580
610    REM
620    REM   END OF PROGRAM
630    REM
640    PRINT D$;"CLOSE EMPLOY"
645    PRINT D$;"CLOSE EMPLO4"
650    STOP
63999 END
```

```
TYPE THE ID NUMBER OF THE RECORD TO BE DELETED
IF FINISHED -- TYPE 99
?104
RECORD REMOVED 104   17          BRAVO           4           40   2


TYPE THE ID NUMBER OF THE RECORD TO BE DELETED
IF FINISHED -- TYPE 99
?202
RECORD REMOVED 202   16          WILSON          4           40   0


TYPE THE ID NUMBER OF THE RECORD TO BE DELETED
IF FINISHED -- TYPE 99
?99


BREAK IN 650
```

To determine whether the program worked, print the "EMPLO4" file. Modify your program that prints the "EMPLO3" file as follows and run it.

```
100   PRINT D$; "OPEN EMPLO4"
110   PRINT D$; "READ EMPLO4"
250   PRINT D$; "CLOSE EMPLO4"
```

101	1	ADAMS	5	40	0
103	12	BAKER	5.6	40	4
108	16	COHEN	6.25	38	0
172	2	JOHNSON	3.75	40	0
198	1	TANNER	4.25	36	0
206	7	LESTER	5.25	40	0
255	12	SCHMIDT	5.6	40	4
281	12	MILLER	6	40	0
313	7	SMITH	4.25	40	4
347	12	GRAY	6	38	0
368	1	WEAVER	3.5	40	2
422	1	WILLIAMS	4	40	0

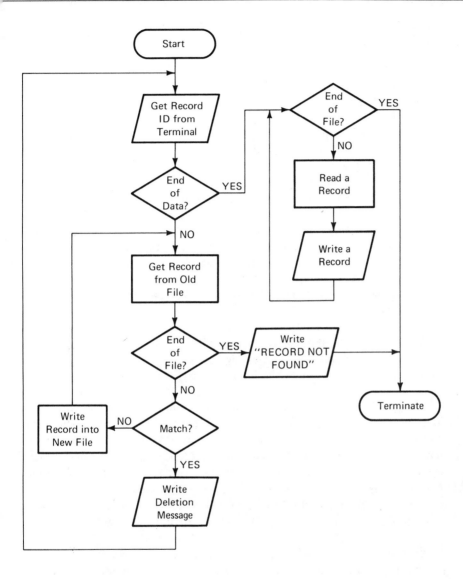

Flowchart for Deleting Records from a File   Figure 6–3

There are no new statements in this program. Just old instructions in a new arrangement. But what an arrangement! Three input statements, four decisions, two prints to a file, and many explanatory REM statements.

When we look at such a program, the mind boggles at the amount of detail. But let's look at it as a computer would see it—one instruction at a time. That way the whole process is simplified.

We start by getting the identification number of a record (employee number) to be deleted from the terminal:

If the data is not finished (ID number is not 99)
> *Then*
>> We read a record from the old file
>> *If* the file is empty
>>> *Then* print the record not found message and terminate
>>> *Else* (there are records in the file)
>>> *If* the keyboard ID matches the record ID from the file
>>>> *Then* the record deleted message is
>>>> printed and we go back to get another
>>>> record from the keyboard
>>> *Else* (record ID does not match keyboard ID)
>>>> The record is printed in the new file
>>>> and we go back to get another record
> *Else* (there are no more records to be deleted)
>> *If* there are no more records in the file (we might have deleted the last record in the file)
>>> *Then* terminate
>>> *Else* Read a record from the file
>>> Print it in the new file
>>> Go back to check end of file (EOF) again.

Notice that when we look at the program from this viewpoint, we do not look forward. Rather, we work with the limited amount of data available at any particular time. By golly, the computer is abysmally ignorant; so, we need to be very precise and consider all possibilities in order to cover all bases in our programs—*before* they are written. Otherwise, if something is overlooked and that particular condition occurs, the program will not work.

Look at this program again. Then review the other examples provided. After that you can practice thinking logically by doing the exercises.

Example
Inventory Example: Delete from the new inventory file ("INVl") the records for Part Numbers 101, 219, and 300. Print the new file.

```
100  REM   THIS PROGRAM DELETES RECORDS FROM THE INVENTORY FILE
110  REM
115  D$ =  CHR$ (4)
120  REM   OPEN FILES
130  REM
140  PRINT D$;"OPEN INV1"
150  PRINT D$;"OPEN INV2"
160  REM
170  REM   GET THE PART NUMBER OF THE ITEM TO BE DELETED FROM THE TERMI
```

```
180    REM
190    PRINT "TYPE THE PART NUMBER OF THE RECORD TO BE DELETED"
200    PRINT "WHEN FINISHED -- TYPE 99"
210    INPUT N1
220    IF N1 = 99 THEN 550
230    REM
240    REM    READ A RECORD FROM THE EXISTING FILE
250    REM
260    PRINT D$;"READ INV1"
265    INPUT N,B,R1,R2,C
270    REM
280    REM    CHECK FOR END OF FILE
290    REM
300    ONERR  GOTO 480
310    REM
320    REM    CHECK TO SEE IF THE RECORD SHOULD BE DELETED
330    REM
340    IF N1 = N THEN 430
350    REM
360    REM   ID NUMBERS NOT EQUAL -- RECORD REMAINS IN FILE
370    REM
380    PRINT D$;"WRITE INV2"
385    PRINT N;",";B;",";R1;",";R2;",";C
390    GOTO 260
400    REM
410    REM   ID NUMBERS EQUAL -- RECORD NOT TRANSFERRED
420    REM
430    PRINT D$
431    PRINT "RECORD REMOVED ";N; SPC( 2);B; SPC( 2);R1,R2; SPC( 2);C
432    REM
435    REM    GET THE NEXT RECORD TO BE REMOVED FROM THE TERMINAL
440    GOTO 190
450    REM
460    REM    END OF FILE FOUND WITH RECORD NOT FOUND
470    REM
480    PRINT D$
485    PRINT "END OF FILE REACHED"
490    PRINT "RECORD ";N1;" NOT FOUND"
500    GOTO 620
510    REM
520    REM    NO MORE RECORDS TO BE DELETED
530    REM    TRANSFER REMAINING RECORDS TO THE NEW FILE
540    REM
550    ONERR  GOTO 620
560    PRINT D$;"READ INV1"
565    INPUT N,B,R1,R2,C
570    PRINT D$;"WRITE INV2"
575    PRINT N;",";B;",";R1;",";R2;",";C
580    GOTO 560
590    REM
600    REM    END OF PROGRAM
610    REM
```

```
620   PRINT D$;"CLOSE INV1"
625   PRINT D$;"CLOSE INV2"
740   STOP
63999 END


]RUN
TYPE THE PART NUMBER OF THE RECORD TO BE DELETED
WHEN FINISHED -- TYPE 99
?101
RECORD REMOVED 101   120   40      45   5
TYPE THE PART NUMBER OF THE RECORD TO BE DELETED
WHEN FINISHED -- TYPE 99
?219
RECORD REMOVED 219   60   60      80   3.25
TYPE THE PART NUMBER OF THE RECORD TO BE DELETED
WHEN FINISHED -- TYPE 99
?300
RECORD REMOVED 300   0   150      70   6.85
TYPE THE PART NUMBER OF THE RECORD TO BE DELETED
WHEN FINISHED -- TYPE 99
?99

BREAK IN 740
```

Modify your program that prints the "INV" file to print the "INV2" file.

112	0	50	10	8.25
226	5	110	90	2.95
235	100	0	50	6.2
347	0	50	20	4.6

BREAK IN 500

Exercises

Account Balance Exercise: Delete from the new customer statement file ("CUST1") the records for customer numbers 2741, 2937, and 3426. Print the new file ("CUST2") with another program.

_____

_____

_____

_____

_____

_____

_____

_____

_____

_____

_____

_____

_____

_____

_____

_____

_____

_____

_____

_____

_____

_____

_____

(Attach additional paper to complete your program.)

Sales Commission Exercise: Delete from the new sales file ("SALES1") the records for salesmen Bill, Tom, and Harry. Print the new file with another program.

_____

_____

_____

_____
_____
_____
_____
_____
_____
_____
_____
_____
_____
_____
_____
_____
_____
_____
_____
_____
_____
_____
_____
_____
_____
_____

(Attach additional paper to complete your program.)

SUMMARY   This chapter did not deal with BASIC statements; it dealt with how to use what you have already learned in order to solve two problems—deleting and adding records.

The use of sequential files, and some of their limitations, becomes apparent in these problems. Sequential files can only be read from the beginning. We cannot start anywhere in the middle. We must start with the first record in the file, and proceed record by record until the desired record is found. Then, and only then, can the operation be performed—adding a record or deleting a record.

If sequential files are so restricted, why then are they so common? The answer is simple—cost. Sequential file processing is efficient when large numbers of active records are involved. Such is the case for many business applications. We can collect a large amount of data and process it all together in a batch.

All of the records are processed in an identical way. The basic logic for sequential processing is simply input-process-output (and repeat the input-process-output sequence until finished). Each transaction receives identical treatment.

In this chapter you have learned more about how to handle sequential files:

- How to add records to the end and to the middle of a file
- How to remove records from a file

In the next chapter this added skill will become useful when you update sequential files.

PROBLEMS

1. Use the file "XK1" from Problem 1 in Chapter 4 (page 94) and add the following records:

ID	Time 1	Time 2
107	35	0
209	40	4
420	40	2

Call the new file "XK2". PRINT the new file.

2. Use the file "TOP" from Problem 3 in Chapter 4 (page 89) and add the following records:

ID	Name
250	Bong
263	Cabot
270	Walters
273	Beck

Call the new file "TOP1". Print the new file.

3. Use the file "XK2" from Problem 1 above and delete records with the following IDs: 101, 209, 281, 422. Call the new file "XK3". Print the new file.

4. Use the file "TOP1" from Problem 2 above and delete records with the following IDs: 247, 262, 263, 273. Call the. new file "TOP2". Print the new file.

7 / Updating Sequential Files

At the end of this chapter you should be able to update sequential files with:

- One transaction record for each master record
- Transaction records missing
- Master records missing
- Multiple transaction records for each master record
- Coded transaction records

So far, you have used one or two files in a program. The two files have generally had records with the same fields. When you have created files, the records have also contained the same fields. In this chapter, sequential files are used; however, the records of the different files will not contain the same number of fields. Updating is the term used to describe the processing and/or programs that take master files and transaction files and create new master files.

The programs in this chapter may appear to be long. Most of the statements in each program are remarks. The programs contain these remarks so that you may follow the logic in the programs more easily.

The payroll example has the file "EMPLOY" that contains records with the following fields: employee number, department number, name, hourly rate, regular hours worked, overtime hours worked. This file has been sufficient for our needs until now. In using this file, you may have thought that for each pay period (week), this file is input by a data entry operator with one record per employee. This is not the way it is done by businesses. If the "EMPLOY" file was prepared this way each week, there would be a great deal of duplication. To have to type employee number, department number, and hourly rate for each employee each week would be a great waste of time, especially if there were thousands of employees.

In order to avoid this duplication, master files and transaction files are used. A master file contains information that does not change often. A transaction file contains information that changes regularly. In the payroll example, the only information about an employee that may change regularly (with each payroll) will be regular and overtime hours worked. As a consequence of this, each employee may have two records in two different files. The first file will contain the information that does not change from pay period to pay period; this is the employee master file. The second file will contain the information that does change regularly; this is the employee transaction file.

An example of typical information contained in an employee master file and transaction file is given in Figure 7–1. The information that changes regularly, regular and overtime hours, appears in the transaction file along with the employee number (for identification of the record). The employee master file contains information that does not change often: department number, name, hourly rate, number of exemptions as well as some other information. The year-to-date information is kept in the master record and,

```
Employee Master File
    Employee Master Records
        • Employee Number
        • Department Number
        • Name
        • Marital Status
        • Hourly Rate
        • Number of Exemptions
        • Year-to-Date Gross Pay (YTD GROSS)
        • Year-to-Date Federal Income Tax Withheld (YTD FIT)
        • Year-to-Date Social Security Withheld (YTD FICA)
Employee Transaction File
    Employee Transaction Record
        • Employee Number
        • Regular Hours Worked
        • Overtime Hours Worked
```

Figure 7–1   Data in Employee Master and Transaction Files

obviously, these amounts will change with each payroll. So, the definition of a master record given above must be modified. A master record contains information that does not often change, as well as summary information. In this case the summary information is year-to-date data. In a business, an employee master record for payroll would contain many more fields, but for brevity, the record defined in Figure 7–1 will be sufficient to illustrate an update.

In programming terms, an update may be thought of as a program that matches transaction records with master records and updates the summary information in the master record. As an integral part of this procedure, a payroll can be prepared as well as any management reports concerning payroll. In this chapter, to compute the federal income tax (FIT), use 20% of gross pay; to compute the FICA amount, use 6.13% of gross pay. Emphasis is placed on the programming logic needed to deal with master and transaction files to perform an update. In a later chapter, the tax information will be given and you will be able to program the exact computations for taxes. There is no field for year-to-date net pay since it can easily be computed (YTD NET PAY = YTD GROSS PAY − YTD FIT − YTD FICA).

Table 7–1 shows the information in the employee master file, "EMPMAS", Table 7–2 shows the information in the employee transaction file, "EMPTRA". You can create the file "EMPMAS" by writing a program that will take the "EMPLOY" file and print on the records of the

Employee Master File

Table 7-1

Employee No.	Dept. No.	Name	Marital Status	Hourly Rate	No. of Exemp.	YTD Gross	YTD FIT	YTD FICA
101	1	Adams	2	5.00	3	1000.00	200.00	61.30
103	12	Baker	1	5.60	2	1288.00	257.60	78.95
104	17	Bravo	2	4.00	4	860.00	172.00	52.72
108	16	Cohen	2	6.25	4	1187.50	237.50	72.79
172	2	Johnson	1	3.75	0	750.00	150.00	45.98
198	1	Tanner	2	4.25	4	765.00	153.00	46.89
202	16	Wilson	2	4.00	5	800.00	160.00	49.04
206	7	Lester	2	5.25	3	1050.00	210.00	64.37
255	12	Schmidt	2	5.60	5	1288.00	257.60	78.95
281	12	Miller	2	6.00	4	1200.00	240.00	73.56
313	7	Smith	2	4.25	3	977.50	195.50	59.92
347	12	Gray	2	6.00	3	1140.00	228.00	69.88
368	1	Weaver	1	3.50	1	752.50	150.50	46.13
422	1	Williams	2	4.00	2	800.00	160.00	49.04

Employee Transaction File

Table 7-2

Employee Number	Regular Hours	Overtime Hours
101	40	0
103	40	4
104	40	2
108	38	0
172	40	0
198	36	0
202	40	0
206	40	0
255	40	4
281	40	0
313	40	4
347	38	0
368	40	2
422	40	0

"EMPMAS" file the following fields: employee number, department number, name, and hourly rate. Make sure that you leave space for the five missing fields. Then write another program or continue in the same program to input from the keyboard the missing fields—marital status, number of exemptions, year-to-date gross pay, year-to-date federal income tax withheld, and year-to-date social security withheld. Marital status is defined as follows: 1 = single, 2 = married. The alternative way to create the "EMPMAS" file is to input all of the data from the keyboard by writing a program as shown in Chapter 4, page 68.

The "EMPTRA" file may be created by writing a program that reads the "EMPLOY" file and places employee number, regular hours, and overtime hours in the "EMPTRA" file. Alternatively, you may write a program that will input the data from the keyboard. The transaction file data is found in Table 7–2.

A program that combines the creation of the "EMPMAS" and "EMPTRA" files is given below.:

```
100   REM   THIS PROGRAM CREATES THE EMPLOYEE MASTER FILE
110   REM   AND THE EMPLOYEE TRANSCTION FILE
120   ONERR  GOTO 260
125   D$ =   CHR$ (4)
130   PRINT D$;"OPEN EMPLOY"
140   PRINT D$;"OPEN EMPMAS"
150   PRINT D$;"OPEN EMPTRA"
155   PRINT D$;"READ EMPLOY"
160   INPUT N,D,N$,H,R,V
165   PRINT D$
170   PRINT "MARITAL STATUS (1 OR 2), EXEMPTIONS FOR   ";N$
180   INPUT M,E
190   PRINT "YTD GROSS, YTD FIT, YTD FICA"
200   INPUT G,F,Fl
225   PRINT D$;"WRITE EMPMAS"
230   PRINT N;",";D;",";N$;",";M;",";H;",";E;",";G;",";F;",";Fl
235   PRINT D$;"WRITE EMPTRA"
240   PRINT N;",";R;",";V
250   GOTO 155
260 Y =   PEEK (222)
265   IF Y = 5 THEN 290
270   PRINT D$
275   PRINT "UNUSUAL ERROR",Y
280   STOP
290   PRINT D$;"CLOSE EMPLOY"
300   PRINT D$;"CLOSE EMPMAS"
310   PRINT D$;"CLOSE EMPTRA"
320   STOP
63999   END
```

In the program, the transaction file with the weekly hours worked will be used to update the master file. Also a list of employees and their gross pay will be printed.

In order to understand the programming involved in an update, the following example illustrates what is required.

Problem Summary

Input
1. Employee master file, "EMPMAS"
2. Employee transaction file, "EMPTRA"

Processing
Match transaction records and master records by employee number. Calculate gross pay, taxes, and net pay.

Output
An updated master file with the new values for year to date fields. Print out a list of employee numbers, their names, their net pay, and the updated master file suitably labelled.

The program therefore has to perform the following steps:

1. Establish a link to the transaction file, master file, and the new master file.

2. Read a transaction record and associated master record.

3. Calculate the taxes and print the employee number, name, and net pay.

4. Update the master record with the payroll data.

5. Write the updated master record into a new master file.

6. Go back to read more records while there is still data in the files.

7. Print out the updated master file.

A program is shown below:

```
100   REM                 UPDATE OF MASTER FILE
105   REM
110   ONERR  GOTO 650
115   D$ =   CHR$ (4)
116   DEF   FN R(X) =  INT (100 * X + 0.5) / 100
120   REM
130   REM               SET UP HEADINGS
140   REM
150   PRINT
160   PRINT "EMPLOYEE","NAME","NET"
170   PRINT "NUMBER"," ","PAY"
180   PRINT
190   REM
200   REM
210   PRINT D$;"OPEN EMPMAS"
220   PRINT D$;"OPEN EMPTRA"
230   PRINT D$;"OPEN EMPMA1"
240   REM
250   REM   READ A TRANSACTION RECORD
260   REM
270   PRINT D$;"READ EMPTRA"
275   INPUT I,R,V
280   REM
290   REM   READ A MASTER RECORD
300   REM
310   PRINT D$;"READ EMPMAS"
315   INPUT N,D,N$,M,H,E,G,F,F1
```

```
320    REM
330    REM    COMPARE IDS
340    REM
350    IF I = N THEN 410
360    IF I > N THEN 310
370    IF I < N THEN 750
380    REM
390    REM    IDS MATCH -- DO COMPUTATIONS FOR UPDATE
400    REM
410 G1 = (R * H) + (V * H * 1.5)
420 F2 = .2 * G1
430 F3 = .0613 * G1
440 P = G1 - F2 - F3
450 G = G + G1
460 F = F + F2
470 F1 = F1 + F3
480 P1 = P1 + P
490    REM
500    REM    PRINT UPDATED MASTER RECORD
510    REM
520    PRINT D$;"WRITE EMPMA1"
525    PRINT N;",";D;",";N$;",";M;",";H;",";E;",";G;",";F;",";F1
528    PRINT D$
530    REM
540    REM    PRINT ID, NAME, NET PAY
550    REM
555 P =   FN R(P)
560    PRINT N,N$,P
570    REM
580    REM    READ A TRANSACTION RECORD
590    REM
600    PRINT D$;"READ EMPTRA"
605    INPUT I,R,V
610    GOTO 350
620    REM
630    REM    *** ERROR CHECK ***
640    REM
650    PRINT D$
655 Y =   PEEK (222)
660    IF Y = 5 THEN 690
665    PRINT "UNUSUAL ERROR",Y
670    PRINT D$;"CLOSE EMPMAS"
672    PRINT D$;"CLOSE EMPTRA"
674    PRINT D$;"CLOSE EMPMA1"
680    STOP
690 L =   PEEK (218) + 256 *   PEEK (219)
695    IF L = 605 THEN 780
700    IF L = 912 THEN 940
710    STOP
720    REM
730    REM    MISSING MASTER RECORD
740    REM
750    PRINT D$
755    PRINT "MASTER RECORD MISSING FOR EMPLOYEE NUMBER",I
760    PRINT D$;"CLOSE EMPMAS"
762    PRINT D$;"CLOSE EMPTRA"
764    PRINT D$;"CLOSE EMPMA1"
770    STOP
780    PRINT D$;"CLOSE EMPMAS"
782    PRINT D$;"CLOSE EMPTRA"
784    PRINT D$;"CLOSE EMPMA1"
790    REM
800    REM    PRINT OUT OF UPDATED MASTER FILE
810    REM
820    PRINT
```

```
830    PRINT
840    PRINT
850    PRINT
860    PRINT "                          UPDATED MASTER FILE"
870    PRINT
880    PRINT D$;"OPEN EMPMA1"
890    PRINT "EMPLOYEE"; SPC( 2);"DEPT","NAME","MARITAL","HOURLY","EX-","YTD","YTD","YTD"
900    PRINT "NUMBER"; SPC( 4);" "," ","STATUS","RATE","EMP","GROSS","FIT","FICA"
910    PRINT D$;"READ EMPMA1"
912    INPUT N,D,N$,M,H,E,G,F,F1
913 G =  FN R(G)
914 F =  FN R(F)
915 F1 =  FN R(F1)
918    PRINT D$
920    PRINT N; SPC( 7);D,N$,M,H,E,G,F,F1
930    GOTO 910
940    PRINT D$;"CLOSE EMPMA1"
950    STOP
63999  END
```

EMPLOYEE NUMBER	NAME	NET PAY
101	ADAMS	147.74
103	BAKER	190.29
104	BRAVO	127.06
108	COHEN	175.44
172	JOHNSON	110.81
198	TANNER	113.02
202	WILSON	118.19
206	LESTER	155.13
255	SCHMIDT	190.29
281	MILLER	177.29
313	SMITH	144.42
347	GRAY	168.42
368	WEAVER	111.17
422	WILLIAMS	118.19

UPDATED MASTER FILE

EMPLOYEE NUMBER	DEPT	NAME	MARITAL STATUS	HOURLY RATE	EX- EMP	YTD GROSS	YTD FIT	YTD FICA
101	1	ADAMS	2	5	3	1200	240	73.56
103	12	BAKER	1	5.6	2	1545.6	309.12	94.74
104	17	BRAVO	2	4	4	1032	206.4	63.26
108	16	COHEN	2	6.25	4	1425	285	87.35
172	2	JOHNSON	1	3.75	0	900	180	55.18
198	1	TANNER	2	4.25	4	918	183.6	56.27
202	16	WILSON	2	4	5	960	192	58.85
206	7	LESTER	2	5.25	3	1260	252	77.24
255	12	SCHMIDT	2	5.6	5	1545.6	309.12	94.74
281	12	MILLER	2	6	4	1440	288	88.27
313	7	SMITH	2	4.25	3	1173	234.6	71.9
347	12	GRAY	2	6	3	1368	273.6	83.86
368	1	WEAVER	1	3.5	1	903	180.6	55.36
422	1	WILLIAMS	2	4	2	960	192	58.85

BREAK IN 950

The easiest way to understand the logic that is required for an update is to begin with the flowchart (Figure 7–2). This flowchart does not represent each line in the program with a box. It focuses on the logic of matching transaction records with master records in (a) and the logic of the error routines in (b). First, a record from the transaction file "EMPTRA" is input then a record from the master file "EMPMAS" is input. In matching the transaction record to the appropriate master record three conditions may

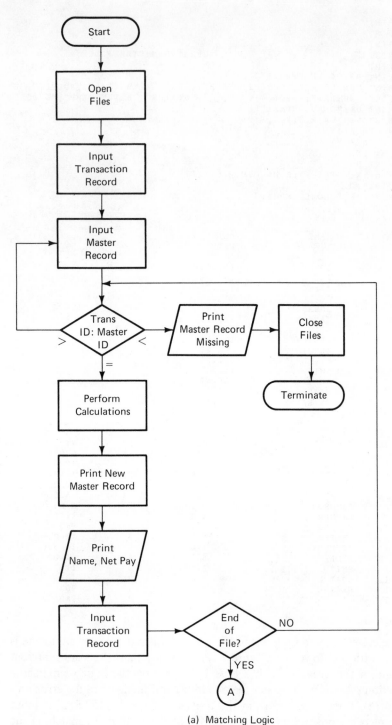

(a) Matching Logic

Figure 7–2   Flowchart of Update Program

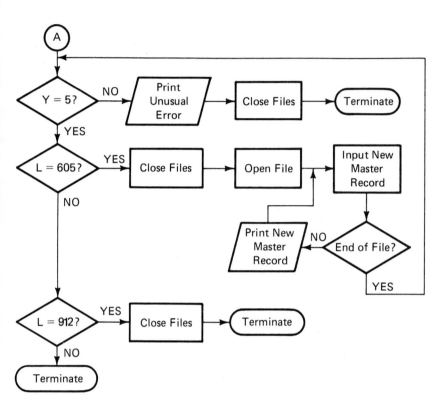

(b) Error Logic (Error Routines)

Flowchart of Update Program (cont'd)   Figure 7-2

occur. The employee number (ID) of the transaction record may be greater than, less than, or equal to the employee number (ID) of the master record.

- If the transaction record ID is greater than the master record ID: Then, there is no transaction and input the next master record. This should not occur since there is one transaction record for each master record.

- If the transaction record ID is equal to the master record ID: Then, perform the update calculations, print the updated (new) masterfile, and print the employee ID, name, net pay. Read the next transaction record.

- If the transaction record ID is less than the master record ID: Then, a master record is missing from the master file. If a master record is missing, a message is generated and the program is terminated.

Note: Remember, the transaction and master files must be in ascending order of employee number (ID).

If the flowchart does not help you understand the program, then let us perform the job (update) manually. There are two files "EMPMAS" and "EMPTRA", assume that they are in separate cabinets. Also assume that the data on each record in both files are on a separate sheet of paper, and that the files are organized in ascending employee number. In order to focus on the problem of matching master and transaction records only the first field, employee number (ID), is shown in Figure 7–3.

Record Number	Master File "EMPMAS" Employee Number	Transaction File "EMPTRA" Employee Number
1	101	101
2	103	103
3	104	104
4	108	108
5	172	172
6	198	198
7	202	202
8	206	206
9	255	255
10	281	281
11	313	313
12	347	347
13	368	368
14	422	422

Figure 7–3   Employee Number Fields for Master and Transaction Records

Manually we would reach into the transaction file and read the first record. Remember, you can only read one record at a time! We then reach into the master file for a record. The IDs match (both are 101). We update the master record with the information on the transaction record and then read the second transaction record. Its ID is 103, the master record ID is still 101 so we read the next master record. Its ID is 103 and we have a match. We update and read the third transaction record—ID is 104. The master ID is still 103, so we read the next (third) master record and have a match. We update and proceed until there are no more records to be processed.

In the program the ONERR condition is reached after the last master record is updated. To be more specific, the ONERR is reached at line 605 where an attempt to read a transaction record encounters the end of file. Then the files are closed and the updated master file ("EMPMA1") is printed.

In the program, a new BASIC instruction appears in line 690.

$$L = PEEK(218) + 256 * PEEK(219)$$

All of the programs that read files test for the end of a file (after the last record) with the ONERR instruction. In all of the prior programs, when the end of a file occurred the program would close the file and terminate. Or, a test value was set so that other functions could be performed before termination. The instruction in 690 allows us to determine the line number in a program where an ERR (in this case an end of file) occurs. The computer determines the value when the program is executed. The logic of the program and a one to one correspondence between master and transaction records will result in the end of file occurring at line 605. L has a value equal to the line number at which the ERR occurs. The test IF L = 605 will allow the execution of line 780 next, and result in a print out of the updated master file. When the end of file is reached, the ONERR will allow the execution of line 650 again and the program will test for L = 605 which is not the case. Then it will test for L = 912 which is the case. So "EMPMA1" will be closed and the program will terminate. A flowchart for the testing of the ERR conditions is found in Figure 7–2(b).

There is one additional new instruction in the program. Line 116 is an example of a function. This function differs from the INT function in that it is defined in the program. So it is called a user defined function. The INT function was ready for you to use because it is part of the BASIC language. The function in the program

116 DEF FN R(X)=INT(100*X+.5)/100

is an example of a user defined function. This function is used to round off decimal numbers to two decimal places (dollars and cents). We have already used the logic of this function in Chapter 5. A function may be defined as any arithmetic statement. Functions are used to eliminate repetition of arithmetic statements and abbreviate typing in much the same way as D$=CHR$(4) was used.

In lines 555, 913, 914, and 915, the function is used to round off numeric fields to dollars and cents so that our output will be more readable.

You may be thinking at this point that all you have to do is read a transaction record and a master record and they will match. This is the case here where there is one, and only one, transaction record for each and every master record. It is rarely the situation!

UPDATING WITH MISSING TRANSACTIONS

The payroll example illustrates an update where there is one transaction record for each master record. There are many instances where there may be more than one transaction record for each master record or no transaction record for a master record. Common examples are credit card statements, sales, inventory, and customer statements.

For the next example, the sales file "SALES" will be used as the master file and the transaction file will be called "SALEST". The data in these files is given in Tables 7–3 and 7–4. If you have the "SALES" file saved, you can run the alphabetic sort given in Appendix B on this file or create a new

"SALES" file with data shown in Table 7–3. The transaction file, "SALEST", must be created. The program should print out an error message if a master record is missing, but it should not terminate.

Table 7–3   Sales Master File "SALES" Sorted Alphabetically By Salesman

Department	Salesman	Gross Sales Year-to-Date	Commission Rate
1	Bill	12050	.05
3	Bob	14690	.05
3	Clyde	7340	.04
3	Harry	9460	.045
1	Joe	5270	.045
2	Phil	11200	.055
2	Tom	6940	.04

Table 7–4   Sales Transaction File "SALEST" Sorted Alphabetically By Salesman

Salesman	Amount of Sale
Bill	1050
Bill	275
Bill	390
Clyde	460
Clyde	290
Harry	1500
Joe	280
Joe	490

Problem Summary

Input
1. Sales commission master file, "SALES"
2. Sales transaction file, "SALEST"

Processing
Match transaction records and master record by salesman's name. Calculate the commissions for the salesmen due on the transaction data.

Output
A list of commissions for the salesmen for their latest sales, an updated master file with the new value of year to date sales, and print out the updated master file.

The program therefore has to perform the following steps:

1. Establish a link to the transaction, master and new master files.
2. Read a transaction record and the associated master record.
3. Calculate the commissions for the latest sales.
4. Print the commissions for the salesmen.
5. Update the master record with the transaction data.
6. Write the updated master record into a new master file.
7. Go back to read more records while there is still data in the files.
8. Print out the updated master file.

See the flowchart (Fig. 7–4) and the following program.

```
100    REM        PROGRAM TO UPDATE SALES
110    ONERR   GOTO 1040
115 D$ =   CHR$ (4)
120    REM
130    REM       SET UP HEADINGS FOR OUTPUT
140    REM
150    PRINT "NAME","COMMISSION"
160    PRINT "------------------------"
170    REM
180    REM   LINK TO FILES
190    REM
200    PRINT D$;"OPEN SALEST"
210    PRINT D$;"OPEN SALMAS"
220    PRINT D$;"OPEN NSALES"
230    REM
240    REM   READ A TRANSACTION RECORD
250    REM
260    PRINT D$;"READ SALEST"
265    INPUT N$,A
270    REM
280    REM   READ A MASTER RECORD
290    REM
300    PRINT D$;"READ SALMAS"
305    INPUT D,S$,G,C
308    PRINT D$
310    REM
320    REM   COMPARE TRANSACTION WITH MASTER
330    REM
340    IF N$ = S$ THEN 410
350    IF N$ > S$ THEN 550
360    IF N$ < S$ THEN 670
370    REM
380    REM   TRANSACTION EQUAL TO MASTER
390    REM   UPDATE THE MASTER
400    REM
410 G = G + A
```

```
420 C1 = A * C
430 REM
440 REM   PRINT NAME AND COMMISSION
450 REM
460 PRINT S$,C1
470 REM
480 REM   READ NEXT TRANSACTION AND GO TO COMPARE
490 REM
500 PRINT D$;"READ SALEST"
505 INPUT N$,A
508 PRINT D$
510 GOTO 340
520 REM
530 REM   TRANSACTION GREATER THAN MASTER
540 REM
550 PRINT D$;"WRITE NSALES"
555 PRINT D;",";S$;",","G;",";C
560 REM
570 REM   GO BACK AND GET ANOTHER MASTER
580 REM
590 GOTO 300
600 REM
610 REM      TRANSACTION LESS THAN MASTER
620 REM      ERROR -- NO MASTER IN FILE
630 REM      WRITE ERROR MESSAGE, THEN
640 REM      READ ANOTHER TRANSACTION AND
650 REM      CONTINUE PROCESSING
660 REM
670 PRINT D$
675 PRINT "***TRANSACTION WITHOUT MASTER*** ";N$,A
680 GOTO 500
690 REM
700 REM   NO MORE TRANSACTIONS -- WRITE REMAINING MASTER RECORDS
720 REM
730 PRINT D$;"WRITE NSALES"
735 PRINT D;",";S$;",";G;",";C
740 PRINT D$;"READ SALMAS"
745 INPUT D,S$,G,C
750 GOTO 730
760 REM
770 REM   UPDATE IS FINISHED -- PRINT THE UPDATED MASTER
780 REM
790 PRINT D$;"CLOSE SALEST"
792 PRINT D$;"CLOSE SALMAS"
794 PRINT D$;"CLOSE NSALES"
800 PRINT D$;"OPEN NSALES"
810 REM
820 REM   PRINT HEADINGS
830 REM
840 PRINT
850 PRINT
```

```
860    PRINT "UPDATED FILE -- NSALES"
870    PRINT "----------------------"
880    PRINT
890    PRINT "TERRITORY","NAME","YTD","COMMISSION"
900    PRINT " "," ","SALES","RATE"
910    PRINT "---------","----","-----","----"
920    REM
930    REM   READ A RECORD AND PRINT
940    REM
950    PRINT D$;"READ NSALES"
955    INPUT D,S$,G,C
958    PRINT D$
960    PRINT D,S$,G,C
970    GOTO 950
980    REM
990    PRINT D$;"CLOSE NSALES"
1000   GOTO 1110
1010   REM   *****************************
1020   REM   *** ERROR CHECKING ROUTINES ***
1030   REM   *****************************
1040   PRINT D$
1045 Y =  PEEK (222)
1050   IF Y = 5 THEN 1080
1055   PRINT "UNUSUAL ERROR",Y
1060   PRINT D$;"CLOSE SALEST"
1062   PRINT D$;"CLOSE SALMAS"
1064   PRINT D$;"CLOSE NSALES"
1070   STOP
1080 L =  PEEK (218) + 256 *  PEEK (219)
1085   IF L = 505 THEN 730
1090   IF L = 745 THEN 790
1100   IF L = 955 THEN 990
1110   STOP
63999  END
```

NAME	COMMISSION
BILL	52.5
BILL	13.75
BILL	19.5
CLYDE	18.4
CLYDE	11.6
HARRY	67.5
JOE	12.6
JOE	22.05

```
UPDATED FILE -- NSALES
----------------------
```

TERRITORY	NAME	YTD SALES	COMMISSION RATE
---------	----	-----	----
1	BILL	13765	.05
3	BOB	14690	.05
3	CLYDE	8090	.04
3	HARRY	10960	.045
1	JOE	6040	.045
2	PHIL	11200	.055
2	TOM	6940	.04

```
BREAK IN 1110
```

The flowcharts and program are different from the payroll update in five ways:

1. Missing transaction records occur.

2. The new master record is printed on the file when the transaction record ID is greater than the master record ID.

3. The matching of IDs is on alphabetic data.

4. The program will not terminate when a master record is missing.

5. Multiple transaction records for each master record occur.

Missing transactions are accounted for in the logic in two places. First, new master records are printed on the file only when the transaction record ID is greater than the master record ID. Second, if the end of the transaction file has been read and master records remain to be processed, line 1085 IF L = 505 THEN 730 and the instructions that follow line 730 take care of this problem.

IDs that consist of alphabetic information (salesman name) are matched in this program. There is no essential difference between matching alphabetic as opposed to numeric IDs as far as the programming is concerned.

The program will not terminate if master records are missing. This problem is solved by printing the appropriate message and reading the next transaction record.

Finally, the program will handle the case where there is more than one transaction record for a master record. This is done by not printing a new master record until the transaction record ID is greater than the master record ID. Also, the accumulation of the gross sales in line 410, G = G + A, will update the gross sales on the master record correctly. The value of G is changed each time a master record is read, while the value of A will be added to it for each transaction record.

The program can best be understood by referring to the flowchart (Figure 7–4), Figure 7–5, and tracing the logic. The first transaction record is

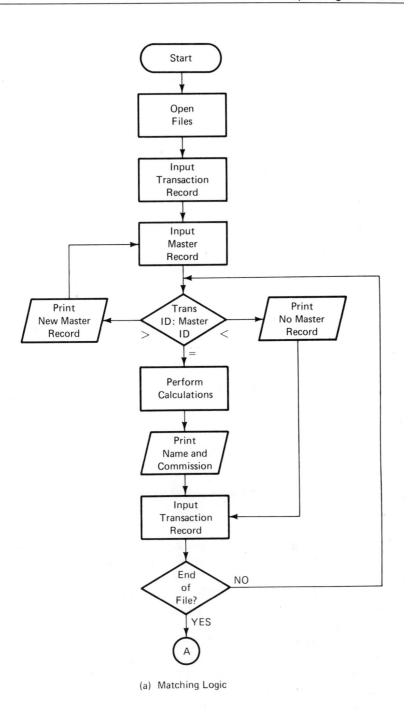

(a) Matching Logic

Flowchart of the Sales Update   Figure 7-4

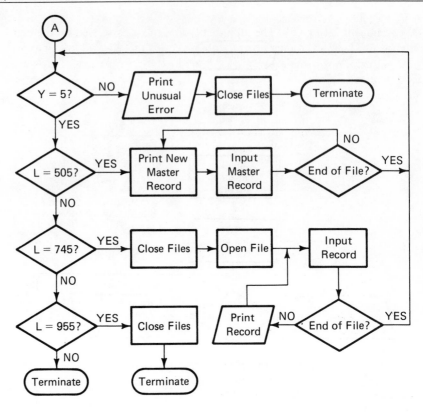

(b) Logic of Error Routines

Figure 7-4   Flowchart of the Sales Update (cont'd.)

input followed by the first master record. The salesman for both these records is Bill. There is a match, the name and commission are printed and the second transaction record is input. The master record ID is Bill and the second transaction record ID is Bill. So the name and commission are printed using the data of the second transaction record. The third transaction record is read. There is another match and the printout of name and commission occurs again. The fourth transaction record is read (Clyde) and the transaction record ID is greater than the master record ID so the master record for Bill, now fully updated by three transaction records, is printed and the second master record is read (Bob). You may wonder how Clyde is greater than Bob. The answer is that the letter "C" is greater, or of higher value, than the letter "B". The alphabet from A to Z is viewed by the computer as just a series of increasing values. It is this fact that allows us to perform alphabetic sorts as in Appendix B, and compare alphabetic fields with IF statements.

Master File SALES		Transaction File SALEST
Record Number	Salesman	Salesman
1	Bill	Bill
2	Bob	Bill
3	Clyde	Bill
4	Harry	Clyde
5	Joe	Clyde
6	Phil	Harry
7	Tom	Joe
8		Joe

Salesman Fields For Master and Transaction Records   Figure 7–5

At this point, we have printed Bill's updated master record, input Bob's master record, and input Clyde's transaction record. Clyde is greater than Bob (TR>MR) so Bob's master record is printed. There were no transaction records for Bob; so his updated master record remains the same and the next master record is input (Clyde). There is a match, name and commission are printed, and the next transaction record is input (five). There is another match, name and commission are printed and the next transaction record is input (Harry). Harry is greater than Clyde, so Clyde's master record is printed and the next master record input (Harry). The logic continues in the above manner until the end of the master file is reached and the program is finished. Note, there are no transactions for Phil or Tom so that the end of file for the transaction file occurs at line 505. The statement IF L = 505 THEN 730 will direct the computer to line 730 and the remaining master records that do not have any transaction records will be printed on the new master file. The two other L statements (1090, 1100) are used to print out the updated master file and produce the required report.

The final example of an update program will use exactly the same logic as the last program, but the transaction file will be more complex. This last example will be an inventory problem. It will use as the master file the file "INVMR". Table 7–5 gives the contents of the master file, Table 7–6 the transaction file, "INVTR".

UPDATING WITH CODED TRANSACTIONS

Table 7–5   Inventory Master File

Part Number	Units on Hand	Cost
101	350	5.00
110	275	7.00
219	90	3.25
226	120	2.95
235	360	6.20
247	140	4.60

Table 7–6   Inventory Transaction File

Part Number	Transaction Code	Quantity
101	1	150
101	2	75
101	2	60
101	2	20
219	2	20
226	1	75
226	1	100
226	2	90
235	2	30
247	1	70

You will have to write programs to create both the transaction and master file. The transaction records have three fields: the part number (ID), a transaction code, and a quantity. The transaction code field has either the number 1 or 2 in it. A transaction code of 1 means that the transaction is a receipt to inventory. A transaction code of 2 means that the transaction is an issuance of goods from inventory. The first transaction record (101,1,150) means that 150 units of part 101 were received in inventory. The third transaction record (101,2,60) means that 60 units of part 101 were issued from inventory.

You may assume that the master file is updated at the end of each week and that the transactions were generated during this week. The files are sorted by part number and you have to write the program for the update. For the *updated* master file, the calculation is as follows:

Units on Hand = Units on Hand (in the old master file)
+ Units received (transaction code 1)
− Units issued (transaction code 2)

Besides updating the master file, one report is to be produced. The report is an "Inventory Valuation Report." It lists the part numbers and the amount of money that is tied up in inventory at the end of the week. It is produced from the updated master file.

Problem Summary

Input
1. Inventory master file, "INVMR"
2. Inventory transaction file, "INVTR"

Processing
Match transaction records and master records by part number. Calculate quantities received and issued by transaction code. Calculate units on hand.

Output
An updated master file, "INVSN", and an inventory valuation report.

The program therefore has to perform the following steps:

1. Establish a link to the transaction file and the master and new master files.

2. Read a transaction record and associated master record.

3. Determine from the transaction code whether the quantity is issued or received.

4. Update the master record.

5. Write the updated master record.

6. Go back to read more records while there is still data in the files.

7. Print out the new master file.

8. Produce the report from the updated master file.

The program follows:

```
100   REM    PROGRAM TO UPDATE INVENTORY
110 D$ =   CHR$ (4)
115   REM
120   REM   LINK TO FILES
130   REM
140   PRINT D$;"OPEN INVTR"
150   PRINT D$;"OPEN INVMR"
160   PRINT D$;"OPEN INVSN"
170   REM
180   REM   READ A TRANSACTION RECORD
190   REM
200   ONERR  GOTO 1260
```

```
210    PRINT D$;"READ INVTR"
215    INPUT P1,T1,Q1
220    REM
230    REM   READ A MASTER RECORD
240    REM
250    PRINT D$;"READ INVMR"
255    INPUT P2,Q2,C2
260    REM
270    REM   COMPARE TRANSACTION WITH MASTER
280    REM
290    IF P1 = P2 THEN 380
300    IF P1 > P2 THEN 560
310    IF P1 < P2 THEN 680
320    REM
330    REM   TRANSACTION EQUAL TO MASTER
340    REM   SO UPDATE THE MASTER
350    REM
360    REM   CHECK IF TRANSACTION IS RECEIPT OR ISSUE
370    REM
380    IF T1 = 2 THEN 470
390    REM
400    REM : T1=1
410    REM
420    Q2 = Q2 + Q1
430    GOTO 510
440    REM
450    REM : T1=2
460    REM
470    Q2 = Q2 - Q1
480    REM
490    REM   READ NEXT TRANSACTION AND GO TO COMPARE
500    REM
510    PRINT D$;"READ INVTR"
515    INPUT P1,T1,Q1
520    GOTO 290
530    REM
540    REM   TRANSACTION GREATER THAN MASTER
550    REM   WRITE UPDATED MASTER RECORD
560    PRINT D$;"WRITE INVSN"
565    PRINT P2;",";Q2;",";C2
570    REM
580    REM   GO BACK AND GET ANOTHER MASTER
590    REM
600    GOTO 250
610    REM
620    REM   TRANSACTION LESS THAN MASTER
630    REM   ERROR -- NO MASTER IN FILE
640    REM   WRITE ERROR MESSAGE, THEN
650    REM   READ ANOTHER TRANSACTION AND
```

```
660    REM    CONTINUE PROCESSING
670    REM
680    PRINT D$
685    PRINT "***TRANSACTION WITHOUT MASTER ";P1,T1,Q1
690    GOTO 510
700    REM
710    REM    NO MORE TRANSACTIONS -- WRITE REMAINING MASTER RECORDS
730    REM
740    PRINT D$;"WRITE INVSN"
745    PRINT P2;",";Q2;",";C2
750    PRINT D$;"READ INVMR"
755    INPUT P2,Q2,C2
760    GOTO 740
770    REM
780    REM    UPDATE IS FINISHED -- PRINT THE UPDATED
790    REM    FILE AND THE REPORT
800    PRINT D$;"CLOSE INVTR"
802    PRINT D$;"CLOSE INVMR"
804    PRINT D$;"CLOSE INVSN"
810    PRINT D$;"OPEN INVSN"
820    REM
830    REM    HEADINGS FOR UPDATED FILE
840    REM
850    PRINT
860    PRINT "    NEW INVENTORY MASTER FILE"
870    PRINT "    ------------------------"
880    PRINT
890    PRINT "PART","UNITS","COST"
900    PRINT "NUMBER","ON HAND"
910    PRINT "------","-------","----"
920    PRINT D$;"READ INVSN"
925    INPUT P,Q,C
928    PRINT D$
930    PRINT P,Q,C
940    GOTO 920
950    PRINT D$;"CLOSE INVSN"
960    PRINT D$;"OPEN INVSN"
970    REM
980    REM    PRINT REPORT HEADINGS
990    PRINT
1000   PRINT
1010   PRINT " INVENTORY VALUATION REPORT"
1020   PRINT " --------------------------"
1030   PRINT
1040   PRINT "PART","DOLLAR"
1050   PRINT "NUMBER","AMOUNT"
1060   PRINT "------","------"
1070   REM
1080   REM    READ A RECORD AND CALCULATE INVENTORY VALUES
```

```
1090   REM
1100 T = 0
1110   PRINT D$;"READ INVSN"
1115   INPUT P,Q,C
1118   PRINT D$
1120 D = Q * C
1130 T = T + D
1140   PRINT P,D
1150   GOTO 1110
1160   REM
1170   REM   END OF DATA -- PRINT TOTALS
1180   REM
1190   PRINT D$
1195   PRINT "------------------------"
1200   PRINT "TOTAL",T
1210   PRINT D$;"CLOSE INVSN"
1220   GOTO 1340
1230   REM   ******************************
1240   REM   *** ERROR CHECKING ROUTINES ***
1250   REM   ******************************
1260   PRINT D$
1265 Y =   PEEK (222)
1270   IF Y = 5 THEN 1300
1275   PRINT "UNUSUAL ERROR",Y
1280   PRINT D$;"CLOSE INVTR"
1282   PRINT D$;"CLOSE INVMR"
1284   PRINT D$;"CLOSE INVSN"
1290   STOP
1300 L =   PEEK (218) + 256 *  PEEK (219)
1305   IF L = 515 THEN 740
1310   IF L = 755 THEN 800
1320   IF L = 925 THEN 950
1330   IF L = 1115 THEN 1190
1340   STOP
63999 END
```

```
       NEW INVENTORY MASTER FILE
       -------------------------
```

PART NUMBER	UNITS ON HAND	COST
101	345	5
110	275	7
219	70	3.25
226	205	2.95
235	330	6.2
247	210	4.6

```
INVENTORY VALUATION REPORT
--------------------------

PART              DOLLAR
NUMBER            AMOUNT
------            ------
101               1725
110               1925
219               227.5
226               604.75
235               2046
247               966
--------------------------
```

The flowchart is the same as the flowchart of the sales update program (Figure 7–4) with one minor exception–the logic for handling the transaction codes. The flowchart for this portion of the program is Figure 7–6. Since the master record inputs the value of Q2, the two statements

$$Q2 = Q2 + Q1$$
$$Q2 = Q2 - Q1$$

will accumulate the value of Q2 updated by the transaction records until the new master record is printed and a new master record is input.

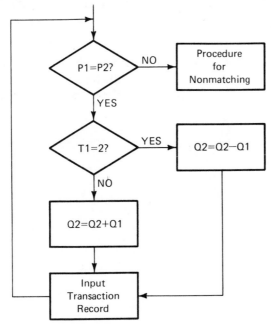

Flowchart of Transaction Code Logic   Figure 7–6

The data for the required report are obtained from the new master file and the report is the last part of the program.

SUMMARY

This chapter covered the updating of sequential files. Descriptions of master files and transaction files to produce a new updated master file were given. Various conditions with respect to the correspondence of master and transaction records were handled by the programs. In each program the third IF statement used to match master and transaction records could have been replaced by a GO TO statement. The IF statement was used to emphasize the logic of matching. The new instruction L = PEEK(218) + 256 * PEEK(219) was discussed and illustrated.

The objective of data processing in a business environment is achieved by the update. Through the update, customer statements, payrolls, accounts receivable, accounts payable and general ledgers are produced on some time cycle, usually once a month.

BASIC Instructions Introduced:

Instruction	*Explanation*
L = PEEK(218) + 256 * PEEK(219)	Gives the line number at which an ONERR condition took place. The field L was arbitrarily chosen to represent the line number. Any other field name may be used.
DEF FN R(X)	Allows the programmer to define mathematical functions to avoid repetitious typing in a program.

1. Modify the first update program (payroll example) so that it will provide   PROBLEMS
   the logic required to:

   a. Handle a missing transaction record.

   b. Continue processing rather than stop after printing the error message
      "MASTER RECORD MISSING FOR EMPLOYEE NUMBER".

   Create and use the following transaction file to test the program.

Employee Number	Regular Hours	Overtime Hours
103	40	4
108	38	0
165	40	0
198	36	0
255	40	4
313	40	4
368	40	2

   Use "EMPMAS" as the master file.

   Print out the updated master file with suitable headings.

   Print out the employee numbers, names and their net pay. Remember
   some employees will receive no pay.

2. Modify the sales update program so that it will print out the total commission due to each salesman, rather than the commission for each sale.
   Also print out the total commission due to all salesmen.

3. Modify the inventory update to print out for each part number the total
   units issued and received.

4. Assume that the payroll transaction file can contain more than one record for an employee. Modify your program in Problem 1 so that it can
   use the following transaction file and perform the update.

Employee Number	Regular Hours	Overtime Hours
104	20	0
104	20	5
108	10	0
198	40	7
202	15	0
202	25	4

202	0	6
206	20	0
206	20	3
313	30	0
313	10	0
313	0	8

There should be a printout for every employee showing number, name, and net pay—even if it is zero. Use one line per employee. Also print out the new master file.

8 / Using Lists and Tables

At the end of this chapter you should be able to:

- Set up lists and tables
- Use lists to accumulate summary output
- Use tables to hold data for reference
- Use lists and tables to hold data for processing

All the transaction processing applications that we have discussed have basically the same pattern. The pattern consists of getting a transaction, doing the required computation for that transaction, outputting required results, and then looping back to get the next transaction. Such processing minimizes the amount of data required by the computer.

But business has problems that require a group of data to be entered at the beginning and used for all transactions. Tax tables come readily to mind. And business also has analytic problems, where all the data has to be available to solve a problem or where data is collected from all transactions and held for output until the end of all transactions. An example of the first type would be a linear programming problem (which is a management science method). An example of the second type would be analytic reports that classify data in categories.

To help solve these types of problems, BASIC provides lists and tables. A list is a series of items in a meaningful grouping or sequence. Employee names in alphabetic sequence would be an example of a list. Total sales in item number sequence might be another example. Any row or column of items constitutes a list.

A table is an arrangement of words, numbers, or signs in parallel columns. It is used to show a set of facts or relationships in a compact and comprehensive form. Income tax tables are a clear example of "an arrangement of ... numbers ... in parallel columns." A table is therefore a grouping of lists. A list is a one-dimensional (row or column, but not both) presentation of data; and a table is a two-dimensional (both rows and columns) presentation of data.

Let's derive a problem from the payroll application to get a feel for the use of lists and tables. Assume that you need to summarize the payroll expense by department. As you recall, there are 20 departments—numbered consecutively from 1 to 20. But sorting the file is a time consuming process. Hence the "EMPLOY" file will not be sorted for this problem. A simple representation of this type of problem is shown in Figure 8–1.

Problem Summary

Input
   "EMPLOY" file
Processing
   Calculate gross pay and accumulate gross pay by department.

Output
Total gross pay by department

The program therefore has to:

1. Link to the "EMPLOY" file.

2. Read a record.

3. Calculate the gross pay.

4. Accumulate gross pay by department number.

5. When all records have been processed, print the departmental gross pay totals.

6. Terminate.

A flowchart (Fig. 8–1), a program to perform these tasks, and the output are shown below:

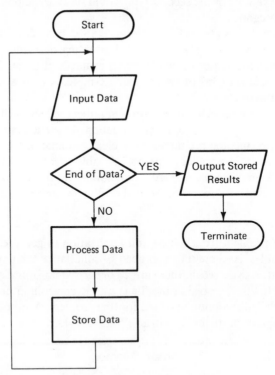

Figure 8–1   Flowchart for Summary Output

```
100   REM    PROGRAM TO ACCUMULATE GROSS PAY BY DEPARTMENT
110   REM
115 D$ =    CHR$ (4)
120   REM    OPEN FILE
130   REM
140   PRINT D$;"OPEN EMPLOY"
150   REM
160   REM   SET UP A LIST TO HOLD DEPARTMENT TOTALS
170   REM
180   DIM T(20)
190   REM
200   REM    READ A RECORD UNTIL OUT OF DATA
220   ONERR  GOTO 360
230   PRINT D$;"READ EMPLOY"
235   INPUT N,D,N$,H,R,V
240   REM
250   REM   CALCULATE AMOUNT OF GROSS PAY
260   REM
270 G = H * R + H * V * 1.5
280   REM
290   REM   ACCUMULATE GROSS PAY BY DEPARTMENT NUMBER
300   REM
310 T(D) = T(D) + G
320   GOTO 230
330   REM
340   REM   CHECK FOR END OF FILE AND PRINT RESULTS
350   REM
360   PRINT D$
365 Y =    PEEK (222)
370   IF Y = 5 THEN 420
375   PRINT "UNUSUAL ERROR",Y
380   GOTO 520
390   REM
400   REM   PRINT DEPARTMENTAL TOTALS WITH HEADINGS
410   REM
420   PRINT "DEPARTMENTAL GROSS PAY TOTALS"
430   PRINT
440   PRINT "DEPARTMENT","GROSS PAY"
450   PRINT "----------","---------"
460   FOR M = 1 TO 20
465 T(M) =    INT (100 * T(M) + .5) / 100
470   PRINT M,T(M)
480   NEXT M
490   REM
500   REM   TERMINATE
510   REM
520   PRINT D$;"CLOSE EMPLOY"
530   STOP
63999   END
```

```
DEPARTMENTAL GROSS PAY TOTALS

DEPARTMENT          GROSS PAY
----------          ----------
1                   663.5
2                   150
3                   0
4                   0
5                   0
6                   0
7                   405.5
8                   0
9                   0
10                  0
11                  0
12                  983.2
13                  0
14                  0
15                  0
16                  397.5
17                  172
18                  0
19                  0
20                  0
```

BREAK IN 530

Now here is a program with some interesting new features:

- The DIM statement in line 180
- The summation in line 310 and the output in 470
- The FOR statement in line 460 and its associated NEXT statement in line 480

Let's look at each of these three items in turn. The DIM statement sets up a list, at least that is what the preceding remark in line 160 says. But what exactly does it do? In this case, line 180 tells the computer to reserve 20 consecutive positions all under the name "T." Previously, one field name served to identify one value. Here, one field name serves to identify many values.

If many values are identified by one name, how can you differentiate between the values? The answer is simple—by position. Line 180 sets up a list of 20 positions, thus:

| T | 1 | 2 | 3 | 4 | 5 | 6 | 7 | 13 | 14 | 15 | 16 | 17 | 18 | 19 | 20 |

To get any one item in the list, we need to specify its position (1–20). The value in the first position would be referred to as T(1). If we wanted the value from the second position, then T(2) is used. The location in the list is specified by enclosing a number, or a field name that has the position desired, in parentheses.

Line 310 refers to T(D). Here the "D" (enclosed in parentheses) specifies which position in T is involved. Hence the Dth position (whatever the department number D may be) of T is referenced. Similarly, in line 470, the reference is to position M (whatever value M may have) in T.

A new BASIC instruction in this program is found in lines 460 and 480. These two lines define a *loop*. A loop is a shorthand way of telling the computer to repeat a series of instructions a certain number of times. Line 460 sets up the loop and gives the loop parameters. The loop parameters tell the computer how often the statements in the loop are to be repeated. Line 480 closes the loop.

In general, the FOR-NEXT statements form loops. The statements within a loop are repeated the number of times specified in the FOR statement by the loop parameters. The loop parameters (in line 460), 1 TO 20, specify that the loop will be repeated twenty times. Each time the loop is repeated, the value of M will be increased by one. By this manner, when M reaches a value of 20, the loop will be repeated one more (final) time.

Line 460 tells the computer to repeat the statements between 460 and 480 (the NEXT M statement) twenty times. In this example, line 470 is performed for M values of 1, 2, 3, 4, 5, 6, 7, 8, 9, 10, 11, 12, 13, 14, 15, 16, 17, 18, 19 and 20 in turn.

Let us look closely at what the program does. First it opens a file for input. This is the file "EMPLOY" from past examples. The file contains employee records with six fields:

- Employee number
- Department number
- Employee name
- Hourly rate
- Regular hours
- Overtime hours

The department number is between 1 and 20. The range of department numbers is important because we want to accumulate gross pay by department. Next a list "T" with 20 positions: one for each of the departments, is set up. Then the program reads a record and calculates gross pay. The department number (D) is used to add the gross pay to that location in T. In other words, whenever the gross pay for a person in department 2 is calculated, it is added to the second position in T. Similarly if the department were 16, gross pay would be added to the sixteenth position in T.

After the end-of-file has been reached, the gross pay for each of the departments is printed in lines 460–480. Notice that line 470 will print M, which stands for the department number, as well as the Mth value of T (which is the departmental gross pay total).

Many problems require the use of reference tables. Income tax tables are the most obvious example. But life insurance companies use actuarial tables; statisticians use statistical tables; and financial analysts use present value or

REFERENCE
TABLES

annuity tables. If you look closely, you can see tables everywhere. Even this book has a table, a table of contents.

Tables hold data for reference. When the data is needed, we look it up in the appropriate table. One problem that requires table referencing is an income tax calculation. A simple representation of this type of problem is shown in Figure 8–2.

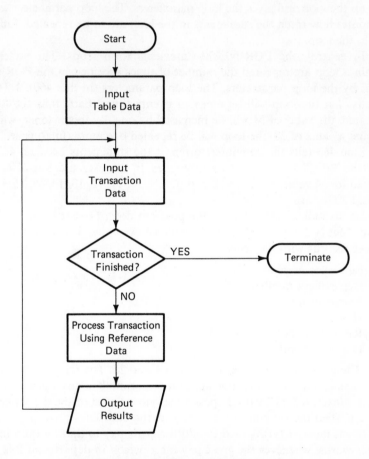

Figure 8–2   Flowchart for Reference Tables

The income tax problem requires two tables: one for single people; another for married people. Both are shown in Table 8–1. But the tables provided by the Internal Revenue Service have to be changed to fit our requirements. The tables need to be consistent. Table 8–2 is the same IRS tables—made consistent by the addition of the first line.

Before the tables can be used in the weekly payroll calculation, they have to be set up. Since tax rates are liable to annual changes, the tax tables are stored in separate files: "SINGLE" for single people; and "MARRID" for married people. The program to get the data into the "SINGLE" file is shown below.

Percentage Withholding Tables   Table 8–1

(a) SINGLE person—including head of household:

If the amount of wages is:	The amount of income tax to be withheld shall be:		of excess over—
Not over $27 0			
Over—	But not over—		
$27	—$63 .....15%		—$27
$63	—$131 ....$5.40 plus 18%		—$63
$131	—$196 ....$17.64 plus 21%		—$131
$196	—$273 ....$31.29 plus 26%		—$196
$273	—$331 ....$51.31 plus 30%		—$273
$331	—$433 ....$68.71 plus 34%		—$331
$433	............$103.39 plus 39%		—$433

(b) MARRIED person—

If the amount of wages is:	The amount of income tax to be withheld shall be:		of excess over—
Not over $46 0			
Over—	But not over—		
$46	—$127 ....15%		—$46
$127	—$210 ....$12.15 plus 18%		—$127
$210	—$288 ....$27.09 plus 21%		—$210
$288	—$369 ....$43.47 plus 24%		—$288
$369	—$454 ....$62.91 plus 28%		—$369
$454	—$556 ....$86.71 plus 32%		—$454
$556	............$119.35 plus 37%		—$556

Weekly Tax Tables   Table 8–2

a. **Single person**—including head of household

Amount of Wages Lower End	Amount of Wages Upper End	Amount to be Withheld	Percentage for Excess over Low End
$ 0	$ 27	$ 0	0
27	63	0	.15
63	131	5.40	.18
131	196	17.64	.21
196	273	31.29	.26
273	331	51.31	.30
331	433	68.71	.34
433	999	103.39	.39

b. **Married person.**

Amount of Wages Lower End	Amount of Wages Upper End	Amount to be Withheld	Percentage for Excess over Low End
$ 0	$ 46	$ 0	0
46	127	0	0.15
127	210	12.15	0.18
210	288	27.09	0.21
288	369	43.47	0.24
369	454	62.91	0.28
454	556	86.71	0.32
556	999	119.35	0.37

```
100   REM   PROGRAM TO SET UP TAX TABLE
110   REM
120   REM   LINK TO FILE
130   REM
135   D$ =  CHR$ (4)
140   PRINT D$;"OPEN SINGLE"
150   REM
160   REM   SET UP TABLE OF 8 ROWS AND 4 COLUMNS
170   REM
180   DIM T(8,4)
190   REM
200   REM   FOR EACH ROW, GET DATA FROM TERMINAL
210   REM
220   FOR R = 1 TO 8
230   PRINT "ENTER LOW AND HIGH WAGES,MINIMUM AND PERCENTAGE"
240   INPUT T(R,1),T(R,2),T(R,3),T(R,4)
250   NEXT R
260   REM
270   REM   PRINT TABLE AND PLACE IT INTO FILE
```

```
280    REM
290    PRINT
300    PRINT
310    FOR L = 1 TO 8
320    PRINT T(L,1),T(L,2),T(L,3),T(L,4)
325    PRINT D$;"WRITE SINGLE"
330    PRINT T(L,1);",";T(L,2);",";T(L,3);",";T(L,4)
335    PRINT D$
340    NEXT L
350    PRINT D$;"CLOSE SINGLE"
360    STOP
63999 END

]RUN
ENTER LOW AND HIGH WAGES,MINIMUM AND PERCENTAGE
?0,27,0,0
ENTER LOW AND HIGH WAGES,MINIMUM AND PERCENTAGE
?27,63,0,.15
ENTER LOW AND HIGH WAGES,MINIMUM AND PERCENTAGE
?63,131,5.40,.18
ENTER LOW AND HIGH WAGES,MINIMUM AND PERCENTAGE
?131,196,17.64,.21
ENTER LOW AND HIGH WAGES,MINIMUM AND PERCENTAGE
?196,273,31.29,.26
ENTER LOW AND HIGH WAGES,MINIMUM AND PERCENTAGE
?273,331,51.31,.30
ENTER LOW AND HIGH WAGES,MINIMUM AND PERCENTAGE
?331,433,68.71,.34
ENTER LOW AND HIGH WAGES,MINIMUM AND PERCENTAGE
?433,999,103.39,.39


0              27             0              0
27             63             0              .15
63             131            5.4            .18
131            196            17.64          .21
196            273            31.29          .26
273            331            51.31          .3
331            433            68.71          .34
433            999            103.39         .39

BREAK IN 360
```

The program gets table data from the terminal and places it into the "SINGLE" file. The details of its operation deserve closer inspection.

Line 180 reserves the spaces for the table T. The dimensions of the table are given in parentheses as 8,4. These dimensions show that the table consists of 8 rows (first dimension) by 4 columns (second dimension). Therefore 32 positions are reserved for T.

The data is entered into the table by the loop in lines 220–250. The "FOR-NEXT" loops the computer through the statements in 230 and 240 eight times. The first time through the loop, R has the value 1. Therefore line 240 gets four values from the terminal and assigns them to row 1 (first dimension: R is 1), columns 1 through 4 in turn.

Then the NEXT R is encountered. The computer adds 1 to R and checks the R value against its limit (the 8 specified in the FOR statement). (Since R is less than 8, lines 230 and 240 are executed.) This time, the data are placed into row 2.

Every time the computer encounters the NEXT R (until R would exceed 8), it adds 1 to R and fills the next successive row of T. After the eighth row has been filled, the looping is finished. The computer continues with the next statement in the program.

Lines 310 through 340 print the data on the terminal and also place it into the SINGLE file. The FOR-NEXT loop sends the computer through the statements in 320 and 330 eight times. For each value of L (1 to 8), it prints that row of the table and places the row into the SINGLE file. Thus the eight rows of T are filed away for future use.

A similar program has to be written to place the data into "MARRID". You can use this program if you change the file name from "SINGLE" to "MARRID".

These two tables are used in the calculation of the taxes for the employees in "EMPTRA". We will also need the master file "EMPMAS" to get the number of exemptions and the year-to-date social security (YTD FICA). Each exemption claimed by the employee deducts $19.23 from taxable wages. And social security deductions are 6.13% up to a limit of $22,900 gross pay.

The old UPDATE program from Chapter 7 serves as the basis for solving this problem. We have modified it to handle the tax tables and the social security calculations.

Problem Summary

Input

"SINGLE" and "MARRID" files for the tax tables

"EMPTRA" file for the weekly earnings

"EMPMAS" file for the deductions and year-to-date FICA

Processing

For each employee: Calculate gross pay, social security (FICA), federal income tax (FIT), and net pay (by subtracting FICA and FIT from gross pay).

Output

The results of the "pay check" calculations, giving employee name and number, gross pay, social security and income tax deductions, and net pay

The updated master file, "EMPMA1"

The program therefore has to
1. Link to the files.
2. Read and hold the tax tables.
3. Get an employee record from "EMPTRA".
4. Find the matching record from "EMPMAS".
5. Calculate gross pay.
6. Determine the amount of the social security deduction:
    a. If YTD gross pay plus weekly gross pay is less than $22,900, *then* all of weekly gross pay is subject to FICA.
    b. If YTD gross pay is less than $22,900, but weekly gross pay added to YTD gross pay makes it greater than $22,900, *then* only that portion of weekly gross pay that brings the YTD up to $22,900 is subject to FICA.
    c. If YTD gross pay is greater than $22,900, *then* no social security is withheld.
7. Calculate taxable income by subtracting deductions from gross pay.
8. Find the applicable tax in the tax tables.
9. Calculate net pay.
10. Update the master record and place it into "EMPMA1".
11. Print the output.
12. Repeat steps 3 through 12 for all other "EMPLOY" records.
13. Terminate.

A program to do all those tasks is shown on the following pages.

```
100   REM              UPDATE OF MASTER FILE
110   ONERR   GOTO 650
120   REM
130   REM              SET UP HEADINGS
140   REM
150   PRINT
160   PRINT "EMPLOYEE","NAME","GROSS","FIT","FICA","NET"
170   PRINT "NUMBER"," ","PAY"
180   PRINT
185   DEF   FN R(X) =   INT (100 * X + 0.5) / 100
190   REM
200   REM
201 D$ =   CHR$ (4)
202   PRINT D$;"OPEN SINGLE"
204   PRINT D$;"OPEN MARRID"
210   PRINT D$;"OPEN EMPMAS"
220   PRINT D$;"OPEN EMPTRA"
230   PRINT D$;"OPEN EMPMA1"
231   REM
232   REM   TAX TABLES
233   REM
234   DIM S(8,4),M(8,4)
235   FOR L1 = 1 TO 8
236   PRINT D$;"READ SINGLE": INPUT S(L1,1),S(L1,2),S(L1,3),S(L1,4)
237   PRINT D$;"READ MARRID": INPUT M(L1,1),M(L1,2),M(L1,3),M(L1,4)
238   NEXT L1
239   REM
240   REM
250   REM              READ A TRANSACTION RECORD
```

```
260   REM
270   PRINT D$;"READ EMPTRA"
271   INPUT I,R,V
280   REM
290   REM          READ A MASTER RECORD
300   REM
310   PRINT D$;"READ EMPMAS"
311   INPUT N,D,N$,M,H,E,G,F,F1
320   REM
330   REM          COMPARE IDS
340   REM
350   IF I = N THEN 410
360   IF I > N THEN 310
370   IF I < N THEN 750
380   REM
390   REM          IDS MATCH -- DO COMPUTATIONS FOR UPDATE
400   REM
405   REM   CALCULATE GROSS PAY
406   REM
410 G1 = (R * H) + (V * H * 1.5)
412   REM   CALCULATE SOCIAL SECURITY
413   REM
414 F3 = 0
415   REM
416   REM   SOCIAL SECURITY IS ZERO IF YTD GROSS OVER 22,900
417   REM
418   IF G > 22900 THEN 433
419   REM
420   REM   SOCIAL SECURITY IS 0.0613 OF WEEKLY GROSS
421   REM   IF YTD GROSS+WEEKLY GROSS LESS THAN 22,900
422   REM
423   IF G + G1 > 22900 THEN 429
424 F3 = G1 * 0.0613
425   GOTO 433
426   REM   SOCIAL SECURITY IS 0.0613 OF DIFFERENCE
427   REM   BETWEEN 22,900 AND YTD GROSS
428   REM
429 F3 = (22900 - G) * 0.0613
430   REM
431   REM   CALCULATE TAXABLE INCOME BY SUBTRACTING EXEMPTIONS
432   REM
433 T = G1 - E * 19.23
434   REM
435   REM   DETERMINE TAX TABLE
436   REM
437   IF M = 2 THEN 452
438   REM
439   REM M IS 1; FIND ROW IN SINGLE TABLE
440   REM
441   FOR R1 = 1 TO 8
442   IF T < = S(R1,2) THEN 447
443   NEXT R1
444   REM
445   REM   CALCULATE TAX
446   REM
447 F2 = S(R1,3) + (T - S(R1,1)) * S(R1,4)
448   GOTO 462
449   REM
450   REM M IS 2; FIND ROW IN MARRID TABLE
451   REM
452   FOR R1 = 1 TO 8
453   IF T < = M(R1,2) THEN 458
454   NEXT R1
455   REM
456   REM   CALCULATE TAX
457   REM
```

```
458 F2 = M(R1,3) + (T - M(R1,1)) * M(R1,4)
459  REM
460  REM   CALCULATE NET PAY
461  REM
462 P = G1 - F2 - F3
463  REM
464  REM   ADD WEEKLY GROSS, FIT AND FICA TO YTD TOTALS
465  REM
466 G = G + G1
467 F = F + F2
470 F1 = F1 + F3
480 P1 = P1 + P
490  REM
500  REM            PRINT UPDATED MASTER RECORD
510  REM
520  PRINT D$;"WRITE EMPMA1"
521  PRINT N;",";D;",";N$;",";M;",";H;",";E;",";G;",";F;",";F1
522  PRINT D$
540  REM            PRINT ID, NAME, NET PAY
550  REM
556 G1 =  FN R(G1):F2 =  FN R(F2):F3 =  FN R(F3):P =  FN R(P)
560  PRINT N,N$,G1,F2,F3,P
570  REM
580  REM            READ A TRANSACTION RECORD
590  REM
600  PRINT D$;"READ EMPTRA"
601  INPUT I,R,V
610  GOTO 350
620  REM
630  REM           *** ERROR CHECK ***"
640  REM
650  PRINT D$
655 Y =  PEEK (222)
660  IF Y = 5 THEN 690
665  PRINT "UNUSUAL ERROR",Y
670  PRINT D$;"CLOSE EMPMAS"
671  PRINT D$;"CLOSE EMPTRA"
672  PRINT D$;"CLOSE EMPMA1"
673  PRINT D$;"CLOSE SINGLE"
674  PRINT D$;"CLOSE MARRID"
680  STOP
690 L =  PEEK (218) + 256 *  PEEK (219)
691  IF L = 601 THEN 780
700  IF L = 911 THEN 940
710  STOP
720  REM
730  REM            MISSING MASTER RECORD
740  REM
750  PRINT D$
755  PRINT "MASTER RECORD MISSING FOR EMPLOYEE NUMBER",I
760  PRINT D$;"CLOSE EMPMAS"
761  PRINT D$;"CLOSE EMPTRA"
762  PRINT D$;"CLOSE EMPMA1"
763  PRINT D$;"CLOSE SINGLE"
764  PRINT D$;"CLOSE MARRID"
770  STOP
780  PRINT D$;"CLOSE EMPMAS"
781  PRINT D$;"CLOSE EMPTRA"
782  PRINT D$;"CLOSE EMPMA1"
783  PRINT D$;"CLOSE SINGLE"
784  PRINT D$;"CLOSE MARRID"
790  REM
800  REM             PRINT OUT OF UPDATED MASTER FILE
810  REM
820  PRINT
830  PRINT
```

```
840    PRINT
850    PRINT
860    PRINT "              UPDATED MASTER FILE"
870    PRINT
880    PRINT D$;"OPEN EMPMA1"
890    PRINT "EMPLOYEE"; SPC( 2);"DEPT","NAME","MARITAL","HOURLY","EX-","YTD","YTD","YTD"
900    PRINT "NUMBER"; SPC( 4);" "," ","STATUS","RATE","EMP","GROSS","FIT","FICA"
910    PRINT D$;"READ EMPMA1"
911    INPUT N,D,N$,M,H,E,G,F,F1
912    PRINT D$
915    H =  FN R(H):G =  FN R(G):F =  FN R(F):F1 =  FN R(F1)
920    PRINT N; SPC( 7);D,N$,M,H,E,G,F,F1
930    GOTO 910
940    PRINT D$;"CLOSE EMPMA1"
950    STOP
63999  END

MAXFILES 5

RUN
```

EMPLOYEE NUMBER	NAME	GROSS PAY	FIT	FICA	NET
101	ADAMS	200	14.91	12.26	172.83
103	BAKER	257.6	37.31	15.79	204.5
104	BRAVO	172	7.36	10.54	154.09
108	COHEN	237.5	18.19	14.56	204.75
172	JOHNSON	150	21.63	9.19	119.18
198	TANNER	153	4.51	9.38	139.11
202	WILSON	160	2.68	9.81	147.51
206	LESTER	210	16.71	12.87	180.42
255	SCHMIDT	257.6	18.35	15.79	223.46
281	MILLER	240	18.64	14.71	206.64
313	SMITH	195.5	14.1	11.98	169.42
347	GRAY	228	19.95	13.98	194.08
368	WEAVER	150.5	17.7	9.23	123.58
422	WILLIAMS	160	11.33	9.81	138.86

UPDATED MASTER FILE

EMPLOYEE NUMBER	DEPT	NAME	MARITAL STATUS	HOURLY RATE	EX- EMP	YTD GROSS	YTD FIT	YTD FICA
101	1	ADAMS	2	5	3	1200	214.91	73.56
103	12	BAKER	1	5.6	2	1545.6	294.91	94.74
104	17	BRAVO	2	4	4	1032	179.36	63.26
108	16	COHEN	2	6.25	4	1425	255.69	87.35
172	2	JOHNSON	1	3.75	0	900	171.63	55.18
198	1	TANNER	2	4.25	4	918	157.51	56.27
202	16	WILSON	2	4	5	960	162.68	58.85
206	7	LESTER	2	5.25	3	1260	226.71	77.24
255	12	SCHMIDT	2	5.6	5	1545.6	275.95	94.74
281	12	MILLER	2	6	4	1440	258.64	88.27
313	7	SMITH	2	4.25	3	1173	209.6	71.9
347	12	GRAY	2	6	3	1368	247.95	83.86
368	1	WEAVER	1	3.5	1	903	168.2	55.36
422	1	WILLIAMS	2	4	2	960	171.33	58.85

```
BREAK IN 950
```

Lines 236, 237, 556, and 915 look strange. They each have more than one BASIC statement on their respective lines. You can put more than one statement per line if you separate each statement with a colon (:). Lines 236 and 237 have two BASIC statements while lines 556 and 915 have four.

The key statements for the table reference are in lines 452–454 for married employees and in lines 441–443 for single employees, where the appropriate row of the table is found. But before we can discuss that, let's look at how the tables were set up in line 234–238.

First, line 234 reserves the space for two tables: S for single and M for married employees. Each table consists of eight rows and four columns. According to the tax tables of the Internal Revenue Service, each row corresponds to a range of income. The columns of the table are as follows:

- Column 1: the low end of the weekly income range
- Column 2: the upper end
- Column 3: the taxes up to the low end
- Column 4: the tax rate for anything above the low end (but below the high end of the range).

Then in lines 235–238 the tables are filled. The field L1 stands for the row number. It is assigned the values 1 through 8 successively by the FOR-NEXT statement. For each value of L1, the four columns of each table are input. So if L1 is 1, then the first row is filled. When L1 is two, the second row of the tables S and M is given values. Once all eight rows are filled, we exit from the loop and start to process the employee records.

Now we can see how to work with these tables. The taxable income has already been computed when we arrived at line 437. The statement in 437 checks whether the single person or married person tax table has to be used. Depending on this test, we go either to line 441 for a single person or to line 452 for a married person.

The taxable income tells us what row of the table is used for the tax calculation. Hence taxable income is compared to the upper end of an income range. Because the ranges are in ascending order, each row holds the data for a weekly income that is less than the upper end of that row, but greater than the upper end of the earlier rows. Since the rows are checked starting with the lowest income, as long as taxable income is greater than the upper end of a range, we have not yet reached the correct row of the table.

Once the right row has been found, then we can use the row number R1 to calculate the taxes. Line 458 calculates the tax for married employees and line 447 calculates the tax for single employees.

Besides the table reference, this program also contains one other complication—the social security calculation. Actually, there is nothing new in lines 414–429; it's just cumbersome because we have to follow the rules of the Internal Revenue Service. All the conditions make it awkward to follow the calculations. The program handles three conditions:

1. Year-to-date greater than $22,900; in which case no social security is calculated (determined in line 418).

2. Year-to-date plus weekly wages less than $22,900; where all of the weekly wages are subject to social security (calculated in line 424).

3. Year-to-date less than $22,900, but year-to-date plus weekly wages greater than $22,900; here the difference between $22,900 and the year-to-date is subject to a social security deduction. (That deduction is calculated in line 429.)

Apple BASIC has the ability to handle up to sixteen files in a program. However, if you have more than three files open simultaneously in a program, you must use the BASIC command MAXFILES with the number of files that the program uses. This command must be given before the run command.

Of course, the actual payroll calculation for a real firm would have many more deductions. Not included in this example are deductions for health insurance, pension plans, payroll savings plans, state and local taxes where required, union dues, etc. But from this example you can appreciate what is needed to do payroll calculations.

Look at the other example that follows.

Inventory Report: Some industries experience rapid price fluctuations. When prices fluctuate rapidly, it is often convenient to establish and maintain separate price tables for parts in inventory. Table 8–3 shows the price table for the parts in inventory.

Example

Inventory Price Table

Table 8–3

Part Number	Price
101	5.25
110	7.00
219	3.25
226	3.10
235	6.20
247	4.85

Management has asked for a report that shows the dollar value of issues and receipts by part number. The issues and receipts are in the transaction file "INVTR".

Problem Summary

Input

"INVTR" file

Price table file, "INVPRC"

Processing

Accumulate subtotals and totals for the dollar amounts issued and received by part number and for the file as a whole.

Output

An inventory report, giving by part number the dollar amount of issues and the dollar amount of receipts.

```
100    REM   PROGRAM TO PRICE ISSUES AND RECEIPTS
101    REM
102    REM   HEADINGS FOR REPORT
103    PRINT
104    PRINT
105    PRINT "    RECEIPTS AND ISSUES REPORT"
106    PRINT
107    PRINT "PART","RECEIPTS","ISSUES"
110    REM
115    D$ =  CHR$ (4)
118    DEF   FN R(X) =  INT (100 * X + 0.5) / 100
120    REM   LINK TO FILES
130    REM
140    PRINT D$;"OPEN INVTR"
150    PRINT D$;"OPEN INVPRC"
160    REM
170    REM   SET UP PRICE TABLE AND GET DATA FROM INVPRC
180    REM
190    DIM P(6,2)
200 R = 0
210    ONERR  GOTO 770
220    PRINT D$;"READ INVPRC"
225    INPUT N,D
230 R = R + 1
240 P(R,1) = N
250 P(R,2) = D
260    GOTO 220
270    REM
280    REM   READ AN INVENTORY TRANSACTION
290    REM
300    PRINT D$;"READ INVTR"
305    INPUT P1,T1,Q1
310    REM
320    REM   SET P9 TO PART NUMBER FOR LATER COMPARISON
330    REM
340 P9 = P1
350    REM
360    REM   DETERMINE PRICE OF PART BY COMPARING P1 TO
370    REM   COLUMN 1 OF TABLE P
380    REM
390    FOR R = 1 TO 6
400    IF P1 = P(R,1) THEN 450
410    NEXT R
```

```
420   REM
430   REM   DETERMINE WHETHER TRANSACTION IS SHIPMENT OR RECEIPT
440   REM
450   IF T1 = 2 THEN 540
460   REM
470   REM   RECEIPT: T1=1
480   REM
490 R1 = R1 + Q1 * P(R,2)
500   GOTO 580
510   REM
520   REM   SHIPMENT: T1=2
530   REM
540 S1 = S1 + Q1 * P(R,2)
550   REM
560   REM   READ NEXT TRANSACTION
570   REM
580   PRINT D$;"READ INVTR"
585   INPUT P1,T1,Q1
590   REM
600   REM   CHECK WHETHER ITS THE SAME PART AS BEFORE
610   REM
620   IF P1 = P9 THEN 390
630   REM
640   REM   PRINT OUT OLD PART NUMBER, RECEIPTS AND SHIPMENTS
650   REM
660   PRINT D$
665   PRINT P9, FN R(R1), FN R(S1)
670   REM
680   REM   SET RECEIPT AND SHIPMENT ACCUMULATORS TO ZERO
690   REM   AND PROCESS TRANSACTION
700   REM
710 R1 = 0
720 S1 = 0
730   GOTO 340
740   REM
750   REM   ERROR CHECKING ROUTINE
760   REM
770   PRINT D$
772 Y =  PEEK (222)
774   IF Y = 5 THEN 780
776   PRINT "UNUSUAL ERROR",Y
778   GOTO 800
780 L =  PEEK (218) + 256 *  PEEK (219)
785   IF L = 225 THEN 300
790   IF L = 585 THEN 800
800   PRINT D$;"CLOSE INVTR"
810   STOP
63999 END

]RUN
```

```
           RECEIPTS AND ISSUES REPORT

PART                RECEIPTS           ISSUES
101                 787.5              813.75
219                 0                  65
226                 542.5              279
235                 0                  186

BREAK IN 810
```

This program generates a report of receipts and shipments by part number from the "INVTR" file. It performs the following tasks:

1. It links to files "INVTR" and "INVPRC" (statements 140 and 150).

2. It reserves room for the price table (statement 190).

3. It gets a part number and a price from "INVPRC" and assigns it to the price table (statements 200–260).

4. It reads the first inventory transaction from "INVTR" (statement 305).

5. It "remembers" the part number (statement 340).

6. It processes the transaction:
   a. It determines which row of the price table has the same part number (statements 390–410).
   b. It determines whether the transaction is a shipment or a receipt (statement 450).
      (1) It accumulates the dollar amount of receipts (statement 490).
      (2) It accumulates the dollar amount of shipments (statement 540).

7. It reads the next transaction (statement 585).

8. If the part number of this transaction is the same as the part number on a prior transaction, then repeat steps 6 and 7 (statement 620).

9. If the part number of this transaction is not the same as the part number of a prior transaction, then print the prior part number receipts and shipments (statement 665); set accumulators for receipts and shipments to zero (statements 710 and 720) and perform steps 5, 6 and 7.

10. It terminates when out of transaction data.

The table reference in this example is in step 6. Let's look at it again to see the details of its operation. The price table P looks as follows:

Column

Row	1	2
1	101	5.25
2	110	7.00
3	219	3.35
4	226	3.10
5	235	6.20
6	247	4.85

Now let's take the first transaction:

Part Number	Transaction Code	Quantity
101	1	150

The FOR-NEXT loop starts R at 1. So in line 400 when we compare the part number (P1) to column 1 of the table, we have a match. Therefore we skip out of the loop (R is still 1 since it was not changed) and use this row number to calculate the dollar value of the receipt in line 490.

That example was too easy. Take another transaction:

Part Number	Transaction Code	Quantity
226	2	90

Again R starts at 1 in line 390. The comparison between P1 (the part number) and the table P (Row 1, Column 1) shows they are not equal. Therefore we come to the NEXT R statement in 410. A one is added to R: R is now 2; and the comparison in line 400 is between P1 (value of 226) and row 2, column 1 of table P (value of 110). Again, they are not equal.

Notice that as R is changed, from 1 to 2, to 3, to 4, the program skips down the first column of P. At each value of R the next row of the table is used in the comparison. Once the proper row has been found, the row number (R) is used with the second column of P to calculate the dollar value of a transaction, either in line 490 or in line 540.

SORTING LISTS AND TABLES

Sometimes we must change the order of a small amount of data. For example, we might want a listing of our employees by descending order of gross pay for labor negotiations. Or we might want product lines in ascending order of sales. Or we might want to rank our customers by volume of sales.

Sorting of files has already been mentioned. Appendix B has the sorts needed. But sometimes the data is in lists or tables, not on a file, and we need to sort it.

Let's assume that we need a list of employees in descending order of net pay. The net pay of the employees has already been calculated in the revised employee payroll program. But the output from that program is in employee number sequence. Our need is in descending order of net pay.

Problem Summary

Input

    Employee number

    Employee name

    Weekly net pay

Processing

    Store the fields in lists. Sort by weekly net pay (in descending order).

Output

    Print employee name and number in descending order of pay.

The program therefore has to:

1. Get the employee data and put it into lists.

2. Sort the list into descending order of net pay.

3. Print the sorted data.

4. Terminate.

A program that performs these tasks is shown below:

```
100   REM   PROGRAM TO SORT LISTS
110   REM
120   REM   SET UP LISTS TO HOLD DATA
130   REM
140   DIM N(100),N$(100),P(100)
150   REM
160   REM   GET THE DATA FROM THE TERMINAL AND PLACE IT INTO
170   REM   THE LISTS
180   REM
190 L = 0
200   PRINT "TYPE EMPLOYEE NUMBER, EMPLOYEE NAME"
210   PRINT "AND NET PAY SEPARATED BY COMMAS"
220   PRINT "WHEN FINISHED --   TYPE 99,AA,99"
230   INPUT N1,M$,P1
240   IF N1 = 99 THEN 340
260 L = L + 1
270   N(L) = N1
280   N$(L) = M$
```

```
290 P(L) = P1
300   GOTO 230
310   REM
320   REM   SORT THE DATA
330   REM
340 U = L - 1
350 F = 0
360   FOR K = 1 TO U
370   REM   COMPARE TWO CONSECUTIVE VALUES
380   REM   IF THEY ARE NOT IN ORDER THEN EXCHANGE
390   IF P(K) > = P(K + 1) THEN 600
400   REM
410   REM   VALUES OUT OF SEQUENCE HENCE EXCHANGE
420   REM
430 T = P(K)
440 P(K) = P(K + 1)
450 P(K + 1) = T
460   REM
470   REM   EXCHANGE NAME AND ID ALSO TO KEEP THEM
480   REM   AND RATES TOGETHER
490   REM
500 T = N(K)
510 N(K) = N(K + 1)
520 N(K + 1) = T
530 T$ = N$(K)
540 N$(K) = N$(K + 1)
550 N$(K + 1) = T$
560   REM
570   REM   SET F TO INDICATE THAT AN EXCHANGE HAS OCCURRED
580   REM
590 F = 1
600   NEXT K
610   REM
620   REM   CHECK IF ANY EXCHANGES HAVE OCCURRED
630   REM
640   IF F = 1 THEN 350
650   REM
660   REM   END OF SORT
670   REM
680   REM   PRINT OUT LISTS WITH HEADINGS
690   REM
700   PRINT "EMPLOYEE","EMPLOYEE","WEEKLY"
710   PRINT "NUMBER","NAME","PAY"
730   FOR K = 1 TO L
740   PRINT N(K),N$(K),P(K)
750   NEXT K
770   STOP
63999 END

]RUN
TYPE EMPLOYEE NUMBER, EMPLOYEE NAME
```

```
AND NET PAY SEPARATED BY COMMAS
WHEN FINISHED --   TYPE 99,AA,99
?101,ADAMS,172.20
?103,BAKER,204.50
?104,BRAVO,154.09
?108.COHEM.204.44
?172,JOHNSON,119.18
?198,TANNER,139.11
?202,WILSON,147.51
?206,LESTER,180.19
?255,SCHMIDT,223.15
?281,MILLER,206.32
?313,SMITH,169.32
?347,GRAY,193.69
?368,WEAVER,123.58
?422,WILLIAMS,138.86
?99,AA,99
EMPLOYEE           EMPLOYEE           WEEKLY
NUMBER             NAME               PAY
255                SCHMIDT            223.15
281                MILLER             206.32
103                BAKER              204.5
108                COHEM              204.44
347                GRAY               193.69
206                LESTER             180.19
101                ADAMS              172.2
313                SMITH              169.32
104                BRAVO              154.09
202                WILSON             147.51
198                TANNER             139.11
422                WILLIAMS           138.86
368                WEAVER             123.58
172                JOHNSON            119.18


BREAK IN 770
```

This program puts data into lists in lines 190–300. Then it sorts the lists in lines 340 to 640. Finally, it prints out the lists in lines 700 to 750. Let's look at each of these actions in turn.

The storage of data starts by setting the field L to zero. L will be used in lines 270 through 290 to indicate the location in a list. Notice that the lists have 100 spaces each (the dimension is set in line 140), although fewer spaces will be needed for our data.

Then line 230 gets the first record for the file. The program adds 1 to L in line 260. L is now 1. Hence in lines 270–290, the first (L value of 1) location of N, N$, and P is filled with the values of N1, M$ and P1 respectively.

Line 300 takes us back to the input of data. As long as there are records in the file, the program reads the data; adds one to L; and places the desired fields into successive locations in the lists. At the end of the data input, L will contain the number of records; L is also the highest position in the lists that has been filled with data.

Lines 340 to 640 sort the data into descending order of weekly pay. The sort is finished when all items are in order. It works by comparing two adjacent positions in the pay list. If they are in sequence, we compare the next two positions. But if two adjacent positions are out of sequence, they are first placed in the proper sequence before the next two positions are compared.

We know that all items are in their proper sequence if we do not have to interchange any items. Whether an interchange has occurred is shown by a field (a "flag" called F in the program). The field is set to zero at the beginning of each pass through the array. When an interchange occurs, it is set to one. Therefore if F is one, we don't know yet that the lists are in their desired sequence. Line 640 tests F, and if F is one, we repeat the process.

We can see the operations of this sort by looking at the first five records of the lists. These records would be in the lists N, N$ and P as follows:

		List	
Position	N	N$	P
1	101	Adams	172.83
2	103	Baker	204.50
3	104	Bravo	154.09
4	108	Cohen	204.75
5	172	Johnson	119.18

Now let's start through the steps of the sort. First, U, a field to hold the upper limit for the comparisons, will be 4. Therefore K, the loop index, will take on values 1 to 4 in turn. Line 350 sets F to zero, because at this stage no exchanges have occurred. Then K is set to 1, and we compare the K (first) position and K + 1 (second) position in the net pay list. They are out of sequence. P(2) is $204.50, and P(1) is $172.83. To put them in proper order, Baker should come before Adams. Hence lines 430 to 450 interchange the values.

Notice that an interchange is a three-step process. If we tried it in two steps, it wouldn't work:

$$P (K) = P (K + 1)$$
$$P (K + 1) = P (K)$$

Why not? Because the computer is a sequential machine. For a K value of 1, the following would happen in the two-step process: Step 1: $P (K) = P (K + 1)$. This means $P (1) = P (2)$ and after the assignment the first two positions of P would look as follows:

Position 1	204.50
Position 2	204.50

Because we put the value from position 2 into the first position, they are both identical. The value in the first position is lost, wiped out, erased. And the second step would put a 204.50 into position 2 again.

The three-step process works, because it puts the value for the first position temporarily somewhere else—in T. Now when a value is placed into P (K), we still have its old value in T as shown below:

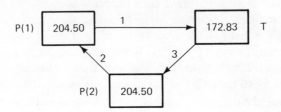

The numbers on the arrows give the sequence in which the assignments have to occur to do the exchange.

At the end of line 450, our lists would look as follows:

N	N$	P
101	Adams	204.50
103	Baker	172.83
104	Bravo	154.09
108	Cohen	204.75
172	Johnson	119.18

As you can see the net pays are in order, but they are not with the right employee name and number. Lines 500–550 interchange the names and ID numbers so that the list will look like this:

N	N$	P
103	Baker	204.50
101	Adams	172.83
104	Bravo	154.09
108	Cohen	204.75
172	Johnson	119.18

Then line 590 sets F to 1 because an interchange has occurred and we are ready for the next K value.

When K is 2, the second (Kth) and third positions of P are compared. They are already in sequence. Therefore we go to the next K value.

When K is 3, we compare the third and fourth position. They are out of sequence. Therefore we interchange and our list would look as follows before the next K value is executed:

N	N$	P
103	Baker	204.50
101	Adams	172.83
108	Cohen	204.75
104	Bravo	154.09
172	Johnson	119.18

When K is 4, the comparison between the fourth (Kth) and fifth (K + 1) values of P shows that they are in sequence.

Since K has now reached its upper limit (the value of U), the looping is finished. But a check with F (in line 640) shows that at least one exchange has occurred. Since the lists may not be in sequence, the program sends us back to 350 for another pass through the data.

At the end of the second pass (K value of 1, 2, 3 and 4), the lists would look as follows:

N	N$	P
103	Baker	204.50
108	Cohen	204.75
101	Adams	172.83
104	Bravo	154.09
172	Johnson	119.18

It takes one more pass to get the data in order and another to assure us that no more interchanges are needed. Then we know that the lists are in the desired sequence.

Notice that the sequence of the items is basically defined by the test in line 390. In this example, the contents of two adjacent positions in the list are compared to see if they are in descending sequence.

It is important that two equal values *not* be exchanged. If the test in 390 was just *greater than* (as opposed to the actual *greater than or equal*), then two values that were equal would be exchanged. And they would be exchanged again in the next pass. And the next. And the next. And the next. In fact, the exchanges would never end.

A situation like that, called an infinite loop, can cost you a lot in computer time. Therefore care must be taken to avoid infinite loops. In this case, the test must be a *greater than or equal,* or *less than or equal,* so that an infinite loop is not generated.

SUMMARY   This chapter has discussed the use of lists and tables. Lists and tables are convenient ways to hold data either for subsequent processing or for output after processing.

In the first example, a list was used to accumulate departmental totals. To use the list, space for the list had to be reserved and labelled. To access individual elements of the list, subscripts giving the location of a position in a list had to be used.

Tables are different from lists, because two subscripts are needed—a row indicator and a column indicator. Two tables were used to determine income taxes for the employees.

Besides lists and tables, this chapter also presented a way to perform looping. The FOR-NEXT construction lets you control how often a set of BASIC statements would be executed.

BASIC Commands Introduced:

Statement	*Explanation*
MAXFILES N	Used when more than three files are open at the same time. N is the number of files.

BASIC Instructions Introduced:

Statement	*Explanation*
DIM Y(X),Z(Q,R)	Sets the lists Y (represented by a letter) to X positions. Defines that Z (represented by a letter) has Q rows and R columns. Individual elements of lists and tables are identified by their location: the position number in a list or the row number *and* column number in a table. X, Q, and R must be numbers.
FOR Y = N TO M ⋮ NEXT Y	Sets up a loop. The FOR statement begins the loop. It sets Y to N (beginning value); the loop will continue until Y has a value greater than M (the upper bound). The NEXT statement closes the loop.

1. Write a program that will generate a summary report of inventory by department from the "INV" file (see Chapter 5). Use a list to hold the inventory cost by department.

2. A machine shop has seven machines. When an order for a part arrives, the sequence in which any of the seven machines will be us mined. To make a part requires four of the seven machines. The time in minutes for each machine to make a part is shown below:

Machine	Time
1	20
2	30
3	12
4	26
5	32
6	17
7	14

a. Write a program to store the data as a table in the "MCHTM" file.
b. The data regarding orders will be input from a terminal. Order data consists of an order number and the numbers of the machines in the required sequence to make the part. The following orders have arrived:

Order Number	Machine Sequence
7442	2,4,5,6
7443	1,5,3,7
7444	1,6,5,4
7445	1,3,6,7

Write a program that will input the "MCHTM" file and the order data; then print the order number and the total time required to process that order.

3. In Problem 2, the time required to transport the orders from one machine to another has been neglected. Modify your program to take transportation times into account in determining the total time to process an order. The transportation time in minutes are as follows:

		To Machine						
		1	2	3	4	5	6	7
	1	0	15	23	7	16	5	19
	2	12	0	16	9	12	17	5
From	3	25	14	0	12	17	12	18
Machine	4	8	12	13	0	9	8	14
	5	19	14	15	11	0	12	10
	6	7	15	10	10	15	0	9
	7	17	8	14	18	12	13	0

Write a program to store the transportation time as a table in the "TRTM" file and modify your program in Problem 2 to include transportation time. Use the same order data as in Problem 2.

4. Change the sort program in this chapter (page 208) so that it will sort in ascending order. Use the net pay data to test the program.

9 / Using Direct Access Files

At the end of this chapter you should be able to:

- Create relative record files
- Read and print relative record files
- Change field values in a relative record record
- Update master records in a relative record file
- Query records in a relative record file

So far, sequential files have been used exclusively for all problems, exercises, and examples. There is one major drawback in using sequential files—every time you want to read any record in a file you must start with the first record and read each record until the desired record is reached. If a file has 2,000 records, and you want to print the 1,995th record, 1,995 records would have to be read to reach the record to be printed. A great deal of time would be wasted reading and testing every record until the one to be printed is reached. The time to reach a record in a sequential file is proportional to the position of the record (first, middle, last) in the file.

You may still wonder why a few seconds may be important. A sequential file of 2,000 records with the same fields as "EMPLOY" was created to test the time required to find and print a record. It took less than a second to read and print the first record. It took over four minutes to read and print the 1,995th record!

In the early days of computers, only sequential files were available. But to reduce the time required to find a record, direct access files were developed. All direct access files share one characteristic—the time to find any record in a file is constant. With direct access files, there is a method to find a record without reading from the beginning of a file.

There is more than one way to create and use direct access files in BASIC. One of the simplest methods is called relative record. It follows the techniques of Chapter 8 where lists and tables were discussed. We shall create a relative record file in almost the same manner as a table is created. An inventory example will be used throughout this chapter to illustrate the use of relative record (direct access) files.

The data for the inventory master file are found in Table 9–1. Note that the part number and the record number are the same! In an actual business, the part number would be a multi-digit number within which the record number would exist or be added to the existing part number after a dash. For example, part number 27364–001 could indicate that part 27364 is record number one. There are other more sophisticated ways of obtaining record numbers from part numbers; but they are beyond the introductory level of this book.

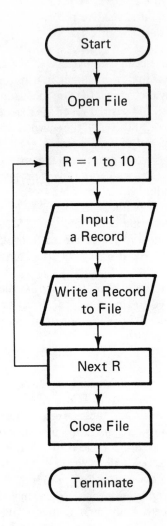

Figure 9-1   Flowchart to Create a Relative Record File

Inventory Master File—"INVMST"   Table 9–1

Part Number	Stock on Hand	Unit Cost
1	590	1.50
2	750	2.75
3	231	1.39
4	395	5.96
5	674	7.23
6	279	6.79
7	942	4.26
8	27	5.49
9	152	1.26
10	420	3.74

Problem Summary

Input

Inventory master file.

Processing

Input the data at execution time.

Output

Instructions for input and a relative record file, "INVMST".

The program consists of the following steps:

1. Link to the relative record file.

2. Input the data.

3. Stop when the data has been entered.

See the flowchart (Fig. 9–1). A program to perform all of these steps is below:

```
100   REM    PROGRAM TO CREATE RELATIVE RECORD FILE
110   REM
115 D$ =   CHR$ (4)
120   REM
130   REM   OPEN THE FILE
140   REM
150   PRINT D$;"OPEN INVMST,L16"
160   REM
170   REM   INPUT A RECORD
180   REM
190   FOR R = 1 TO 10
```

```
200    PRINT "TYPE PART NUMBER, STOCK ON HAND, UNIT COST"
210    INPUT A1,A2,A3
220    PRINT D$;"WRITE INVMST,R";R
230    PRINT A1;",";A2;",";A3
240    PRINT D$
250    NEXT R
260    REM
270    REM  FINISH
280    REM
290    PRINT D$;"CLOSE INVMST"
300    STOP
63999  END
```

Before discussing the program, there is a very important concept that must be understood. The creation of a relative record file results in a file on the diskette that is similar to a table. The rows of the table correspond to records in the file. The record is identified by its row number which is the same as the record number since each row consists of one record.

Relative record files are referred to in a program in the same way as sequential files. The only difference will be expansion of some file commands that you have already used. Line 150 PRINT D$; "OPEN INVMST, L16" tells the computer to open a relative record file "INVMST" and that the length of each record is a maximum of 16 characters. The 16 was determined as follows: 2 characters for the part number, 3 characters for the stock on hand and 4 characters for the unit cost (the decimal point counts as a character). This only adds to 9 characters. When you type a record into the computer you use commas after you enter the part number and stock on hand. You also press "RETURN" at the end of a record. The two commas and the "RETURN" count as 3 characters, resulting in a total of 12 characters. Sixteen characters were specified in the open statement. The remaining four characters were left in order to leave room for expansion of the fields if and when it may become necessary.

In line 220 PRINT D$; "WRITE INVMST, R";R a relative record with record number R will be written on the file. The R will change its value, each time the FOR-NEXT loop (lines 190–250) changes the R value from 1 to 10. In these lines ten records will be typed in from the keyboard and written on the file.

Upon completion of the data input, you have set up and stored the relative record file "INVMST" as if it were a table. The file looks like Figure 9–2.

READING AND PRINTING A RELATIVE RECORD FILE

The program to read and print out the inventory master file is given below. It is a very simple program.

Column

Row	1	2	3
1	1	590	1.50
2	2	750	2.75
3	3	231	1.39
4	4	395	5.96
5	5	674	7.23
6	6	279	6.79
7	7	942	4.26
8	8	27	5.49
9	9	152	1.26
10	10	420	3.74

Table   A (10,3)

The Relative Record File—"INVMST"

Figure 9-2

```
00   REM     THIS PROGRAM READS AND PRINTS THE RELATIVE RECORD FILE INVMST
10   REM
15   D$ =   CHR$ (4)
20   REM
30   REM   PRINT HEADINGS FOR REPORT
40   REM
50   PRINT "PART","STOCK","UNIT"
60   PRINT "NUMBER","ON HAND","COST"
70   PRINT
75   REM
80   REM   LINK TO FILE
90   REM
00   PRINT D$;"OPEN INVMST,L16"
10   REM
20   REM   PRINT OUT THE FILE
30   REM
40   FOR R = 1 TO 10
50   PRINT D$;"READ INVMST,R";R
60   INPUT A1,A2,A3
70   PRINT D$
80   PRINT A1,A2,A3
90   NEXT R
00   REM
10   REM   FINISH
20   REM
30   PRINT D$;"CLOSE INVMST"
40   STOP
3999   END
```

In lines 150 and 160 the headings for the output are printed. Next, the file is opened. Lines 240 through 290 print the file, row by row. The only new instruction is an extension of the file read.—Line 250 PRINT D$; "READ INVMST,R";R is used the same way as in the write statement. The R indicates the record number to be read.

CHANGING
VALUES IN A
RELATIVE
RECORD FILE

It is necessary to change values in an inventory master record due to price changes and adjustments. The stock on hand has to be adjusted because a manual count of stock on hand just took place. The following records have to be adjusted for stock on hand or cost.

Table 9–2

Changes to the Inventory Master File

Part Number	Stock on Hand	Unit Cost
1	600	2.00
9	152	1.40
6	230	7.00
3	231	1.50
10	500	4.00
5	674	7.25

Since "INVMST" is a direct access file, you do not have to order the changes by record (part) number.

Problem Summary

Input
Inventory master file, "INVMST"

Processing
Find the record to be changed. Input the new values.

Output
The inventory master file, "INVMST", with the appropriate records changed.

See the flowchart (Fig 9–3). A program follows:

```
100   REM   THIS PROGRAM CHANGES VALUES IN A RECORD OF A RELATIVE RECORD F
110   REM
115 D$ =   CHR$ (4)
120   REM
130   REM   OPEN THE FILE
140   REM
150   PRINT D$;"OPEN INVMST,L16"
160   REM
170   REM   INPUT RECORD NUMBER (PART NUMBER)
180   REM
190   PRINT "WHAT IS THE RECORD NUMBER? TYPE 9999 TO END"
200   INPUT R
210   REM
220   REM   TEST FOR END OF INPUT
230   REM
240   IF R = 9999 THEN 470
```

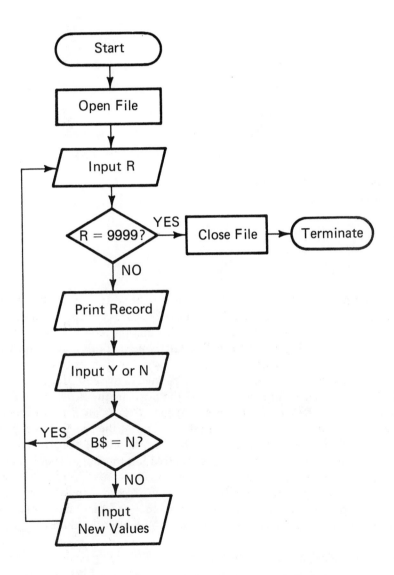

Flowchart for Changing a Record   Figure 9-3

```
250    REM
260    REM   GET THE RECORD AND PRINT IT OUT
270    REM
280    PRINT D$;"READ INVMST,R";R
290    INPUT A1,A2,A3
300    PRINT D$
310    PRINT "IS THIS THE RECORD TO BE CHANGED?"
320    PRINT A1,A2,A3
330    REM
340    REM   IS THIS THE CORRECT RECORD?
350    REM
360    PRINT "TYPE Y IF YES, N IF NO"
370    INPUT B$
380    IF B$ = "N" THEN 190
390    REM
400    REM   CORRECT THE VALUES
410    REM
420    PRINT "TYPE THE NEW VALUES: STOCK ON HAND, UNIT COST"
430    INPUT A2,A3
440    PRINT D$;"WRITE INVMST,R";R
450    PRINT A1;",";A2;",";A3
455    PRINT D$
460    GOTO 190
470    PRINT D$;"CLOSE INVMST"
480    STOP
63999  END
```

The program opens "INVMST" as a relative record file in line 150. Next, the record (part) number is input in line 200. A test for the end of data input is on line 240. It is important to check that the record to be changed is the one found. It is printed out in line 320. Note that this line prints out the entire record. Then a Y or an N is input to verify that the record printed out is the record to be changed. The Y or N is tested in line 380. If the input is Y, then the new values for stock on hand and price are input. Upon input, the values in the "INVMST" file are changed. That is all that is necessary. Next, the record number is requested. The end of the program is signalled by input of 9999 for record number. The file is closed and the program ends.

You should notice that the time required to print out a record after the record (part) number is given, is the same for all records. There is no need to read from the beginning of the file to reach any record. After you have input the changes given in Table 9–2, run the program that prints out "INVMST". The file should look like Table 9–3 after the changes:

UPDATING
MASTER
RECORDS IN A
RELATIVE
RECORD FILE

The next logical step, after you have mastered changing records in a relative record file, is to update the file. The update described below produces an instantaneously updated master file. There is no transaction file. Each transaction record updates its appropriate master record as soon as it is entered. In order to add a touch of realism to the update of the inventory

Inventory Master File After Changes   Table 9–3

Part Number	Stock on Hand	Unit Cost
1	600	2.00
2	750	2.75
3	231	1.50
4	395	5.96
5	674	7.25
6	230	7.00
7	942	4.26
8	27	5.49
9	152	1.40
10	500	4.00

master file "INVMST", assume that there are two computer terminals in the area where inventory is kept. The first terminal is located at the unloading area where shipments are received from suppliers. The second terminal is located by the loading area where items are shipped (issued) to the company's customers.

The first terminal is used to enter any receipts to inventory as soon as they are placed in inventory. The second terminal is used to enter any shipments (issues) from inventory.

The update program to handle direct access files is much simpler than the inventory update program in Chapter 7. A transaction code will be used to indicate a receipt to inventory (code = 1) and a shipment from inventory (code = 2). A transaction consists of three fields: the code, part number, and amount. If a shipment transaction (code = 2) has an amount greater than the stock on hand, the order cannot be filled. The program should cancel the shipment and keep the old value of the stock on hand. The transaction data can be found in Table 9–4.

Transaction Data to Update "INVMST"   Table 9–4

Transaction Code	Part (Record) Number	Quantity
1	9	50
2	2	500
1	10	200
1	5	75
2	9	50
1	1	40
1	2	100
2	8	50

Problem Summary

Input

Inventory master file, "INVMST" (Table 9-3)

Transactions

Processing

Determine the transaction code and update the appropriate master record.

Output

An updated master file.

See the flowchart (Fig 9-4). A program appears below:

```
100    REM     THIS PROGRAM UPDATES THE RELATIVE RECORD FILE INVMST
110    REM
115    D$ =    CHR$ (4)
120    REM
130    REM   OPEN THE FILE
140    REM
150    PRINT D$;"OPEN INVMST,L16"
160    REM
170    REM   INPUT THE TRANSACTION CODE
180    REM
190    PRINT "TYPE THE TRANSACTION CODE:"
200    PRINT "   1 IS A RECEIPT TO INVENTORY"
210    PRINT "   2 IS A SHIPMENT FROM NVENTORY"
220    PRINT "TYPE 9999 TO END"
230    INPUT T
240    REM
250    REM   TEST TO END DATA INPUT
260    REM
270    IF T = 9999 THEN 590
280    PRINT "TYPE THE PART NUMBER, QUANTITY"
290    INPUT M,Q
295    PRINT D$;"READ INVMST,R";M
300    INPUT A1,A2,A3
305    PRINT D$
308    REM
310    REM   TEST FOR RECEIPT
320    REM
330    IF T = 1 THEN 540
340    REM
350    REM   SHIPMENT
360    REM
370    A2 = A2 - Q
390    REM
400    REM   TEST FOR POSITIVE STOCK ON HAND
410    REM
420    IF A2 >  = 0 THEN 560
```

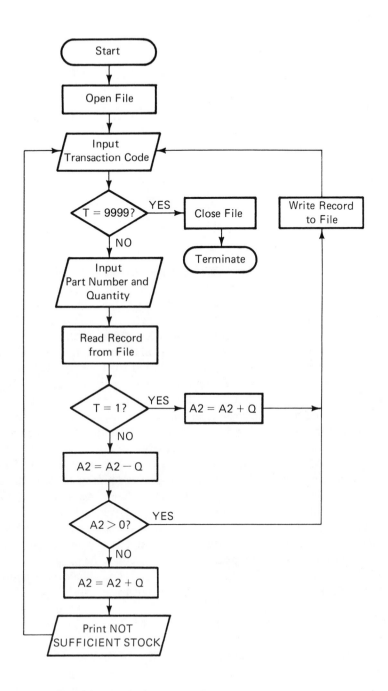

Flowchart of Direct Access Update

Figure 9–4

```
430   REM
440   REM   NOT ENOUGH STOCK ON HAND
450   REM    CANCEL ORDER
470   REM
480   A2 = A2 + Q
490   PRINT "*** NOT SUFFICIENT STOCK *** ONLY ";A2;" UNITS ON HAND"
500   PRINT "SHIPMENT CANCELLED -- NOTIFY CUSTOMER"
510   GOTO 190
520   REM   RECEIPT TRANSACTION
530   REM
540   A2 = A2 + Q
560   PRINT D$;"WRITE INVMST,R";M
565   PRINT A1;",";A2;",";A3
568   PRINT D$
570   GOTO 190
580   REM
590   PRINT D$;"CLOSE INVMST"
600   STOP
63999   END
```

In the program, "INVMST" is opened. In line 230 the transaction code is input, followed by the test to end data input. The transaction part (record) number and quantity are input next in line 290. After reading the record from "INVMST", the test for the transaction code is at line 330. If the transaction is a shipment from inventory (code = 2), then lines 340 through 510 are executed. If there is enough stock on hand, A2, to make the required shipment, then the stock on hand is adjusted for the shipment in line 370: A2 = A2 − Q. If Q is greater than the stock on hand, A2, then the newly assigned value of A2 in line 370 will be negative. For example, the stock on hand is 20 and you wish to ship 30 units, there would be −10 units in stock on hand. Line 420 tests for this condition. If the condition (stock on hand is less than zero) exists, then the old value of stock on hand is replaced in line 480, A2 = A2 + Q, and the shipment is cancelled (lines 490 and 500).

If the transaction is a receipt to inventory (code = 1), then in line 540 the quantity received is added to the stock on hand, A2 = A2 + Q, and that record is written on "INVMST". Then another transaction code is entered.

The writing of the updated master record occurs at lines 560 and 565 where A2 is assigned a value contingent upon the transaction code and other tests. The update program uses the same concept as the program to change a record. As soon as a transaction is entered, the master record is updated. The last transaction will result in a shipment being cancelled.

After the update program is run with the transactions given in Table 9–4, run the program that prints the "INVMST" file. The file should look like Table 9–5.

A relative record master file is organized by ascending record number. The transactions may be entered in any order. The time required to update a master record is the same, regardless of its location in the file, because relative record files are one form of direct access files.

The "INVMST" File After Updating   Table 9–5

Part Number	Stock on Hand	Unit Cost
1	640	2.00
2	350	2.75
3	231	1.50
4	395	5.96
5	749	7.25
6	230	7.00
7	942	4.26
8	27	5.49
9	152	1.40
10	700	4.00

If transactions are entered from the two terminals in the inventory area as stock is received and shipped, then the master file is updated in real-time. Real-time updating means the master files contain the latest up-to-the-second information. This is especially important when dealing with inventory. In order to have real-time updating, direct access files must be used. Real-time updating may be contrasted with batch updating, which has a time cycle (a day, a week, or a month) for the running of the update program. The update programs in Chapter 7 were examples of batch updating. The transactions were accumulated in a file during the time cycle. Then they were sorted and the update program was run at the end of the cycle.

If the update is in real-time, then any time you retrieve and print a record of the master file, it contains the latest stock on hand. This is very useful when you consider that a company has a sales department. Salesmen need to know the latest inventory levels in order to give customers reasonable delivery dates. Assume, in our inventory example, that there is a third terminal in the sales department. When a salesman writes an order for a customer, he phones the sales department to determine whether sufficient stock is on hand to fill the order. The program that retrieves and prints master records is called a query program. "Query" is a short form for "inquire". The program is the same as the first part of the program for changing a record.

QUERYING RECORDS IN A RELATIVE RECORD FILE

Problem Summary

Input
   Part (record) number
   Inventory master file, "INVMST"
Processing
   Retrieve a master record.

Output
Print the appropriate master record.

```
100   REM    QUERY PROGRAM
110   REM
115 D$ =    CHR$ (4)
120   REM
130   REM   OPEN THE FILE
140   REM
150   PRINT D$;"OPEN INVMST,L16"
160   PRINT "WHAT IS THE PART NUMBER?"
170   PRINT "TYPE 9999 TO END"
180   INPUT R
190   REM
200   REM   TEST FOR END OF DATA INPUT
210   REM
220   IF R = 9999 THEN 330
230   PRINT D$;"READ INVMST,R";R
240   INPUT A1,A2,A3
250   PRINT D$
260   REM
270   REM  PRINT OUT RECORD
280   REM
290   PRINT "PART","STOCK","UNIT"
300   PRINT "NUMBER","ON HAND","COST"
310   PRINT A1,A2,A3
320   GOTO 160
330   PRINT D$;"CLOSE INVMST"
340   STOP
63999 END
```

```
WHAT IS THE PART NUMBER?
TYPE 9999 TO END
?9
PART              STOCK              UNIT
NUMBER            ON HAND            COST
9                 152                1.4
WHAT IS THE PART NUMBER?
TYPE 9999 TO END
?1
PART              STOCK              UNIT
NUMBER            ON HAND            COST
1                 640                2
WHAT IS THE PART NUMBER?
TYPE 9999 TO END
?5
PART              STOCK              UNIT
NUMBER            ON HAND            COST
5                 749                7.25
```

```
WHAT IS THE PART NUMBER?
TYPE 9999 TO END
?10
PART                STOCK               UNIT
NUMBER              ON HAND             COST
10                  700                 4
WHAT IS THE PART NUMBER?
TYPE 9999 TO END
?9999

BREAK IN 340
```

The sales department would run this program to see if a customer's order could be filled. In a sophisticated company, the salesman would have portable terminals that use a telephone to reach the computer. Also the programs would be more complex in order to allow a salesman to reserve stock and to ship partial orders.

SUMMARY

In this chapter one type of direct access file is introduced. The programs necessary to handle a relative record file were given. In essence, a relative record file can be treated as a table where the rows represent records and the columns represent fields. The example throughout this chapter was inventory, not payroll. Inventory was selected because it represents a good example of the requirement for real-time updating. The real-time example was illustrated by an update where, as soon as a transaction was generated, the master file was updated. The final section dealt with an inquiry program that reads and prints records from a relative record file.

BASIC Instructions Introduced:

Instruction	Explanation
PRINT D$; "OPEN filename,LXX"	Opens a relative record file with records of length XX.
PRINT D$; "READ filename,R";N	Reads relative record N
PRINT D$; "WRITE filename,R";N	Writes relative record N

PROBLEMS   1. Modify the first program in this chapter so that you can stop an input session and continue entering the data at any point in the file without having to re-enter all the earlier records. To test your program, create a file "I11".

2. Create a relative record file, "CUMST", with eight records as follows:

Customer Number	Current Balance
1	$257.26
2	194.40
3	276.00
4	0.00
5	51.27
6	29.32
7	426.25
8	972.36

3. Write a program that will print the "CUMST" file as described in Problem 2.

4. Write a program that will update the "CUMST" file. There are three types of transactions: payments, purchases, and returns. Payments should be subtracted from the current balance (Transaction code = 1). Purchases should be added to the current balance (TR CODE = 2). Returns should be subtracted from the current balance (TR CODE = 3). If customers have a current balance less than zero, a message should be printed to issue a refund check to the customer. Use the following transactions to test your program:

Transaction Code	Customer Number	Amount
1	5	51.27
1	1	200.00
2	4	57.26
1	3	250.00
2	8	320.21
3	5	23.27
1	2	194.40
2	1	72.73
3	7	157.29

5. Write an inquiry program for the "CUMST" file, so that customers may call and be given their latest balance.

10 / Use and Design of Complex Programs

At the end of this chapter you should be able to:

- Use "canned" programs
- Recognize the role of structured programming

Programming is the expensive aspect of computer systems. It is also the most time-consuming. Without programs the computer cannot solve problems. However, once a program has been written and debugged (i.e., the errors have been removed), then using these programs to help solve recurring problems is simple.

In progressing through this book, you have built a program library. If a problem should develop that is similar to those you've already solved, you don't have to write a brand new program. Merely modify the appropriate program to meet the new requirements and it can aid in arriving at a solution. In effect, your program library is a toolbox. Simple changes to your tools allow you to solve most data processing problems.

You may have access to programs other than those you've written. Any number of sources may have contributed skills and energies to fill your toolbox: the vendor of your computer system, an independent consultant, other people in your organization, or other organizations in your industry.

At times it is difficult to transfer programs from one system to another. The procedures and problems of one organization may not match the procedures and problems of another organization. In other cases the transfer of programs is easy. Statistical, scientific, and engineering programs transfer easily from one organization to another. No matter what organization uses them, the rules for performing statistical computations remain the same. The programming of natural laws is not affected by the organization involved. And mathematical calculations are not a matter of opinion or preference $(2 + 2 = 4$ no matter who is involved, where the calculation is performed, or what we wish the result to be). Therefore once a statistical, scientific, or engineering program has been written, it can be copied and used by many organizations.

This chapter discusses how to use programs that have been written elsewhere. A statistical program serves as an example of a "canned" program. The chapter also discusses some elements of style that make a program easier to read and modify.

Programs developed by one organization that are transferred as a whole to another organization are called "canned" or "packaged" programs. No modification of the program logic is involved, although some statements may have to be changed to fit your system.

Once the program has been changed so that it will run on another system, it can be used by anybody with access to that system. A person provides the problem context and the data, runs the appropriate program, and interprets the output. Problem specification, data collection, selection of an appropriate program for solution, and interpretation of output are the key elements for the successful use of canned programs. But these elements are beyond the scope of this book. Here we shall focus on how to enter the data and run a canned program.

Linear regression is a statistical technique for determining the relationship between two variables. (Regression analysis is covered in statistical textbooks.) LINREG is a program that performs linear regression. A copy of this program is shown below:

```
1    GOTO 630
200    DATA   7E22,5E22
205    READ Q1
210    DIM D(100,20)
215    PRINT
220 I = 0
225 I = I + 1
230    READ D(I,1),D(I,2)
235    IF D(I,1) <  > 7E22 THEN 225
240 Q2 = I - 1
245 S9 = 0
250    IF Q1 = 1 THEN 270
255    IF Q1 = 2 THEN 325
260    IF Q1 = 3 THEN 395
265    GOTO 220
270 S9 = 1
275    GOSUB 490
280    PRINT "LINEAR:    Y=A+B*X    WITH A=";Q8;" AND B=";Q9
285    GOSUB 565
290    FOR J = 1 TO Q2
295 W7 = Q8 + Q9 * D(J,1)
300 Z7 = W7 - D(J,2)
305 Q4 = 100 * Z7 / D(J,2)
310    PRINT D(J,1),D(J,2),W7,Z7,Q4
315    NEXT J
320    GOTO 999
325    FOR J = 1 TO Q2
330 D(J,2) =   LOG (D(J,2))
335    NEXT J
340    GOSUB 490
345    PRINT "EXPONENTIAL:    Y=A*EXP(B*X)    WITH A="; EXP (Q8);" AND B=";
350    GOSUB 565
355    FOR J = 1 TO Q2
360 W7 =   EXP (Q8 + Q9 * D(J,1))
365 W8 =   EXP (D(J,2))
370 Z7 = W7 - W8
375 Q4 = 100 * Z7 / W8
380    PRINT D(J,1),W8,W7,Z7,Q4
385    NEXT J
390    GOTO 999
395    FOR J = 1 TO Q2
```

```
D(J,1) =  LOG (D(J,1))
D(J,2) =  LOG (D(J,2))
 NEXT J
 GOSUB 490
 PRINT "POWER:    Y=A*(X^B)    WITH A="; EXP (Q8);" AND B=";Q9
 GOSUB 565
 FOR J = 1 TO Q2
W7 =  EXP (D(J,1))
W8 =  EXP (D(J,2))
W9 =  EXP (Q8) * W7 ^ Q9
Q4 = W9 / W8 - 1
Z7 = W9 - W8
 IF Q4 < 0 THEN 470
Q4 =  INT (1000 * Q4 + 0.5) / 10
 GOTO 475
Q4 =  INT (1000 * Q4 - 0.5) / 10
 PRINT W7,W8,W9,Z7,Q4
 NEXT J
 GOTO 999
Q3 = 0
Q4 = 0
Q5 = 0
Q6 = 0
Q7 = 0
 FOR J = 1 TO Q2
Q3 = Q3 + D(J,1)
Q4 = Q4 + D(J,2)
Q5 = Q5 + D(J,1) * D(J,2)
Q6 = Q6 + D(J,1) ^ 2
Q7 = Q7 + D(J,2) ^ 2
 NEXT J
Q9 = (Q2 * Q5 - Q3 * Q4) / (Q2 * Q6 - Q3 ^ 2)
Q8 = (Q4 - Q3 * Q9) / Q2
 RETURN
Q0 = (Q2 * Q5 - Q3 * Q4) /  SQR ((Q2 * Q6 - Q3 ^ 2) * (Q2 * Q7 - Q4 ^ 2))
 PRINT
 IF S9 = 0 THEN 590
 PRINT "COEFFICIENTS:   ";
 GOTO 595
 PRINT "INDICIES:    ";
 PRINT "CORREL = ";Q0;"    DETERM = ";Q0 ^ 2
 PRINT
 PRINT "COMPARISON OF ACTUAL Y'S WITH Y'S ESTIMATED FROM EQUATION: "
 PRINT
 PRINT "X-ACTUAL","Y-ACTUAL","Y-ESTIM","DIFFER","PCT-DIFF"
 PRINT
 RETURN
 PRINT
 PRINT "THIS IS A LINEAR REGRESSION PROGRAM FOR DATA IN TWO"
 PRINT "VARIABLES, X AND Y.  FROM INPUT POINTS, DESCRIBED BY"
 PRINT "THEIR X AND Y COORDINATES, AN EQUATION IS PRODUCED THAT"
 PRINT "BEST FITS THESE POINTS IN THE LEAST-SQUARES SENSE.  TO"
```

```
655    PRINT "USE THE PROGRAM, TYPE THE FOLLOWING:"
660    PRINT
665    PRINT "      1 DATA K"
670    PRINT "            (WHERE K=1 FOR LINEAR, 2 FOR EXPONENTIAL,"
675    PRINT "            AND 3 FOR POWER FUNCTION TO BE FITTED.)"
680    PRINT "      2 DATA X(1),Y(1),X(2),Y(2),.....,X(N),Y(N)"
685    PRINT "            (WHERE X(1),Y(1) IS THE FIRST POINT, X(2),"
690    PRINT "            Y(2) IS THE SECOND AND SO ON UNTIL ALL"
695    PRINT "            POINTS HAVE BEEN ENTERED.  ADDITIONAL DATA"
700    PRINT "            STATEMENTS 3-199 MAY BE USED AS NEEDED.)"
705    PRINT
710    PRINT "THEN TYPE 'RUN'."
999    STOP
63999  END
```

You can use LINREG by calling it up (LOAD LINREG), entering your data, and typing RUN. But data entry for LINREG, as well as many similar programs, is different from how it was handled in earlier parts of this book. Data is entered with DATA statements that are part of the program. LINREG provides instructions for entering data:

```
LOAD LINREG

RUN

THIS IS A LINEAR REGRESSION PROGRAM FOR DATA IN TWO
VARIABLES, X AND Y.  FROM INPUT POINTS, DESCRIBED BY
THEIR X AND Y COORDINATES, AN EQUATION IS PRODUCED THAT
BEST FITS THESE POINTS IN THE LEAST-SQUARES SENSE.  TO
USE THE PROGRAM, TYPE THE FOLLOWING:

    1 DATA K
            (WHERE K=1 FOR LINEAR, 2 FOR EXPONENTIAL,
            AND 3 FOR POWER FUNCTION TO BE FITTED.)
    2 DATA X(1),Y(1),X(2),Y(2),.....,X(N),Y(N)
            (WHERE X(1),Y(1) IS THE FIRST POINT, X(2),
            Y(2) IS THE SECOND AND SO ON UNTIL ALL
            POINTS HAVE BEEN ENTERED.  ADDITIONAL DATA
            STATEMENTS 3-199 MAY BE USED AS NEEDED.)

THEN TYPE 'RUN'.
```

This RUN shows what has to be entered in DATA statements. A DATA statement is a non-executable BASIC instruction that holds data for a program. It starts with a line number, the word DATA, and then the individual data values separated by commas. For example:

$$1 \text{ DATA } 3.7, 4.2, 3.9, 2.5, 6$$

The DATA statement holds five values. They may be the values for five fields of a record, or they may be five values for one field. Either way, DATA statements hold a stream of values that are used one after another.

Data values in DATA statements are assigned to fields by READ statements. Look at LINREG, line 205 and line 230. Both contain the BASIC instruction READ. Line 205, READ Q1, being the first READ, assigns the first value found in any DATA statements to Q1. Line 230, READ D(I,1),D(I,2), assigns the next data value to D(I,1) and the following value to D(I,2).

Once an item of data has been assigned, the next READ uses the item of data that follows. Every READ "uses up" data values. Although data can be distributed over many DATA statements, they must follow the *order* of the READ statements. The READ statements follow the stream of data, using up data values in sequence.

Now we can run LINREG. First, call up the program. Then enter the data as specified by the instructions:

```
1    DATA    1
2    DATA    719,3756
3    DATA    1384,5100
4    DATA    995,4950
5    DATA    231,894
6    DATA    462,480
7    DATA    486,1908
8    DATA    1299,5388
9    DATA    233,240
10   DATA    189,468
11   DATA    759,1662
12   DATA    112,96
13   DATA    1252,5334
14   DATA    677,786
15   DATA    295,648
```

Then type the word "RUN", and it generates the output.

```
LINEAR:    Y=A+B*X    WITH A=-662.487627 AND B=4.50729427

COEFFICIENTS:   CORREL = .927247143   DETERM = .859787265

COMPARISON OF ACTUAL Y'S WITH Y'S ESTIMATED FROM EQUATION:
```

X-ACTUAL	Y-ACTUAL	Y-ESTIM	DIFFER	PCT-DIFF
719	3756	2578.25695	-1177.74305	-31.3563112
1384	5100	5575.60764	475.607639	9.32563999
995	4950	3822.27017	-1127.72983	-22.7824208
231	894	378.697349	-515.302651	-57.6401176
462	480	1419.88232	939.882325	195.808818
486	1908	1528.05739	-379.942613	-19.9131348
1299	5388	5192.48763	-195.512373	-3.6286632
233	240	387.711938	147.711938	61.5466407

189	468	189.39099	−278.60901	−59.5318398
759	1662	2758.54872	1096.54872	65.9776608
112	96	−157.670669	−253.670669	−264.24028
1252	5334	4980.6448	−353.355204	−6.62458199
677	786	2388.95059	1602.95059	203.937734
295	648	667.164183	19.1641822	2.95743552

BREAK IN 999

The interpretation of this output and its use in decision making will determine the value of LINREG. But that aspect is peripheral to our focus. Notice how easy it is to use the program: Enter the data, type run, and the program can generate reams upon reams of output.

Other statistical programs are just as easy to use. Just enter the data and the program does the rest. It is not necessary to know anything about statistics or about computer programming to use these programs for analysis. Therein lies the power, as well as the danger, of using computers. Anybody, whether knowledgeable in the technique used or not, has the technique available if he can enter data and type RUN. But knowledge of the problem context, of the validity of the data, and of the technique of analysis is required to derive the proper conclusions from such use of canned programs.

Another example of a canned program is the file sort in Appendix B. Again, the detailed instructions of the program are unimportant. What is important is knowing how to use it properly to do the desired job.

Similar to canned programs, but at a much lower level, are functions. Functions perform one specific task in a program. For example, the INT function used in Chapter 6, gives the integer portion of a number. Functions are usually indicated by a three-letter keyword. Table 10-1 lists the mathematical functions available in BASIC.

STRUCTURED PROGRAMMING

Structured programming is a systematic way of designing a program. It is a philosophy of design to make a program readable and easy to change.

Structured programming breaks a program into a number of pieces, called modules. Each module performs one task. Since the modules are smaller than the whole program, each piece is easier to understand, easier to code, and easier to change. But breaking a program into modules requires planning. Structured programming emphasizes planning of what a program does and how its modules are related. All modules should be clearly specified before coding. All variables should be clearly defined and their roles in the various modules identified. Obviously this planning is not cheap and requires careful coordination between programmers.

Structured programming recognizes three types of sequences of instruc-

Mathematical Functions   Table 10–1

Function*	Explanation
Y = ABS(X)	Assigns to Y the absolute value of X.
Y = ATN(X)	Assigns to Y the arc tangent of X; Y is expressed in radians.
Y = COS(X)	Assigns to Y the cosine of X; X is in radians.
Y = EXP(X)	Assigns to Y the value of e raised to the X power; where e is 2.71828.
Y = INT(X)	Assigns to Y the greatest integer in X which is less than or equal to X.
Y = LOG(X)	Assigns to Y the natural logarithm of X.
Y = RND(X)	Assigns to Y a random number uniformly distributed between 0 and 1.
Y = SGN(X)	Assigns to Y the value 1 preceded by the sign of X.
Y = SIN(X)	Assigns to Y the sine of X; X is in radians.
Y = SQR(X)	Assigns to Y the square root of X.
Y = TAN(X)	Assigns to Y the tangent of X; X is in radians.

* Y stands for the name of any field; and X can be a field or a formula, but must be enclosed in parentheses.

tions—simple sequence, selection, and looping. Any program can be composed using one or a combination of these elementary types. For example:

Simple sequence

```
100 LET R = 3.00
110 LET H = 40
120 LET P = R*H
130 PRINT P
```

Selection	100 IF T = 2 THEN 300
Alternative 1	200 Q2 = Q2 + Q1
(false)	210 GO TO 400
Alternative 2	300 Q2 = Q2 − Q1
(true)	400 ....
Loop	100 FOR R1 = 1 TO 8
	⋮
	200 NEXT R1

A simple sequence has no GO TO. Each statement follows the preceding statement until the sequence is finished.

A selection consists of an IF–THEN and its two possible groups of instructions. One of these two possible groups is selected when the IF–THEN is true. The other is selected when the IF–THEN is false.

A loop repeats a group of instructions until a specified condition has been met.

Of course the alternatives of a selection or the group of instructions in a loop may contain subsidiary selections or loops. Ideally each type of module should have one entry and one exit with no backtracking. The flow of a program should be top to bottom (except for loops.) GO TO's that jump back to previously executed code should be eliminated.

To clarify the relationship between the elements of a program, structured programming uses indentations and additional comments (REM statements) to highlight the structure of a program. Indentation shows which elements fit together. Comments aid in understanding both the logic (what the program does) and the structure (how the program is organized.)

Let's look at some examples to clarify these ideas. First, look at the SORT program in Chapter 8. It performs three major tasks that can be diagrammed as follows in Figure 10–1.

This program can be rewritten to make the structure stand out. A rewritten version follows:

```
100   REM   ************************************************************
110   REM   * PROGRAM NAME: LIST SORT                                  *
120   REM   *                                                          *
130   REM   * THIS PROGRAM --                                          *
140   REM   *   1. GETS DATA FROM A TERMINAL AND STORES THEM IN        *
150   REM   *      LISTS                                               *
160   REM   *   2. SORTS THE LISTS IN DESCENDING ORDER OF NET PAY      *
170   REM   *   3. PRINTS THE SORTED LISTS                             *
180   REM   *                                                          *
190   REM   * PROGRAMMER NAME: A.N.LYST                                *
200   REM   * DATE: APRIL 1, 1979                                      *
```

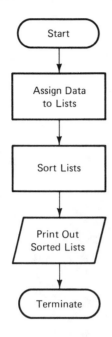

SORT Program

Figure 10-1

```
210   REM   *                                                        *
220   REM   * FIELD NAMES:                                           *
230   REM   *    F......EXCHANGE FLAG -- SET TO 1 WHEN AN            *
240   REM   *           EXCHANGE HAS OCCURRED; 0 OTHERWISE           *
250   REM   *    K......INDEX OF FOR-NEXT LOOP                       *
260   REM   *    L......POINTER TO A LOCATION IN A LIST DURING       *
270   REM   *           DATA ENTRY; THE NUMBER OF ITEMS IN A LIST    *
280   REM   *           AFTER DATA ENTRY                             *
290   REM   *    M$.....EMPLOYEE NAME ENTERED FROM TERMINAL          *
300   REM   *    N()....LIST TO HOLD EMPLOYEE NUMBER                 *
310   REM   *    N1.....EMPLOYEE NUMBER ENTERED FROM TERMINAL        *
320   REM   *    N$()...LIST TO HOLD EMPLOYEE NAME                   *
330   REM   *    P()....LIST TO HOLD EMPLOYEE NET PAY                *
340   REM   *    P1.....EMPLOYEE NET PAY ENTERED FROM TERMINAL       *
350   REM   *    T......TEMPORARY STORAGE OF A NUMERIC VALUE         *
360   REM   *           DURING AN EXCHANGE                           *
370   REM   *    T$.....TEMPORARY STORAGE OF EMPLOYEE NAME           *
380   REM   *           DURING AN EXCHANGE                           *
390   REM   *********************************************************
400   REM
410   DIM N(100),N$(100),P(100)
420   REM
430   REM  GET DATA FROM TERMINAL AND PUT THEM INTO THE LISTS
440   REM
450 L = 0
```

```
460    REM  *** BEGIN DATA ENTRY LOOP
470    PRINT "TYPE EMPLOYEE NUMBER, EMPLOYEE NAME,"
480    PRINT "AND NET PAY -- SEPARATED BY COMMAS."
490    PRINT "WHEN FINISHED -- TYPE 99,AA,99"
500    INPUT N1,M$,P1
510    REM  -----> EXIT FROM LOOP WHEN DATA ENTRY FINISHED
520    IF N1 = 99 THEN 640
530    REM  ASSIGN DATA TO ARRAYS
540    L = L + 1
550    N(L) = N1
560 N$(L) = M$
570    P(L) = P1
580    REM  *** ENDIF 520
590    GOTO 470
600    REM  *** END DATA ENTRY LOOP
610    REM
620    REM  SORT THE LISTS INTO DESCENDING NET PAY ORDER
630    REM
640    U = L - 1
650    REM  *** BEGIN SORT LOOP
660 F = 0
670    FOR K = 1 TO U
680    REM
690    REM  COMPARE TO ADJACENT VALUES OF NET PAY
700    REM  IF THEY ARE NOT IN ORDER, EXCHANGE THEM
710    REM
720    IF P(K) >  = P(K + 1) THEN 900
730    REM
740    REM      NET PAY VALUES OUT OF SEQUENCE, HENCE EXCHANGE
750    REM
760 T = P(K)
770 P(K) = P(K + 1)
780 P(K + 1) = T
790 T = N(K)
800 N(K) = N(K + 1)
810 N(K + 1) = T
820 T$ = N$(K)
830 N$(K) = N$(K + 1)
840 N$(K + 1) = T$
850    REM
860    REM        SET EXCHANGE FLAG (F) TO 1
870    REM
880 F = 1
890    REM    *** ENDIF 720
900    NEXT K
910    REM  -----> EXIT FROM SORT LOOP WHEN F=0
920    IF F = 1 THEN 660
930    REM  *** END SORT LOOP
940    REM
950    REM  PRINT HEADINGS AND SORTED LISTS
960    REM
970    PRINT "EMPLOYEE","EMPLOYEE","WEEKLY"
```

```
980   PRINT "NUMBER","NAME","PAY"
990   PRINT "------","----","---"
1000  REM  *** BEGIN PRINT LOOP
1010  FOR K = 1 TO L
1020  PRINT N(K),N$(K),P(K)
1030  NEXT K
1040  REM  *** END PRINT LOOP
1050  END
```

As another example, compare the inventory update in Chapter 7 on page 179 with the structured version of the same program shown below.

```
100  REM   **************************************************************
110  REM   * PROGRAM NAME: INVENTORY UPDATE                            *
120  REM   *                                                           *
130  REM   * THIS PROGRAM --                                           *
140  REM   *   1. UPDATES THE OLD INVENTORY MASTER FILE:               *
150  REM   *         READS INVENTORY TRANSACTION RECORDS               *
160  REM   *         READS OLD INVENTORY MASTER RECORDS                *
170  REM   *         UPDATES MASTER RECORDS WITH TRANSACTIONS          *
180  REM   *         WRITES NEW (UPDATED) MASTER RECORDS               *
190  REM   *   2. PRINTS THE NEW (UPDATED) MASTER FILE                 *
200  REM   *   3. PRINTS AN INVENTORY VALUATION REPORT                 *
210  REM   *                                                           *
220  REM   * PROGRAMMER NAME: P. GRAMMER                               *
230  REM   * DATE: APRIL 1, 1980                                       *
240  REM   *                                                           *
250  REM   * FIELD NAMES:                                              *
260  REM   *    C....UNIT COST OF PART INPUT FROM UPDATED MASTER       *
270  REM   *    C2...UNIT COST OF PART INPUT FROM OLD MASTER FILE      *
280  REM   *    D....DOLLAR VALUE OF PART                              *
290  REM   *    P....PART NUMBER INPUT FROM UPDATED MASTER FILE        *
300  REM   *    P1...PART NUMBER INPUT FROM TRANSACTION FILE           *
310  REM   *    P2...PART NUMBER INPUT FROM OLD MASTER FILE            *
320  REM   *    Q....QUANTITY ON HAND INPUT FROM UPDATED MASTER        *
330  REM   *    Q1...QUANTITY OF TRANSACTION INPUT FROM                *
340  REM   *         TRANSACTION FILE                                  *
350  REM   *    Q2...QUANTITY ON HAND INPUT FROM TRANSACTION FILE      *
360  REM   *    T....TOTAL DOLLAR VALUE OF INVENTORY                   *
370  REM   *    T1...TRANSACTION CODE INPUT FROM TRANSACTION FILE      *
380  REM   *         CODE VALUES:  1 = RECEIPT                         *
390  REM   *                       2 = ISSUE                           *
400  REM   **************************************************************
410  REM
420  ONERR  GOTO 1710
445  D$ =  CHR$ (4)
450  REM
460  REM   LINK TO FILES
470  REM
480  PRINT D$;"OPEN INVTR"
490  PRINT D$;"OPEN INVMR"
```

```
500    PRINT D$;"OPEN INVSN"
510    REM
520    REM   READ A TRANSACTION RECORD
530    REM
540    PRINT D$;"READ INVTR"
545    INPUT P1,T1,Q1
550    REM
560    REM   READ A MASTER RECORD
570    REM
580    PRINT D$;"READ INVMR"
585    INPUT P2,Q2,C2
590    REM  *** BEGIN UPDATE LOOP
600    REM
610    REM   IF TRANSACTION EQUALS MASTER
620    REM
630    IF P1 = P2 THEN 670
640    GOTO 820
650    REM      THEN UPDATE MASTER
660    REM       IF TRANSACTION IS A RECEIPT
670    IF T1 = 1 THEN 700
680    GOTO 730
690    REM       THEN ADD TRANSACTION QUANTITY TO QUANTITY ON HAND
700 Q2 = Q2 + Q1
710    GOTO 780
720    REM       ELSE SUBTRACT QUANTITY FROM QUANTITY ON HAND
730 Q2 = Q2 - Q1
740    REM       ***ENDIF 670
750    REM
760    REM       READ A TRANSACTION RECORD
770    REM
780    PRINT D$;"READ INVTR"
785    INPUT P1,T1,Q1
790    REM  -----> EXIT WHEN OUT OF TRANSACTION RECORDS
800    GOTO 630
810    REM       ELSE IF TRANSACTION GREATER THAN MASTER
820    IF P1 > P2 THEN 850
830    GOTO 960
840    REM       THEN WRITE UPDATED MASTER
850    PRINT D$;"WRITE INVSN"
855    PRINT P2;",";Q2;",";C2
860    REM
870    REM       READ A MASTER RECORD
880    REM
890    PRINT D$;"READ INVMR"
895    INPUT P2,Q2,C2
900    REM  ------> EXIT WHEN OUT OF MASTER RECORDS
910    GOTO 630
920    REM       ELSE TRANSACTION LESS THAN MASTER
930    REM
940    REM       WRITE ERROR MESSAGE -- NO MASTER IN FILE
950    REM
```

```
960     PRINT D$
965     PRINT "***TRANSACTION WITHOUT MASTER ";P1,T1,Q1
970     REM
980     REM       READ A TRANSACTION RECORD
990     REM
1000    PRINT D$;"READ INVTR"
1005    INPUT P1,T1,Q1
1010    REM     *** ENDIF 820
1020    REM   -----> EXIT WHEN OUT OF TRANSACTION RECORDS
1030    GOTO 630
1040    REM       *** END UPDATE LOOP
1050    REM
1060    REM       TRANSFER REMAINING RECORDS FROM OLD TO NEW MASTER
1070    REM
1080    REM       *** BEGIN TRANSFER LOOP
1090    PRINT D$;"WRITE INVSN"
1095    PRINT P2;",";Q2;",";C2
1100    PRINT D$;"READ INVMR"
1105    INPUT P2,Q2,C2
1110    REM   ------> EXIT WHEN OUT OF MASTER RECORDS
1120    GOTO 1090
1130    REM       *** END TRANSFER LOOP
1140    REM
1150    REM       PRINT THE UPDATED MASTER FILE
1160    REM
1170    PRINT D$;"CLOSE INVTR"
1172    PRINT D$;"CLOSE INVMR"
1174    PRINT D$;"CLOSE INVSN"
1180    PRINT D$;"OPEN INVSN"
1190    REM
1200    REM       HEADINGS FOR UPDATED FILE
1210    REM
1220    PRINT
1230    PRINT "   NEW INVENTORY MASTER FILE"
1240    PRINT "   ------------------------"
1250    PRINT
1260    PRINT "PARTS","UNITS","COST"
1270    PRINT "NUMBER","ON HAND"
1280    PRINT "------","-------","----"
1290    REM *** BEGIN PRINT LOOP
1300    PRINT D$;"READ INVSN"
1305    INPUT P,Q,C
1308    PRINT D$
1310    PRINT P,Q,C
1320    REM   ------> EXIT WHEN OUT OF NEW MASTER RECORDS
1330    GOTO 1300
1340    REM *** END PRINT LOOP
1350    REM
1360    REM   PRINT INVENTORY VALUATION REPORT
1370    REM
1380    PRINT D$;"CLOSE INVSN"
```

```
1390    PRINT D$;"OPEN INVSN"
1400    REM
1410    REM  HEADINGS FOR VALUATION REPORT
1420    REM
1430    PRINT
1440    PRINT
1450    PRINT " INVENTORY VALUATION REPORT"
1460    PRINT " --------------------------"
1470    PRINT
1480    PRINT "PART","DOLLAR"
1490    PRINT "NUMBER","AMOUNT"
1500    PRINT "------","------"
1510    REM
1520 T = 0
1530    REM  *** BEGIN INVENTORY VALUATION LOOP
1540    PRINT D$;"READ INVSN"
1545    INPUT P,Q,C
1548    PRINT D$
1550 D = Q * C
1560 T = T + D
1570    PRINT P,D
1580    REM  ------> EXIT WHEN OUT OF DATA
1590    GOTO 1540
1600    REM  *** END INVENTORY VALUATION LOOP
1610    REM
1620    REM  PRINT TOTAL VALUATION
1630    REM
1640    PRINT D$
1645    PRINT "------------------------"
1650    PRINT "TOTAL",T
1660    PRINT D$;"CLOSE INVSN"
1670    GOTO 1800
1680    REM  ******************************
1690    REM  *** ERROR CHECKING ROUTINES ***
1700    REM  ******************************
1710    PRINT D$
1715 Y =  PEEK (222)
1720    IF Y = 5 THEN 1760
1725    PRINT "UNUSUAL ERROR",Y
1730    PRINT D$;"CLOSE INVTR"
1732    PRINT D$;"CLOSE INVMR"
1734    PRINT D$;"CLOSE INVSN"
1740    STOP
1750    REM
1760 L =  PEEK (218) + 256 *  PEEK (219)
1765    IF L = 785 THEN 1090
1770    IF L = 1105 THEN 1170
1780    IF L = 1305 THEN 1380
1790    IF L = 1545 THEN 1640
1800    STOP
63999 END
```

In both of the structured programming examples all THEN's and GOTO's should be printed at the far right hand side of the line on which they appear. Since the Apple packs all BASIC instruction lines to the far left, it was not possible to make the programs look more like "normal" structured programs.

Now make your evaluations. Which of the two versions of a program did you find easier to understand? In your opinion, which was easier to write? Since REM statements make a program larger and take time to write and enter (they only exist for the benefit of the reader—the computer ignores them), consider the following: Is the cost in time, effort, and added storage requirements less than, equal to, or greater than the benefit of readability? Only you can make that decision for yourself and your organization.

BASIC Instructions Introduced: SUMMARY

Instruction	Explanation
READ X,Y,Z	Assigns values to fields from DATA statements (X,Y,Z are arbitrary field names)
DATA 5,2,7	Used to hold data for fields in READ statements

11 / Advanced Concepts

At the end of this chapter you should be able to:

- Use full screen editing
- Use the graphics capability on the Apple
- Use EXEC files
- Format reports

Editing consists of changing data or programs once they are in the computer. From your first introduction to BASIC, you realize that the editing of programs is a very important function. Until that happy day when you no longer make errors in typing or logic, editing will continue to be one of the most important and often used functions of the computer.

On the simplest level, editing in BASIC is predicated on line numbers and consists of the ability to: (1) Replace a line (by retyping it), (2) Delete a line (by typing its number followed by a return), and (3) Insert a line between two existing lines (by giving it an appropriate line number). These editing functions work because of the way in which the Apple responds to a LIST or RUN. In either case, the Apple will arrange all lines in ascending order of line number before obeying the command given. If it encounters a second reference to the same line number, it forgets about the first reference. Because of this, it does not matter in what order you enter your BASIC program as long as the line numbers are chosen so that their value indicates where each goes logically. For example:

If You Enter	The Apple Uses
100 END	40 FOR I=1 TO 5
50 PRINT I	50 PRINT I
40 FOR I=1 TO 5	60 NEXT I
60 NEXT I	63999 END
63999 END	
100	

While you can accomplish any editing task using only simple editing, there are easier, less time consuming ways to get most jobs done.

A very powerful editing technique available on the Apple is known as *full screen editing*. Full screen editing gives you the capability of entering anything that is currently displayed on the screen (or a modification of anything displayed) without retyping it. This capability is very useful when: (1) You have just entered a long, complicated line and realize toward the end that there is a mistake toward the beginning; (2) You wish to modify a program and change the name of a field or file each time that it occurs; and (3) You have several similar statements to type, such as OPENing or CLOSEing a file.

Full screen editing is based on the ability to control the cursor (that blinking, white block that always indicates where the next character is going to be typed on the screen). There are two situations in which you need to move the cursor: (1) You wish to position the cursor at a particular point on the screen where you wish to perform an edit, and (2) You wish to move the cursor over a string of characters on the screen with the same effect as though you had just typed them.

In the first case (*positioning*), you must use the escape (ESC) key followed by an A to move one space to the right (ignoring any characters overtyped), a B to move one space to the left, a C to move one line down and a D to move one line up. To move the cursor several positions, you must type ESC followed by the appropriate letter, ESC letter, etc.

Once the cursor is positioned at the desired location (normally at the beginning of the line to be edited), the forward ($\rightarrow$) and backward ($\leftarrow$) arrows are used to move the cursor over the characters to be entered or deleted. Any character to be corrected is simply retyped. When the line is correct, type RETURN and the new line will be entered into your program just as though you had typed it from scratch.

As an example, suppose that you typed the following line and have not yet pressed RETURN (the position of the cursor is indicated by a +):

$$]10 \; A=2.141592654*R^2+$$

You notice that the first digit in the number should have been a "3" instead of a "2". To correct this problem, use the $\leftarrow$ to backspace the cursor until it is positioned on top of the "2". Type "3" and then use the $\rightarrow$ to move the cursor over the rest of the line. Then press RETURN.

In this example, it was not necessary to retype any character but the incorrect one. Since the rest of the line was already displayed on the screen, you just had to run the cursor over it and hit RETURN.

As a second example of full screen editing, suppose that you have typed the same line as above, but have already hit the RETURN. What you see on the screen is:

$$]10 \; A=2.141592654*R^2$$

$$]+$$

In this case the cursor must be positioned before the arrows can be used. Since the cursor is now under the "1", it is necessary to move it up two lines. Do this by typing ESC D,ESC D. It should now be on top of the "1". Use the $\rightarrow$ to run the cursor over until it is on top of the "2", type "3", and continue with $\rightarrow$ to cover the rest of the line. Then type RETURN. You have just corrected and reentered line 10 with a minimum of effort.

Consider now the situation in which three files "EMPLOY", "EMPTRA" and "EMPMA1" must be opened in a program. You may, of course, type all three OPEN statements, or you can use full screen editing to make the job easier. To do so, type the first OPEN statement as follows:

]10 PRINT D$; "OPEN EMPLOY"

]+

Now type ESC D twice to position the cursor on top of the "1", type "2" (to change the line number), and use the → to run the cursor over to the "L" in EMPLOY. Type "TRA", hit the → once to pick up the quotation mark, then RETURN. You have just entered the line 20 PRINT D$;"OPEN EMPTRA". Use the same technique to enter line 30 PRINT D$;"OPEN EMPMA1". Type LIST to make sure that all is well.

As a final example, suppose that you have a program in memory with the following typing error in line 10:

10 PNT A,B$,C

To correct this problem, first LIST 10 to display the bad line. You will see:

]LIST

10 PNTA,B$,C

]+

Notice in this case that the cursor is below the "0" because of the prompt character. Type ESC D,ESC D,ESC B to position the cursor on top of the "1" and use the → to run over to a position on top of the "N" in PNT. Now type ESC D to move the cursor up above the line, type "RI' to insert the missing characters in the word PRINT, then type ESC C,ESC B,ESC B to reposition the cursor back over the "N" in PNT. Now use the → to complete the line as before. Notice that it does not matter that what you see on the screen seems meaningless. What matters is the sequence of characters that you run the cursor over or type. Remember that characters covered using the ESC are ignored. A little practice with full screen editing will give you a tool that will save many hours of needless typing.

Most large computers have editing software (programs) as their principal form of editing. These powerful programs allow you to: (1) Enter programs; (2) Delete, replace, and insert whole lines; (3) Delete, replace, and insert text within a line without retyping it; and (4) Search a specified group of lines (or the whole program) for each occurrence of a particular series of characters and leave the series as is, change it, or delete it as you wish. The computer term for a series of characters is a *string*. Since alphabetic fields are nothing more than series of characters, they are called strings. This last feature is extremely useful. If you have this capability, then you can do any edit with a minimum of effort.

The Apple has both full screen editing and editing software available. The editing software, however, must be purchased separately.

The two principal editing programs on the Apple are the PROGRAM LINE EDITOR distributed by SYNERGISTIC SOFTWARE and the APPLE WRITER distributed by Apple. The PROGRAM LINE EDITOR is primarily oriented toward editing single lines at a time. Within a line, most of the editing functions mentioned above can be performed.

The APPLE WRITER is the most general editor currently available on the Apple. It is a word processor and cannot be used to edit BASIC programs. All of the editing functions mentioned above and many others are available in APPLE WRITER. With it you can move text from one location in a file to another location, insert files of text into a document, delete individual words or lines or paragraphs, and print out the resulting text on a printer with titles, automatically incrementing page numbers, etc. The APPLE WRITER is a very powerful program for editing papers, books, etc.

GRAPHICS ON THE APPLE

The situation often arises in business in which you would like to present some data in graphical form. Graphs of sales, inventory levels, production, etc., are commonly done. The Apple has considerable graphics capability built into the BASIC language. Consider the situation in which you would like to graph sales figures for the last 24 months. The following program solves this problem and illustrates the principal statements involved in low resolution graphics, one of the two graphics modes available on the Apple.

In low resolution graphics mode, the Apple separates the screen into a 40 column by 40 row graphics pad at the top and four lines of text at the bottom. The BASIC statement GR in line 120 accomplishes this division and initializes the graphics mode.

Any point on the graphics pad can be referenced by giving its column and row position. The upper lefthand corner is column 0 and row 0 (referred to as 0,0), the lower left is 0,39, etc. Before a point can be plotted or a line can be drawn, its color must be specified. Low resolution graphics allows 16 colors. They are:

0	Black	8	Brown
1	Magenta	9	Orange
2	Dark Blue	10	Grey
3	Purple	11	Pink
4	Dark Green	12	Green
5	Grey	13	Yellow
6	Medium Blue	14	Aqua
7	Light Blue	15	White

In line 130 of the program, the color dark blue (2) is selected.

Output from Low Resolution Graphics Example   Figure 11-1

```
100   REM   PROGRAM TO ILLUSTRATE LOW RESOLUTION GRAPHICS
110   REM
115   REM   INITIALIZE LOW RES GRAPHICS
118   REM   SET COLOR TO DARK BLUE
120   GR
130   COLOR= 2
140   REM   DRAW BORDER AROUND SCREEN
150   REM
160   HLIN 0,39 AT 0: HLIN 0,39 AT 39
170   VLIN 0,39 AT 0: VLIN 0,39 AT 39
180   REM   SET COLOR TO ORANGE FOR PLOTTING
190   REM
200   COLOR= 9
210   REM   READ 24 MONTHS OF SALES DATA AND DRAW BAR GRAPH
220   REM
230   FOR I = 1 TO 24
240   READ X
245 P = 38 * X / 34
250   VLIN 38,(39 - P) AT I
260   NEXT I
270   DATA   12,15,18,27,31,26,17,21,34,7,11,24
280   DATA   14,16,20,25,32,28,18,23,30,10,13,28
63999  END
```

Now that the graphics mode is initialized and a color has been selected, you are ready to plot points or draw lines on the graphics pad. In line 160, two horizontal lines (HLIN) are drawn. The first extends from column 0 to column 39 in row 0. In effect this line forms the top border of the graphics pad. The second HLIN statement draws the bottom border of the pad. The statements in line 170 finish drawing the borders by filling in first the left, then the right border. From this you can see just how easy it is to use low resolution graphics. All you have to do is figure out where you wish to draw a line and the Apple does the rest. Plotting points is even easier. Just type PLOT followed by a point reference. For example, PLOT 20,30 will plot a single point at the intersection of column 20 and row 30.

Let's get back to our program. We have drawn the borders of the graph so far. What is necessary now is to read each sales figure, scale it so that it will fit on the graph (remember the largest bar we can draw without running into bottom or top borders is 38 blocks high), and then plot it. Lines 230 through 260 accomplish this. In line 240 a value is read into the field X. Line 245 scales this value so that the largest value of X (34 in this example) will require a 38 block bar (the largest possible). This scaling statement will work no matter what size the data are. If they are small, the statement will expand them to occupy the space available. If they are large, it will shrink them to fit.

Line 250 is the trickiest line in the program. It is the line that draws the lines that form the bars on the graph. Because we have already used up row 39 as part of the border, the first block in any bar will be in row 38. Let's suppose that we have a bar 10 blocks high to draw. Such a bar would extend from row 38 to row 29 in its column. In general, it would extend from row 38 through row (39-P) in column I. That is exactly what the statement in line 245 says. This statement is only complicated because the graphics pad on the Apple is upside down from the way in which you are used to seeing a graph. When you studied graphs in school, the origin (the 0,0 point) was always in the lower left corner, not in the upper left corner as the Apple sees it.

As a variation to this program, try replacing line 250 with the statement PLOT I,(39-P). This gives a similar graph except that only the points on the top of the bars are plotted.

When you are finished viewing the results of a low resolution graphics run, type TEXT to return the screen to normal. Even after typing TEXT, there is a lot of garbage left on the screen. To get a nice, clear screen, type escape (ESC) followed by a shift-P and then RETURN.

High resolution graphics is similar in concept to low resolution graphics. The main difference is that the high resolution graphics pad is 280 columns by 160 rows. This allows much finer work to be done including lines connecting any two points on the graphics pad, not just horizontal and vertical lines. The following program shows how high resolution graphics might be used in the previous example.

This high resolution example is very similar to the low resolution example given above. The major differences are due to the increased number of points on the graphics pad.

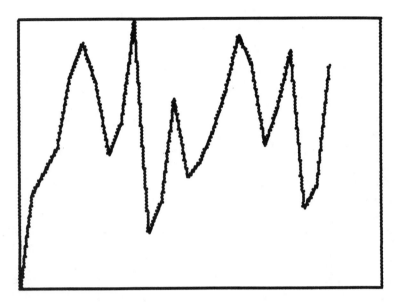

Output from High Resolution Graphics Example   Figure 11–2

```
100  REM    PROGRAM TO ILLUSTRATE HIGH RESOLUTION GRAPHICS
110  REM
115  REM    INITIALIZE HIGH RES GRAPHICS
118  REM    SET COLOR TO WHITE
120  HGR
130  HCOLOR= 7
140  REM    DRAW BORDER AROUND SCREEN
150  REM
160  HPLOT 0,0 TO 279,0: HPLOT 0,159 TO 279,159
170  HPLOT 0,0 TO 0,159: HPLOT 279,0 TO 279,159
190  REM
200  HPLOT 1,158
210  REM  READ 24 MONTHS OF SALES DATA AND DRAW BAR GRAPH
220  REM
230  FOR I = 1 TO 24
240  READ X
245 P = 158 * X / 34
250  HPLOT   TO (10 * I),(159 - P)
260  NEXT I
270  DATA   12,15,18,27,31,26,17,21,34,7,11,24
280  DATA   14,16,20,25,32,28,18,23,30,10,13,28
63999  END
```

In line 120, high resolution mode is initialized by the statement HGR. In line 130 the color for the border is chosen to be white. In high resolution mode, only eight colors are allowed as follows:

0 Black	4 Black
1 Green	5 Orange
2 Violet	6 Blue
3 White	7 White

White (7) is the best color to choose in order to obtain the clearest graph.

In line 160 the top and bottom borders are drawn. As before, the origin (0,0) is in the upper lefthand corner of the graphics pad. Also as before, points are referenced by column number and row number. Line 170 draws the side borders.

Lines 230 through 260 read in the data (X), scale it, and graph it as in the previous example. Line 245 scales X so that its largest value (34) will be 158 points high. This is the highest position available since the borders take up two of the 160 available positions.

In line 250 the tops of what were the bars in the previous example are connected by HPLOT. Initially a point is plotted in column 1, row 158 (in line 200). This is the point in the lower left corner of the graphics pad (taking account of the borders). This point is plotted first because the HPLOT statement in line 250 draws a line from the previous point plotted to the coordinates given after the "TO". The coordinates used with the HPLOT in line 250 are the same as those used in the PLOT modification in the previous example with one exception. The $10*I$ is necessary to spread the points apart enough to be seen. Try running this program with coordinates I,(159-P) and see what happens.

A final problem that is relevant in both graphics modes is that of labelling the axes on the graphical results. Unfortunately, there is no easy way to accomplish this without a special attachment to the Apple which allows graphics and text to be mixed on the graphics pad. This is a shortcoming in Apple graphics, but it can be overcome by using a general plotting program distributed by Apple called APPLE PLOT. APPLE PLOT will allow you to produce professional looking graphical output with a minimum of effort. Figures 11–3 and 11–4 are examples of APPLE PLOT outputs.

After you have spent some time developing a graphics application, you probably will want to have a copy of your work on paper. This does not represent a problem for the Apple. You will need a special printer, however, with graphics capability. Two possibilities are the SILENTYPE, an inexpensive printer with graphics capabilities, and the WATANABE WX4671 plotter.

The Apple's graphics capability is substantial. The examples in this section are not intended to make you a graphics expert, but to whet your appetite for the type of work that you can do on your Apple.

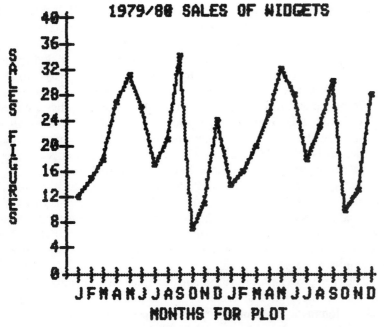

APPLE PLOT Standard Graph

Figure 11–3

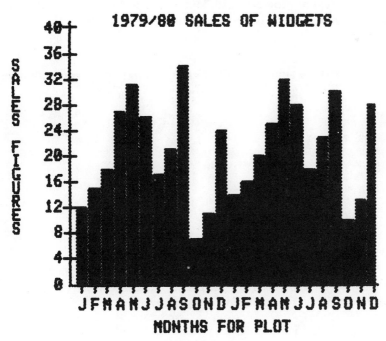

APPLE PLOT Bar Chart

Figure 11–4

USE OF
EXEC FILES

In many computer applications it is necessary to have a clerk who probably has little knowledge of programming run a series of programs one after another. In such situations, it is best to tell the computer the order of the programs to be run in order to save time as well as insure that the proper programs are run in the correct sequence. Such a series of programs together with the instructions concerning their order is known as a *turnkey system*.

To implement turnkey systems on the Apple, EXEC files are used. An EXEC file is an ordinary data file in which each record is a BASIC command, a BASIC statement, or data for an INPUT statement. Instead of running an EXEC file, you EXEC it with the result that each record is treated just as though it had been entered from the keyboard.

As an example of the use of EXEC files, suppose that you wish to produce two reports from EMPLOY. For the first, the data in EMPLOY must be sorted in ascending order on numeric field 1. For the second, the data in EMPLOY must be sorted in descending order on alphabetic field 3. The two reports are identical except for the order of the data and so the same report program is to be used in each case.

The sort program used is the one described in Appendix B. When it is run, it asks via INPUT statements for the field to be sorted, whether the field is alphabetic or numeric, whether the sort is to be in ascending or descending order, and the name of the file to be sorted. It produces an output file called SORT.FIL.

The report program reads a file called TRANSIN and produces a labelled report. Here is a listing of the report program.

```
10    REM   REPORT PROGRAM
20    REM
30    PRINT "EMPLOYEE","DEPARTMENT","EMPLOYEE","HOURLY","REGULAR","OVERTIME"
40    PRINT "NUMBER","NUMBER","NAME","RATE","HOURS","HOURS"
50    PRINT
100   D$ =   CHR$ (4)
105   ONERR  GOTO 160
110   PRINT D$;"OPEN TRANSIN"
120   PRINT D$;"READ TRANSIN"
125   INPUT N,D,N$,H,R,V
130   PRINT D$
140   PRINT N,D,N$,H,R,V
150   GOTO 120
160   PRINT D$;"CLOSE TRANSIN"
63999 END
```

There is nothing new or unusual about this program.

You wish to have this whole procedure of sort 1, report, sort 2, report run automatically. To create the EXEC file, called TRANS, capable of performing this task, use the following program.

```
100   REM   CREATE TRANSACTION PROCESSING EXEC FILE
110   REM
120 D$ =   CHR$ (4)
130   PRINT D$;"OPEN TRANS"
140   PRINT D$;"WRITE TRANS"
150   PRINT "RUN SORT UTILITY"
152   PRINT "1"
154   PRINT "N"
156   PRINT "A"
158   PRINT "EMPLOY"
160   PRINT "RENAME SORT.FIL,TRANSIN"
170   PRINT "RUN REPORT"
175   PRINT "DELETE TRANSIN"
180   PRINT "RUN SORT UTILITY"
182   PRINT "3"
184   PRINT "A"
186   PRINT "D"
188   PRINT "EMPLOY"
190   PRINT "RENAME SORT.FIL,TRANSIN"
200   PRINT "RUN REPORT"
205   PRINT "DELETE TRANSIN"
210   PRINT D$;"CLOSE TRANS"
63999   END
```

This program is similar to programs used previously to create data files except that BASIC commands make up most of the records that are written to the file TRANS. The only lines that are different are lines 152 through 158 and 182 through 188. These lines supply the information that will be requested by the sort program in the order in which it will be requested. For example, lines 152 through 158 tell the sort program that field 1 is to be sorted (line 152) numerically (line 154) in ascending order (line 156) in file EMPLOY (line 158). This information is included in the EXEC file because, while an EXEC file is active, INPUT statements in running programs look into the EXEC file for the values of the required fields, not to the terminal. You must have the correct responses in the correct order contained in the proper spot in the EXEC file. In other words, when a running program comes to an INPUT statement, the next record in the EXEC file will be used as the response to that INPUT statement.

This program to create the EXEC file TRANS should be saved in case the EXEC file is destroyed. Then RUN it to create TRANS. Once this has been accomplished, any time that you wish to run the two sorts and reports, all you have to do is type EXEC TRANS, sit back, and relax. If you suffer from a touch of voyeurism, type MON C,I,O before you EXEC TRANS and the Apple will print each command from the EXEC file as well as the details of each file reference performed. Unless you are printing all this on a printer for future reference, you should probably also type SPEED=150 so that you are able to read what is printed on your screen. When it is all over, don't forget to return things to normal by typing NOMON C,I,O and SPEED=255.

Here is the output from the EXEC TRANS.

```
 EXEC TRANS
]
THIS PROGRAM SORTS A SPECIFIED FIELD IN A SEQUENTIAL TEXT FILE
         (A MAXIMUM OF 100 RECORDS CAN BE SORTED)


THIS PROGRAM SORTS DISK FILES
TO BUILD A SEQUENTIALLY SORTED FILE


POSITION OF FIELD TO BE SORTED; 1,2,3, ETC.
SORT ON ALPHABETIC (A) OR NUMERIC (N) KEY
ASCENDING (A) OR DESCENDING (D)
ENTER FILE NAME

*********  LOADING  ***************
*********  SORTING FILE  *********
*********  SORTED FILE  **********

101,1,ADAMS,5,40,0
103,12,BAKER,5.6,40,4
104,17,BRAVO,4,40,2
108,16,COHEN,6.25,38,0
172,2,JOHNSON,3.75,40,0
198,1,TANNER,4.25,36,0
202,16,WILSON,4,40,0
206,7,LESTER,5.25,40,0
255,12,SCHMIDT,5.6,40,4
281,12,MILLER,6,40,0
313,7,SMITH,4.25,40,4
347,12,GRAY,6,38,0
368,1,WEAVER,3.5,40,2
422,1,WILLIAMS,4,40,0

]
]
```

EMPLOYEE NUMBER	DEPARTMENT NUMBER	EMPLOYEE NAME	HOURLY RATE	REGULAR HOURS	OVERTIME HOURS
101	1	ADAMS	5	40	0
103	12	BAKER	5.6	40	4
104	17	BRAVO	4	40	2
108	16	COHEN	6.25	38	0
172	2	JOHNSON	3.75	40	0
198	1	TANNER	4.25	36	0
202	16	WILSON	4	40	0
206	7	LESTER	5.25	40	0
255	12	SCHMIDT	5.6	40	4
281	12	MILLER	6	40	0
313	7	SMITH	4.25	40	4
347	12	GRAY	6	38	0
368	1	WEAVER	3.5	40	2
422	1	WILLIAMS	4	40	0

```
]
]
THIS PROGRAM SORTS A SPECIFIED FIELD IN A SEQUENTIAL TEXT FILE
         (A MAXIMUM OF 100 RECORDS CAN BE SORTED)


THIS PROGRAM SORTS DISK FILES
TO BUILD A SEQUENTIALLY SORTED FILE
```

```
THIS PROGRAM SORTS DISK FILES
TO BUILD A SEQUENTIALLY SORTED FILE


POSITION OF FIELD TO BE SORTED; 1,2,3, ETC.
SORT ON ALPHABETIC (A) OR NUMERIC (N) KEY
ASCENDING (A) OR DESCENDING (D)
ENTER FILE NAME

**********  LOADING  ***************
**********  SORTING FILE  *********
**********  SORTED FILE  **********

202,16,WILSON,4,40,0
422,1,WILLIAMS,4,40,0
368,1,WEAVER,3.5,40,2
198,1,TANNER,4.25,36,0
313,7,SMITH,4.25,40,4
255,12,SCHMIDT,5.6,40,4
281,12,MILLER,6,40,0
206,7,LESTER,5.25,40,0
172,2,JOHNSON,3.75,40,0
347,12,GRAY,6,38,0
108,16,COHEN,6.25,38,0
104,17,BRAVO,4,40,2
103,12,BAKER,5.6,40,4
101,1,ADAMS,5,40,0

]
]
```

EMPLOYEE NUMBER	DEPARTMENT NUMBER	EMPLOYEE NAME	HOURLY RATE	REGULAR HOURS	OVERTIME HOURS
202	16	..LSON	4	40	0
422	1	WILLIAMS	4	40	0
368	1	WEAVER	3.5	40	2
198	1	TANNER	4.25	36	0
313	7	SMITH	4.25	40	4
255	12	SCHMIDT	5.6	40	4
281	12	MILLER	6	40	0
206	7	LESTER	5.25	40	0
172	2	JOHNSON	3.75	40	0
347	12	GRAY	6	38	0
108	16	COHEN	6.25	38	0
104	17	BRAVO	4	40	2
103	12	BAKER	5.6	40	4
101	1	ADAMS	5	40	0

```
]
]
```

Nicely formatted output is essential in serious business applications. A report produced by the methods described in Chapter 5 is fine as a training exercise, but it still does not look perfect.

Many computers implement output formatting in the form of the PRINT USING statement. As of Version 3.3, Apple DOS does not yet have this most important tool. So that you might have access to output formatting, we have written the following routine which can be included in any of your programs with minimal difficulty.

OUTPUT
FORMATTING

```
1   DEF   FN R(X) =   INT (10 ^ NN * X + 0.5) / 10 ^ NN
6000 AA$ =  STR$ ( FN R(AA))
6050   IF NN < = 0 THEN 7250
6100   FOR II = 1 TO  LEN (AA$)
6200   IF  MID$ (AA$,II,1) = "." THEN 7000
6300   NEXT II
6400 AA$ = AA$ + "."
6500 II = II + 1
7000 YY = NN -  LEN ( MID$ (AA$,II + 1))
7050   IF YY < = 0 THEN 7250
7080   FOR JJ = 1 TO YY
7100 AA$ = AA$ + "0"
7200   NEXT JJ
7250 NN =  LEN (AA$)
7260   PRINT  SPC( PP - NN - RR);AA$;
7270 RR = PP
7300   RETURN
8000 AA$ =  MID$ (AA$,1,PP + 1 - NN)
8020   PRINT  SPC( NN - RR - 1);AA$;
8040 RR = PP
8050 JJ = PP + 1 - NN -  LEN (AA$): IF JJ > 0 THEN  PRINT  SPC( JJ);
8100   RETURN
```

In order to use this routine, you must supply the following information. For each numeric field: (1) the name of the field (AA), (2) the number of digits after the decimal to be printed (NN), (3) the rightmost print position that the field will occupy on the page (PP), and (4) GOSUB 6000. For each alphabetic field, you must supply: (1) the name of the field (AA$), (2) the leftmost print position that the field will occupy (NN), (3) the rightmost print position for the field (PP), and (4) GOSUB 8000.

The following is an example of formatting using the same program that was given at the end of Chapter 5.

```
1   DEF   FN R(X) =   INT (10 ^ NN * X + 0.5) / 10 ^ NN
100   REM  THIS PROGRAM ACCUMULATES TOTALS FOR REGULAR HOURS
110   REM  OVERTIME HOURS AND TOTAL WAGES IN THE EMPLOY FILE
115 D$ =  CHR$ (4)
120   PRINT
130   PRINT
140   PRINT  TAB( 29);"PAYROLL REPORT"
150   PRINT
160   PRINT
170   PRINT "EMPLOYEE   DEPT        NAME        HOURLY    REGULAR    OVERTIME    GROSS"
180   PRINT "NUMBER     NUMBER                  RATE      HOURS      HOURS       PAY"
190   PRINT "---------------------------------------------------------------------"
200   PRINT D$;"OPEN EMPLOY"
210 R1 = 0
```

```
220 V1 = 0
230 W1 = 0
240  PRINT D$;"READ EMPLOY"
245  INPUT N,D,N$,H,R,V
248  PRINT D$
250  ONERR  GOTO 330
260 R1 = R1 + R
270 V1 = V1 + V
280 W = H * R + 1.5 * H * V
290 W1 = W1 + W
295 H =   FN R(H):W =   FN R(W)
300 RR = 0
301 NN = 0:PP = 6:AA = N: GOSUB 6000
302 NN = 0:PP = 14:AA = D: GOSUB 6000
304 NN = 21:PP = 29:AA$ = N$: GOSUB 8000
307 NN = 2:PP = 34:AA = H: GOSUB 6000
309 NN = 0:PP = 44:AA = R: GOSUB 6000
311 NN = 0:PP = 53:AA = V: GOSUB 6000
313 NN = 2:PP = 66:AA = W: GOSUB 6000
314  PRINT
315  GOTO 240
320  REM  ERROR CHECKING ROUTINE
330 Y =   PEEK (222)
335  IF Y = 5 THEN 360
340  PRINT "UNUSUAL ERROR",Y
360  PRINT D$;"CLOSE EMPLOY"
370  PRINT "*************************************************************"
380  PRINT "TOTALS";:RR = 6
381 NN = 0:PP = 44:AA = R1: GOSUB 6000
383 NN = 0:PP = 53:AA = V1: GOSUB 6000
385 NN = 2:PP = 66:AA = W1: GOSUB 6000
386  PRINT
390  GOTO 63999
6000 AA$ =   STR$ ( FN R(AA))
6050  IF NN <  = 0 THEN 7250
6100  FOR II = 1 TO  LEN (AA$)
6200  IF  MID$ (AA$,II,1) = "." THEN 7000
6300  NEXT II
6400 AA$ = AA$ + "."
6500 II = II + 1
7000 YY = NN -  LEN ( MID$ (AA$,II + 1))
7050  IF YY <  = 0 THEN 7250
7080  FOR JJ = 1 TO YY
7100 AA$ = AA$ + "0"
7200  NEXT JJ
7250 NN =  LEN (AA$)
7260  PRINT  SPC( PP - NN - RR);AA$;
7270 RR = PP
7300  RETURN
8000 AA$ =  MID$ (AA$,1,PP + 1 - NN)
8020  PRINT  SPC( NN - RR - 1);AA$;
8040 RR = PP
8050 JJ = PP + 1 - NN -  LEN (AA$): IF JJ > 0 THEN  PRINT  SPC( JJ);
8100  RETURN
63999  END
```

PAYROLL REPORT

EMPLOYEE NUMBER	DEPT NUMBER	NAME	HOURLY RATE	REGULAR HOURS	OVERTIME HOURS	GROSS PAY
101	1	ADAMS	5.00	40	0	200.00
103	12	BAKER	5.60	40	4	257.60
104	17	BRAVO	4.00	40	2	172.00
108	16	COHEN	6.25	38	0	237.50
172	2	JOHNSON	3.75	40	0	150.00
198	1	TANNER	4.25	36	0	153.00
202	16	WILSON	4.00	40	0	160.00
206	7	LESTER	5.25	40	0	210.00
255	12	SCHMIDT	5.60	40	4	257.60
281	12	MILLER	6.00	40	0	240.00
313	7	SMITH	4.25	40	4	195.50
347	12	GRAY	6.00	38	0	228.00
368	1	WEAVER	3.50	40	2	150.50
422	1	WILLIAMS	4.00	40	0	160.00

```
*******************************************************************
```

TOTALS				552	16	2771.70

Lines 300 to 314 and 380 to 386 in this program supply the necessary information to a formatting subroutine. A subroutine is a section of a program that is needed in several different parts of the program. Instead of repeating it, it is entered once and then "called" whenever it is needed. The GOSUB 6000 statement is used to "call" the subroutine. GOSUB is similar to GO TO except that the computer remembers in what line the subroutine was "called" and returns to the statement following the "calling" line when the subroutine finishes with a RETURN statement (line 7300).

Colons are used to separate two or more statements on the same line. Without this facility, the printing part of the example program would be almost as long as the remainder of the program.

The PRINT statements in lines 314 and 386 are necessary so that the next field printed will be on a new line. Without these PRINT statements, all the output would run together and be very difficult to read.

Finally, the field RR must be set equal to zero before each line is printed. This is done in line 300 for the body of the report. Line 386 initializes RR at 6 since the word TOTALS is printed before any field names. The subroutine uses the field name RR to keep track of position on each printed line.

When you use this subroutine there are a few precautions to follow. First, the following field names are used in the subroutine and so should not also be used in your program: AA, AA$, NN, II, JJ, PP, and RR. Use of any of these field names in your program could result in error messages when you use the subroutine.

The second precaution relates to the fact that precise output formatting puts an additional burden on you. You must plan carefully in advance exactly how you wish the output page to look. You also must allow sufficient space for the value of each field to be printed (remember that decimal points take up one space also). One of the best methods of planning is to use a piece of graph paper to lay out the report as you want it to appear. From there it is easy to determine the information necessary to feed the subroutine.

A little care should give you output that you would be proud to give to anyone as an example of what you can do with a computer.

SUMMARY

In this chapter four different uses of the Apple have been covered. You have been shown how to use the full screen editor. The graphics capability of the Apple—both high resolution and low resolution—has been discussed. APPLE PLOT examples were given. The use of EXEC files to run a series of programs automatically was shown. Finally, you have seen how to produce reports that are perfectly formatted.

BASIC Commands Introduced:

	Explanation
EXEC filename	Causes lines in filename to be treated as if they were typed from the keyboard.
MON C,I,O	Prints on screen the execution of an EXEC file and details of each file reference.
NOMON C,I,O	Stops the MON command.
SPEED=X	Slows printing to the screen so that it may be read. X=0—slowest, X=255—fastest.
TEXT	Clears computer from graphics mode.

BASIC Instructions Introduced:

Statement	*Explanation*
COLOR=X	Selects the color (X is a number) for use in low resolution plotting.
GOSUB X RETURN	Defines a subroutine that starts on line X and ends with the RETURN.
GR	Initializes for low resolution graphics.
HCOLOR=X	Selects the color (X is a number) for high resolution graphics.

HGR	Initializes for high resolution graphics.
HLIN X,Y AT Z	Draws a horizontal line from column X to column Y in row Z.
HPLOT X,Y TO U,V	Draws a line between column X row Y and column U row V.
HPLOT TO X,Y	Draws a line from the previous HPLOT point to column X row Y.
PLOT X,Y	Plots a single point in column X, row Y.
VLIN X,Y AT Z	Draws a vertical line from row X to row Y in column Z.

12 / Conclusion

At the end of this chapter you should be able to:

- Recognize the differences between batch, on-line, and real-time
- Understand the problems of a first-time user
- Understand trends in software and hardware for small business computer systems

In this concluding chapter, the payroll program that has been the main example throughout the book will be discussed and put in perspective with regard to other programs that are commonly found in business. The concepts of batch versus real-time programs will be discussed, as well as first-time user organizations. As a conclusion, we present an article that focuses, from the management perspective, on the first-time user and his dilemmas regarding computers.

One of the vehicles for teaching programming in each chapter has been the payroll program. It has grown from a very elementary program to a program that has most of the elements found in an actual payroll program that a business might use. In its present form it is still missing some major elements. For example, it will not write paychecks, nor keep track of some data needed for quarterly tax payments by the employer. The intent of the authors in using payroll as the major example throughout was simple—to pick an application that everyone either is, or can become, familiar with.

All of the programs that appear in this book, with the exception of Chapter 9, are for batch processing. In its simplest terms, batch processing means that transactions are allowed to accumulate before they are used to update master records. Batch processing implies a time cycle—how often the master file is updated. Transactions will accumulate until the update. Batch processing also implies the use of sequential files.

On-line processing is something you have been doing throughout this book. When you type a program at a terminal, you are on-line. The computer accepts or makes comments each time you enter a command or a line of a program. This interaction between a computer and user is referred to as on-line. Other examples of on-line processing are all of the programs that require data entry. The data is entered by you or a data entry operator in an on-line mode.

Files may be considered on-line or off-line. When a file is not being used, it can be stored outside the computer system. When files in computer readable form are removed from the system, they are off-line. They are brought on-line when they need to be used.

The final type of processing is real-time. In real-time, as soon as any transaction occurs, it is entered into the computer system, and the transaction updates the appropriate master record. In Chapter 9, the inventory example illustrated real-time processing. It is necessary to have real-time processing when there is a limited supply or a need for up-to-the-second information. Airline reservation systems were among the first and largest real-time applications.

ROUTINE
BUSINESS
APPLICATIONS

Payroll was one of the first manual systems to be computerized. After payroll, most accounting systems were computerized. These include invoicing, accounts receivable, accounts payable, general ledger, and financial statements. After the accounting area was computerized, the other functional areas of business proceeded with applications. Marketing, production, inventory, distribution, and finance are areas that have large numbers of computer applications. The accounting area was computerized first because it was the easiest. The rules by which bookkeeping is performed are explicit and relatively simple. These characteristics lend themselves to relatively easy computerization.

In simple terms, you have performed two distinct functions in producing the programs in this book. The two functions are: systems analysis and programming.

Systems analysis deals with defining a problem (application). Most of the systems analysis was done for you in defining the program requirements. However, you had to perform some of this function in designing and writing your programs. It is the systems analysis component that is the most difficult in converting from manual to computer systems.

As indicated above, the systems analysis function for accounting applications is simple compared to other areas in a business. As a result, the accounting area was the first highly affected by computers. This is why most of the programs in this book are accounting oriented. In contrast, the systems analysis function for a production/control system is very difficult.

FIRST-TIME
USERS

With the price of computers decreasing dramatically, more and more organizations are using computers. Organizations that have never used computers are called first-time users. There are thousands of horror stories about computers and first-time users. This is not to say that organizations experienced with computers do not also have horror stories; but, first-time users are a special case.

Most first-time users rely on different computer manufacturers' salesmen to provide them with the information they need to choose a computer. Usually, no one in the organization has had any experience with computers. A situation that can be considered analogous to this is as follows: Assume that a cardiologist has recommended that a pacemaker be implanted in a patient. The patient then calls the various manufacturers' representatives for presentations. The patient then selects a model.

It is obvious in the previous analogy that the patient cannot make a rational choice. The same is true of a first-time user selecting a computer based on the sales presentations of manufacturers' representatives. The newspapers are full of reports of trials where users are suing manufacturers, or vice versa, because of basic misunderstandings regarding the computer hardware, software, or both. The best route for a first-time user is to hire someone with computer expertise—either as an employee or consultant. By not choosing either of these alternatives, the use of the computer in an organization might result in greater trauma than necessary.

Computer
Price Trends
and
First-Time User
Organizations

The price of computers has dropped dramatically. No longer are large sums required to get the benefits of computer power. Mini computer systems can be bought for as little as $25,000 or $10,000. Alternatively, you can rent a mini computer system for less than $1,000 per month. An Apple microcomputer complete with two disk drives and a letter quality printer can be purchased for under $5,000. The small price tag lets small organizations, with three to 25 employees, obtain their first computer. And it lets large organizations distribute their data processing capabilities throughout the organization. Therefore, the number of computers in use by business firms is expected to increase considerably.

But both cases (first-time use in small business and distributed processing in large organizations) represent the introduction of computers to people who before had little or no contact with computers. Therein lies a danger. Unless managers prepare themselves and their people now, they may not be ready to meet the challenge when it comes.

Technical Background: Computers have been around for over 30 years. They've been commercially used since the mid-fifties. However, their cost, at that time, limited them to large-scale operations. This is no longer the case. With the advent of minicomputers in the '60s and microcomputers in the '70s, the cost of computers has fallen. Now even small organizations can afford computers.

Furthermore, the trend of smaller, cheaper, more powerful computers is expected to continue. New equipment is continually being developed and introduced to the market. The technological cauldron continues to bubble. New devices will continue to be developed. The cost of computers will drop even further.

But the cost of computers is *not* the cost of computer systems. Similarly, the cost of computation is *not* the cost of problem solving. The computer is a small essential part of a computer system. And computation is a small part of problem solving.

Computer systems are needed to help in solving problems. Computer systems consist of people, of hardware, and of software. Equipment is required for the input, storage, manipulation, and output of data and instructions. Software is required to specify how the equipment should do its work.

The hardware is the tool, the software is the logic for using the tool. Both aspects, hardware and software, are discussed in the following two sections.

Hardware: Managers are faced with a wide variety of choices when they consider hardware. The market is flooded with alternatives. For example, the August 1978 issue of *Datamation*[1] contained a survey covering 57 systems from 46 manufacturers. But that is only a small fraction of what is available. More extensive and comprehensive listings are available in *Auerbach Reports* and *Datapro Reports*.

The equipment itself presents a wide spectrum of alternatives. From the $600 TRS–80 from Radio Shack to the $115,000 (starting price) HP 3000, a whole range of price/performance options are available. Which options to choose depends on the needs of an organization.

The low end of the cost spectrum, such as the $600 computer from Radio Shack, offers systems which are too small for most businesses. They have a CRT (cathode ray tube, a TV screen), a keyboard for entering commands, and a cassette tape recorder to store data and instructions. But these facilities are not enough. Business systems need more main storage, more auxiliary storage, and most important, hardcopy output.

Main storage for microcomputers ranges from 16KB–64KB (KB = kilobyte, roughly one thousand characters—used as a measure of storage capacity for a computer system). Larger main storage capacity is expected to be available in the near future. But useable operating systems facilities require from 20–25KB of main storage. And the application programs will need additional space for efficient operations. Therefore, 48KB of main storage should be considered a minimum for a business system.

Floppy disks provide economic auxiliary storage.[2] Each regular floppy disk holds about 250,000 characters. But at least two (and possibly four) floppy disk drives will be needed to hold the data and instructions. Multiple disk drives are also necessary to provide back up for files and programs.

A printing device is needed for the output of invoices, reports, etc. Although 15 cps (characters per second) printers are available, that equipment is too slow for most business applications. Typical requirements are better served by a line printer capable of printing at least 50 lines per minute. Otherwise the output from the system will be inordinately delayed. But even at 50 lines per minute, the printer can be exasperatingly slow.

Considering these additions and their associated programs, a mini computer useable by a small business will cost between $15,000 and $25,000.[3] If

---

[1] Nancy Krottek, "Mini and Micro Computer Survey," *Datamation,* Vol. 24, No. 8 (Aug. 1978), pp. 113–130.

[2] M. Steifel, "Floppy Disk Systems," *Mini-Micro Systems,* Vol. 11, No. 10 (Nov. 1978), pp. 37–51.

[3] Richard G. Canning and Barbara McNurtin, "MICROS Invade the Business World," *Datamation,* Vol. 24, No. 8 (Aug. 1978), pp. 93–95; and Neil D. Kelley, "Small Business Computers: Some New Options for Uses," *Infosystems,* Vol. 25, No. 10 (Oct. 1978), pp. 59–69.

a company is very small—750 customers, 100 vendors, and generates less than 300 statements per month—then an Apple for under $5,000 with a business software package for $625 will probably suffice.

The described configuration (48–64KB main storage, 500KB–1000KB floppy disk auxiliary storage, keyboard-CRT, and 50 lpm printer) is toward the low end of the spectrum for small computer systems. Depending on the needs of an organization, larger systems may be necessary.

Software: Software is the set of programs that makes a computer work. Without software a computer system is merely a knick-knack that eats electricity. A computer system needs two types of software—systems software and applications software. Systems software is the programs that operate the computer. Applications software uses systems software in the solution of business problems.

Every computer vendor provides systems software to operate their machine. The software includes operating systems, assemblers, compilers, interpreters, and various utilities, such as sort/merge. In general, the systems software provided with a machine is adequate, although software support continues to be a problem area.[4]

However, application software is another story. Application software, unlike systems software, does not deal directly with the computer. It uses the computer (and its systems software) for business data processing and for generating management reports. Application software requires an understanding of business problems, not of computers. Hence, computer vendors have been able to provide systems software that does the required job; but there is a dearth of applications software.

To be sure, most of the standard accounting applications are generally available. Such applications include programs for general ledger, payroll, accounts receivable (both open item and balance forward), accounts payable, and fixed asset accounting. But other application areas are less well developed. Order entry, sales analysis, sales forecasting, inventories, materials requirements planning, and master production scheduling are currently available only for some computer systems. But independent program development is filling the void. Within the next two to three years, adequate application software should become widely available. Skarbek's Software Directory—Apple contains a catalog of all Apple software that is currently available.

In the meantime, an organization will have to satisfy its needs for application software in other ways. The organization can develop its own specialized applications or contract for them. In either case, higher level programming languages speed the development of business applications.

---

[4] "The Small Systems Market: A Survey," *Datamation,* Vol. 24, No. 12 (Nov. 1978), pp. 108–132.

Currently, two languages, BASIC and FORTRAN, are generally available on small business computers.

BASIC is the most widely supported higher level programming language. BASIC (Beginners All-Purpose Symbolic Instruction Code) has the advantage of being easy to learn and use. It is interactive: This means that instructions can be entered and changed instantly. The immediate response of interactive systems eases the program development process. BASIC is interpretive: Each instruction is immediately changed into machine code. Interpreters typically require less main storage than compilers; therefore, less hardware is needed.

The other major, higher-level language that is extensively supported is FORTRAN. FORTRAN (FORmula TRANslator) requires a compiler and hence more main storage than a BASIC interpreter. It is excellent for analytic applications (engineering, scientific and management science problems).

COBOL (COmmon Business Oriented Language) and RPG (Report Program Generator) compilers are available on some systems. Support of other languages, such as PASCAL, APL, ALGOL, etc., is sporadic. Therefore, only BASIC and FORTRAN can be considered for generalized application development.

Success of a small computer system is not determined by the choice of hardware and software alone. Success takes a plan and people to unlock the power inherent in small computer systems.

Plan for Computers

The low price of computer systems tempts many managers. They have heard about the speed and accuracy of computers. They have heard about the prodigious storage capacity of computers. And they have heard about the almost miraculous way of providing information.

At the same time, managers have heard about bad experiences with computers. These horror stories deal with the inflexibility of computerized systems. They tell of problems in understanding computer professionals. And they tell of wasted effort, money, and manpower.

But the truth in either case, the glowing success story and the abysmal horror story, does not lie with the equipment. The computer is merely a tool. It can support either success or failure. Which will result depends on how it is used and what it is used for.

Management control of computer use determines whether or not a computer system supports organizational objectives. Hence, managers must know what the organizational objectives are before they can set the objectives for computer use. Then actual usage can be compared to the stated objectives to see if the system is effective.

Setting objectives for the use of computers is an important step. It should be done before an organization gets a system. But that requires identifying not only where the organization wants to go, but also where the organization is at present. Analysis of current operations identifies the areas where computers can be used to greatest benefit.[5]

In the analysis, two types of questions need to be asked:

1. What are the data processing needs of the organization?
2. What are the information needs of management?

While the computer system can be designed to perform data processing efficiently and while it can answer management's cry for information, the ability of the computer system to respond to either need is only as good as the clarity and precision of the questions that it is asked. An ambiguous question will result in an amorphous design that leaves everybody dissatisfied. And such dissatisfaction perpetuates the horror stories.

Therefore, the organization must determine its data processing needs. Ask where computers can make a contribution to organizational operations. Are there problems in responding to customer questions? On-line inquiry systems should be able to speed up the answers. Are there problems with the accuracy of inventory records? Computers are noted for their accuracy. (Once a program has been debugged, all calculations will be consistent.) Have you inadvertently missed discount periods on vendor invoices? Set up a computerized tickling file so the system won't let you *accidentally* overlook a payment due date. Do you have too many stockouts? Delayed billings? Reports two to three weeks after the end of a period? Administrative people snowed by a blizzard of paper? Clerical people devoted solely to compiling reports for regulatory agencies? All of these problems, when carefully addressed, can be solved with the use of computer systems.

But these questions need to be addressed in detail. For each problem area detailed questions have to be asked, to provide the needed precision for computerized processing. What reports and documents have to be generated? How often? And how many? What are the input data? What is their volume and frequency? How much data has to be stored? How many files, what size, frequency of access, etc. These questions focus on the details of analysis. But these details are needed to explore a prospective problem area. A thorough description of the problem ensures that your organization adds to the number of success stories, not to the horror stories.

The use of computers is a business decision.[6] The low price of computer systems makes computer power available to small organizations and to individual departments in large organizations. To obtain the full benefits of

[5] H. Bromberg, "The Consequences of Minicomputers," *Datamation,* Vol 24, No. 12 (Nov. 1978), pp. 98–103; Canning and McNurtin, loc. cit.; W. A. Saxon and Morris Edwards, "Decision Model for Distributed Processing," *Infosystems,* Vol 25, No. 9 (Sept. 1978), pp. 88–91; W. A. Saxon and Morris Edwards, "Inside the Distributed DP Model," *Infosystems,* Vol. 25, No. 10 (Oct. 1978), pp. 112–224; and Donald T. Winski, "Distributed Systems—Is Your Organization Ready?" *Infosystems,* Vol 25, No. 9 (Sept. 1978), pp. 38–42.

[6] Winski, loc. cit.

computerized speed, accuracy and memory, an organization needs to plan. The plan should consider where and how the computer can be put to use. And in order to plan, an organization must know what its needs are. Therefore, a foundation for the use of a computer system has to exist before the computer system can be used successfully.

Prepare your People

The introduction of a computer system into an organizational unit is a dramatic change. The computer system changes the nature of the work performed by people. It changes the flow of work through an organizational unit. And therefore the relationships between people are changed.

Even small changes in procedures can be traumatic for some people. But first-time computerization has more impact than a small change in procedures. Therefore, people have to be prepared through orientation and training sessions for the new system. Don't limit the sessions to clerical people. Management also needs to know what it can and cannot expect from a new computer system.

Once the requirements have been defined, once a plan for computer use has been established, once a commitment for hardware and software acquisition has been made, once a specific system has been chosen and purchased, then intensive preparation for the upcoming change can start. (Note that we are recommending training and orientation sessions prior to the actual delivery of the computer system.) At this time the organization knows the details of the system to be delivered and how it will be used. Therefore, it can focus its training where it will do the most good.

Small business computers are generally easy to operate and use. Hence, in most cases it will not be necessary to hire computer professionals. In larger organizations an adequate staff exists already to support the needs of management. In small organizations, managers will have to do some of the work themselves and contract outside the organization for the more technical aspects. But in either case, the training and orientation sessions should prepare the people for interaction with computer systems professionals. Hence, some understanding of the terminology and capabilities of computers in general has to be provided by these sessions.

The low cost of small computer systems has led to predictions of almost exponential growth in the number of organizations using them. Rather than being a matter of *whether,* it becomes a matter of *when.* When will your workplace have a computer system? Given this inevitability, then preparation now will pay off in the future. Getting your people prepared now makes the path of transition to a new system smoother.

Of course, with the passage of time, more and more people will already be familiar with computers. Business schools require introductory courses in data processing or information systems for their graduates. They learn the terminology of computers. They learn about the capabilities and limitations of hardware. And they learn how to program computers in BASIC. Since BASIC is so widely supported on small business computer systems, the students will be ready to make a contribution to any organization that is contemplating the use of a small business computer.

CONCLUSION

Low cost computer systems are a reality. But a manager should not be hypnotized by the cost of hardware. To make a computer system successful takes more than computing equipment. Success takes software, tailored to the needs of a business. It takes people who are trained to operate the hardware and people who are trained to use it. But most of all, it takes management—managers who are committed to planning for computerization, managers who set objectives and control computer usage, and managers who are willing to devote themselves to the successful introduction of change.

Appendices

SUMMARY OF BASIC COMMANDS AND INSTRUCTIONS   APPENDIX A

Summary of BASIC Commands:

CATALOG	Lists the names of programs in the user save area (catalogue).
DELETE	Eliminates a program from the diskette.
LIST	Gives a printout (listing) of the program.
LOAD	Asks for a copy of a program from the diskette.
NEW	Tells the system that the operator is about to type in a new program.
RENAME	Gives a new name to a program on the diskette.
RUN	Executes a program, i.e., commands a computer to do what the program instructions tell it to do.
SAVE	Puts a copy of the program onto the diskette under the current program name.

Summary of BASIC Instructions:

PRINT D$; "CLOSE filename"	Closes file and stores it on the diskette.
DATA 5,2,7	Used to hold data for fields in READ statements.
DIM Y(X),Z(Q,R)	Sets the lists Y (represented by a letter) to X positions; defines that Z (represented by a letter) has Q rows and R columns; individual elements of lists and tables are identified by their location: position number in a list; row number *and* column number in a table.
END	Indicates the physical end of a program.

PEEK(218)+256*PEEK(219)
>   Gives the line number at which an ONERR condition took place.

FOR Y = N TO M
⋮
NEXT Y
>   Sets up a loop; the FOR statement begins the loop; it sets Y to M (beginning value); the loop will continue until Y has a value greater than M (the upper bound); the NEXT statement loses the loop.

GOTO nnn
>   Tells the system to go to line number nnn for the next instruction.

Y = PEEK(222)
IF Y = n THEN line number
>   Tells the computer that if the error encountered is n, then processing should resume at the line number given.

IF x THEN nnn
>   If x is true then go to line nnn for the next instruction, otherwise (if x is false) go to the next line in sequence.

PRINT D$; "READ filename"
INPUT fieldnames
>   Reads a record from file number n; the file is identified by its file number. Records are separated by their fieldnames.

INPUT X,Y
>   Takes numeric values for fields X and Y from the keyboard.

INPUT X$, Y$
>   Gets alphabetic values for fields X$ and Y$ from the keyboard.

INT(X)
>   Makes the value X into an integer (whole number).

LET X = Y
>   Places the value of Y into the memory location X.

ONERR GO TO line number
>   Tells the computer to go to *line number* when an error is encountered.

PRINT D$; "OPEN filename"
>   Opens the file identified by the filename; the filename can be from 1 to 30 characters.

PRINT D$; "WRITE filename"
PRINT #n fieldname;"",";fieldname2;"",";etc.

<table>
<tr><td></td><td>Writes a record on filename; the fields of the record will be separated by commas.</td></tr>
<tr><td>PRINT X,Y</td><td>Displays the values of X and Y.</td></tr>
<tr><td>PRINT "XYZ"</td><td>Displays the alphabetic information XYZ.</td></tr>
<tr><td>READ X,Y,Z</td><td>Assigns values to fields from DATA Statements (X,Y,Z are arbitrary field names).</td></tr>
<tr><td>REM</td><td>Prints remarks for programmer; ignored by the computer.</td></tr>
<tr><td>STOP</td><td>Tells the system to stop.</td></tr>
</table>

Arithmetic operations:

$X + Y$	Add X to Y
$X - Y$	Subtract Y from X
$X*Y$	Multiply X by Y
X/Y	Divide X by Y
$X \wedge Y$	Raise X to the Y power

Comparison operators:

$X = Y$	Equal (if X equals Y, this comparison is true).
$X<Y$	Less than (if X is strictly less than Y, this comparison is true).
$X< = Y$	Less than or equal to (if X is less than *or* equal to Y, this comparison is true).
$X>Y$	Greater than (if X is strictly greater than Y, this comparison is true).
$X> = Y$	Greater than or equal to (if X is

greater than *or* equal to Y, this comparison is true).

X<>Y

Not equal to (if X is greater than or less than—that is, not equal to—Y, this expression is true).

APPENDIX B

SORTING

Records may be sorted either alphabetically or numerically for many applications. In order to use the sort program given in this appendix, it is important to understand something about the program:

1. The file to be sorted is unchanged at the end of the sort.

2. The sorted file at the conclusion of the program is called "SORT.FIL".

3. You must rename the "SORT.FIL" with the RENAME command as soon as the sort is finished. It will automatically be saved.

In the chapter on totals and subtotals, it is necessary to sort the "EMPLOY" file by department number; then it becomes the "EMPLDP" file.

A listing of the sorting program, an example running the program, and a command to rename "SORT.FIL" follow:

```
1    DIM KY$(100),SR$(100)
2    ONERR  GOTO 9000
4    PRINT "THIS PROGRAM SORTS A SPECIFIED FIELD IN A SEQUENTIAL TEXT FILE"
5    PRINT "          (A MAXIMUM OF 100 RECORDS CAN BE SORTED)"
10   REM       BUBBLE SORT
20   REM
30   PRINT : PRINT
40   PRINT "THIS PROGRAM SORTS DISK FILES"
45   PRINT "TO BUILD A SEQUENTIALLY SORTED FILE"
50   PRINT : PRINT
60   INPUT "POSITION OF FIELD TO BE SORTED; 1,2,3, ETC.  ";FP
65   IF FP < 1 THEN 60
70   INPUT "SORT ON ALPHABETIC (A) OR NUMERIC (N) KEY     ";AA$
72   IF AA$ = "A" THEN 80
74   IF AA$ = "N" THEN 80
76   GOTO 70
80   INPUT "ASCENDING (A) OR DESCENDING (D)                ";AD$
81   IF AD$ = "A" THEN 85
82   IF AD$ = "D" THEN 85
83   GOTO 80
85   REM    *** MAIN ROUTINE
90 D$ =  CHR$ (4)
210  INPUT "ENTER FILE NAME   ";FI$
220  PRINT D$;"OPEN ";FI$
230  PRINT D$;"OPEN SORT.FIL"
240  GOSUB 300
250  GOSUB 400
260  GOSUB 500
270  PRINT D$;"CLOSE ";FI$
275  PRINT D$;"CLOSE SORT.FIL"
280  GOTO 63999
300  REM   ***** LOADING FILE *****
```

```
302   PRINT
305   PRINT "**********  LOADING  ***************"
308 I = 0
309   PRINT D$;"READ ";FI$
310 I = I + 1
330   GOSUB 600
335 CC = FK
340   IF L2 = 0 THEN 9032
370 KY$(I) =  MID$ (SR$(I),L1,L2)
380   GOTO 310
390   RETURN
400   REM  *****  SORTING FILE  *****
410   PRINT "**********  SORTING FILE  **********"
415   FOR J = 1 TO I - 2
418   FOR K = J + 1 TO I - 1
420   IF AD$ = "D" THEN 427
421   IF AA$ = "A" THEN 425
422   IF  VAL (KY$(J)) <  VAL (KY$(K)) THEN 470
423   GOTO 434
425   IF KY$(J) < KY$(K) THEN 470
426   GOTO 434
427   IF AA$ = "A" THEN 430
428   IF  VAL (KY$(J)) >  VAL (KY$(K)) THEN 470
429   GOTO 434
430   IF KY$(J) > KY$(K) THEN 470
434 H1$ = SR$(J)
435 SR$(J) = SR$(K)
440 SR$(K) = H1$
450 H1$ = KY$(J)
455 KY$(J) = KY$(K)
460 KY$(K) = H1$
470   NEXT K
475   NEXT J
480   RETURN
500   REM  ***** LISTING SORTED FILE *****
515   PRINT "**********  SORTED FILE  **********"
518   PRINT
520   FOR J = 1 TO I - 1
525   PRINT D$;"WRITE SORT.FIL"
530   PRINT SR$(J)
535   PRINT D$
540   PRINT SR$(J)
545   NEXT J
599   RETURN
600   REM  ***** READ RECORD, FIND KEY FIELD ****
605 LO = 1:FD = 0:FK = 0
615   GET B$
620 FD = FD + 1
625   IF B$ =  CHR$ (13) THEN 640
630 SR$(I) = SR$(I) + B$
635   IF B$ < > "," THEN 615
640 FK = FK + 1
642 OL = LO
645 LO = FD + 1
650   IF FP < > FK THEN 670
655 L1 = OL
660 L2 = LO - OL - 1
670   IF B$ < >  CHR$ (13) THEN 615
675   RETURN
9000   REM  ***** ERROR ROUTINE *****
9010   REM
9020 Y =  PEEK (222)
9025 L =  PEEK (218) + 256 *  PEEK (219)
9028   IF Y < > 5 THEN 9045
9030   GOTO 250
9032   PRINT : PRINT
```

```
9034    PRINT "*** FIELD POSITION = ";FP;" FILE ";FI$;" HAS ONLY ";CC;" FIELDS ***"
9036    PRINT
9038    PRINT D$;"CLOSE ";FI$
9040    PRINT D$;"CLOSE SORT.FIL"
9042    GOTO 55
9045    IF Y = 6 THEN 210
9050    PRINT CHR$ (7);"UNUSUAL ERROR ";Y;" IN ";L
9060    GOTO 270
63999   END
```

```
]RUN
THIS PROGRAM SORTS A SPECIFIED FIELD IN A SEQUENTIAL TEXT FILE
          (A MAXIMUM OF 100 RECORDS CAN BE SORTED)


THIS PROGRAM SORTS DISK FILES
TO BUILD A SEQUENTIALLY SORTED FILE


POSITION OF FIELD TO BE SORTED; 1,2,3, ETC.   2
SORT ON ALPHABETIC (A) OR NUMERIC (N) KEY     N
ASCENDING (A) OR DESCENDING (D)               A
ENTER FILE NAME  EMPLOY

**********  LOADING  ***************
**********  SORTING FILE  **********
**********  SORTED FILE  ***********

422,1,WILLIAMS,4,40,0
368,1,WEAVER,3.5,40,2
198,1,TANNER,4.25,36,0
101,1,ADAMS,5,40,0
172,2,JOHNSON,3.75,40,0
313,7,SMITH,4.25,40,4
206,7,LESTER,5.25,40,0
347,12,GRAY,6,38,0
281,12,MILLER,6,40,0
255,12,SCHMIDT,5.6,40,4
103,12,BAKER,5.6,40,4
202,16,WILSON,4,40,0
108,16,COHEN,6.25,38,0
104,17,BRAVO,4,40,2

]RENAME SORT.FIL,EMPLDP
```

In the update chapter, the "SALES" file had to be sorted alphabetically by salesman name. An example running the program, and the renaming of "SORT.FIL" follow:

```
THIS PROGRAM SORTS A SPECIFIED FIELD IN A SEQUENTIAL TEXT FILE
          (A MAXIMUM OF 100 RECORDS CAN BE SORTED)


THIS PROGRAM SORTS DISK FILES
TO BUILD A SEQUENTIALLY SORTED FILE


POSITION OF FIELD TO BE SORTED; 1,2,3, ETC.   2
SORT ON ALPHABETIC (A) OR NUMERIC (N) KEY     A
ASCENDING (A) OR DESCENDING (D)               A
ENTER FILE NAME   SALES
```

```
**********  LOADING  ***************
**********  SORTING FILE  **********
**********  SORTED FILE  ***********

1,BILL,12050,5
3,BOB,14690,.05
3,CLYDE,7340,.04
3,HARRY,9460,.045
1,JOE,5270,.045
2,PHIL,11200,.055
2,TOM,6940,.04
```

SELECTED ERROR MESSAGES   APPENDIX C

In the ONERR statement, the error that is usually tested for is error number 5 (Y = 5). If another error should occur, the statement PRINT "UNUSUAL ERROR" will be printed with an error number. The following is an abbreviated list of error numbers and an interpretation of their meaning:

CODE	DOS MESSAGE
0	NEXT without FOR
1	Language not available
2,3	Range error
4	Disk write protected
5	End of data in file
6	File not found
7	Column mismatch
8	I/O error
9	Disk full
10	File locked
11	Syntax error
12	No buffers available
13	File type mismatch
14	Program too large
15	Not direct command
16	Syntax error
22	RETURN without GOSUB
42	Out of data
53	Illegal quantity
69	Overflow
77	Out of memory
90	Undefined statement
107	Bad subscript
120	Redimensioned array

CODE	DOS MESSAGE
133	Division by zero
163	Type mismatch
176	String too long
191	Formula too complex
224	Undefined function
254	Bad response to INPUT statement
255	Control C interrupt attempted

APPENDIX D   HOW TO . . .

Problem	Solution
Stop a printout on the terminal or printer	Depress the C key while pressing CTRL
Stop execution of a program if nothing seems to be happening	Depress the C key while pressing CTRL
Renumber lines in a BASIC program	Your computer may have a resequence program. Try typing RUN RENUMBER. If the program exists, it will ask for beginning line number and interval. Input of &F100,I10 will result in the program being renumbered so that the first statement is 100 and lines are numbered consecutively 100,120,130, etc. All GO TO and other statements that contain line numbers are automatically changed.
Delete programs from the catalog	DELETE PROGRAMNAME
Delete data files from the catalog	DELETE FILENAME
Delete lines from a program	DEL 180–270: This will cause lines 180–270 of the program in your work space to be deleted DELETE 120: Line 120 will be deleted.
List a data file	Write a program that lists and prints it.

APPENDIX E   INITIALIZATION OF DISKETTES

Your diskette must be initialized by Apple DOS before you can save programs on it. In order to initialize a diskette, you must perform the following steps:

1. Locate the MASTER diskette that is supplied with your Apple. Place it in the disk drive and "boot" the system from it.

2. Remove the MASTER and place the diskette to be initialized in the drive.

3. Type NEW to clear the Apple's memory.

4. Enter the BASIC program that you wish to be executed as the last step of the "booting" process. It will be saved on the diskette under the name HELLO. For example,

> 10 PRINT " MY APPLE SYSTEM"
> 20 PRINT " CREATED JULY 17, 1980"
> 63999 END

5. Type INIT HELLO. The disk drive light will come on and remain on for about two minutes while your disk is being initialized. When the light goes out, your diskette is ready for use. Test it by "booting DOS" from it.

MORE ABOUT DISKETTES   APPENDIX F

Some additional information about Apple diskettes is useful for actual applications. The diskette's recording surface is logically made up of 35 concentric circles called *tracks*. Each of these tracks is comprised of 13 equal length sectors. Each sector holds 256 bytes of information (one byte is the space required to hold one letter, number, or special symbol).

In Apple BASIC, four tracks are reserved for system use, leaving 31 tracks (403 sectors or 103,168 bytes) for user files (programs and data files). In DOS Version 3.3, the same physical diskettes will have 31 sixteen sector tracks of useable space for a total of 496 useable 256-byte sectors.

You can determine how many sectors are being used by a particular SAVEd program by giving the CATALOG command. In response to this command, each program generates one line of output as follows:

A 002 MYPROG

In this example, MYPROG is identified as an Applesoft BASIC (A) program occupying two sectors on the diskette. In addition to Applesoft which is floating point BASIC, other abbreviations are T for a data file, I for an integer BASIC program and B for a binary file. By reviewing the space taken for your files, you can begin to develop a feeling for how much information can be stored on a diskette.

The Apple can support up to six disk drives simultaneously. This would be more than adequate for all but the most data intensive applications.

On the inside of the Apple are a number of "slots" into which various peripheral equipment can be plugged. Three slots are set aside for disk drives. A card called a *disk controller* plugged into each of these slots runs two disk drives (referred to as D1 and D2). Usually the first disk controller is plugged into slot six (S6), the second into S5, and the third into S4.

If you are lucky enough to have several disk drives, you must specify which one is intended in any disk reference (SAVE, DELETE, LOAD, etc.). For example, to request a catalog from the diskette in drive 2, slot 5, the command would be

CATALOG,S5,D2

If no slot and drive are specified, S6 and D1 are assumed by the Apple. Thus, if you have only one disk drive, SAVE MYPROG would put MYPROG on the diskette in slot 6, drive 1.

If you have a CORVUS WINCHESTER disk drive attached to your system, you have ten million bytes of storage space. The CORVUS disk is usually controlled through a card in slot 6. If you also have a floppy disk drive, it will normally be in slot 4.

To protect your diskette from inadvertent replacement of programs and data, you can use the "write protect" feature. There is a rectangular slot cut out of the paper jacket in each diskette. As long as this slot is open, you can SAVE programs on the diskette and LOAD programs from it. If you cover up this slot with a piece of the special tape supplied with your Apple, you will be able to LOAD programs, but not SAVE them. In this condition, the diskette is "write protected" since nothing can be written onto it.

Index